IMAGES
*of America*

# JEWISH ANN ARBOR

*On the cover:* **RABBI HAROLD WHITE.** Rabbi White served the Ann Arbor community from 1962 to 1968, a period of both growth and significant change. During his tenure, Beth Israel became affiliated with the Conservative Judaism movement. At the same time, members interested in a Reform Judaism approach established a new congregation, Temple Beth Emeth. (BIC.)

IMAGES
*of America*

# JEWISH ANN ARBOR

Richard Adler and Ruth Adler

ARCADIA
PUBLISHING

ISBN 0-7385-4021-8

Published by Arcadia Publishing
Charleston SC, Chicago IL, Portsmouth NH, San Francisco CA

Printed in the United States of America

Library of Congress Catalog Card Number: 2006920222

For all general information contact Arcadia Publishing at:
Telephone 843-853-2070
Fax 843-853-0044
E-mail sales@arcadiapublishing.com
For customer service and orders:
Toll-Free 1-888-313-2665

Visit us on the Internet at http://www.arcadiapublishing.com

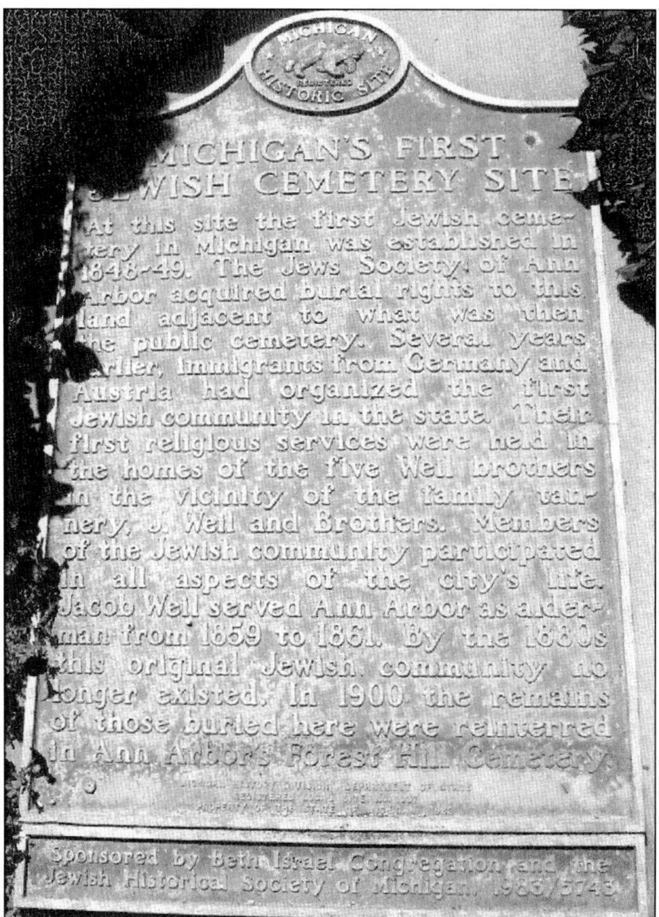


**FIRST PUBLIC JEWISH CEMETERY IN MICHIGAN.** This commemorative plaque is located in the ground at the corner of Huron and Fletcher Streets east of Horace H. Rackham Building. A plaque in Detroit's Elmwood Cemetery also notes the defined half-acre at the Detroit site, dedicated in January 1851, to be "Michigan's Oldest Jewish Cemetery." At the time of the application for the Elmwood historical marker, Leonard Simons, considered the "mentor" of the Jewish Historical Society and a major figure in the Detroit area community for decades, believed the Ann Arbor cemetery to have been privately owned by the Weil family.

# Contents

# ACKNOWLEDGMENTS

Numerous individuals provided guidance, suggestions, and help in completing this history. Melissa Basilone, our project editor at Arcadia, showed patience with our questions and problems. Helen Aminoff was a storehouse of knowledge. Her earlier research into local Jewish history provided the basis for much of what we discovered about the Weil family and included in the text. Others who provided useful information as well as personal photographs included Rabbi Harold White, former religious leader at Beth Israel; Rabbi Robert Dobrusin, current rabbi at Beth Israel; Rabbi Robert Levy, spiritual leader at Temple Beth Emeth; local historian Susan Wineberg; Phoebe Amante and Carol Finerman, current president of Beth Israel; Sheryl Fagin; Ceil Pear; Alan Haber; and Clara Seymour.

We would also like to acknowledge Rose Adler for her patience and help in providing a sense of order in assembling the photographs used in this book. Finally, the members of our family who also provided input: Sally Adler, Steven Adler, and Rebekah Gamble.

Photograph Sources:
JHSM—Permission of Jewish Historical Society of Michigan
BHL—Courtesy of Bentley Historical Library
BIC—Courtesy of Beth Israel Congregation
TBE—Courtesy of Temple Beth Emeth

# INTRODUCTION

There are few early accounts of a Jewish presence in the Michigan territory prior to the beginning of the 19th century; those for whom a record does exist represent a microcosm of the larger historical flow of traders or settlers. As was true in much of what was then western wilderness, the fur trade dominated exploration of the territory. Merchants, and ultimately settlements, followed these pioneers as they migrated along the rivers and forests of the region. Tensions often developed into open conflicts between the earliest French explorers and the British who followed. And lest one forget, the land itself was already occupied by a variety of Native American tribes, many of which aligned themselves with one side of the European settlers or the other. As a result, forts were established, often at the confluence of rivers or lakes. The two most prominent of these early settlements became Fort Pontchartrain (Detroit) and Fort Michilimackinac.

The first recorded Jew in the territory was Ezekial Solomon. An immigrant from Berlin, then in the German state of Prussia, Solomon arrived at Fort Michilimackinac around 1761. While his purpose in coming to the colonies is unknown, it was likely similar to that of many immigrants of the time, a desire to escape the conflicts of the period.

Whatever his reasons, Solomon was one of at least five Jewish traders who joined the British army, and with the end of the war, remained in the territory as fur traders. Among his fellow travelers was Chapman Abraham, who in 1762 became the first recorded Jew in Detroit. (Abraham is sometimes listed as Abraham Chapman. But documents containing his signature indicate Abraham was his surname.) Both Solomon and Abraham had spent time in the captivity of local natives; while Solomon was eventually released in Ottawa following payment of a ransom, Abraham survived only because his violent temper appeared to show him as "mad."

During these years, portions of Upper Canada (Ontario) and the northern portion of Michigan Territory were referred to by the British as the "Upper Country," and trade was open primarily for Christians. "Israelite" traders or merchants were required to sign a pledge upon their arrival in Montreal in which they agreed to follow the laws and regulations as set down by the business communities in Lower Canada (Montreal or Quebec). An exception was made for Abraham due to the distance he was forced to travel, and he was provided a 20-day grace period in which to sign.

In 1825, the Erie Canal was opened for traffic, shortening the period of travel from the east to the Michigan territory from two months down to a week. As a result, a wave of mostly German immigrants entered the territory. Attracted by the rich farmland in the area west of Detroit, as well as the availability of grazing land, many of these immigrants settled in the villages of Woodruff's Grove (Ypsilanti) and Ann Arbor. The convenience of "modern" travel contributed to the settlement of the region, which in 1836 became part of the new state of Michigan. In 1835, a federal highway known as the Chicago Road (now U.S. 12) was opened, linking Detroit and Chicago. Three years later, the railroad stretched from Detroit to Ypsilanti.

Politics (including an early, although unsuccessful, attempt to site the state capital in Ann Arbor following statehood in 1836), as well as the establishment of a state university in the growing village, added to the rapid influx of immigrants into the area. By 1845, the county of Washtenaw listed some 3,000 residents. At least a few of these were the first Jewish settlers in the area. Of course, present-day identification of a traveler or resident as a Jew is primarily by inference, one generally based upon the name of the person. For example, Alexander Cohen in early 19th-century Detroit was probably Jewish; Isaac Moses, a member of the Masonic Lodge in Detroit, may have been. While precise numbers cannot be ascertained, by the end of the decade the Washtenaw County community was large enough to maintain a minyan and a small Orthodox community.

The village of Annarbour first appeared on a map prepared by its two founders, John Allen and Elisha Rumsey, when in 1824, the men purchased some 640 acres located near a river approximately 30 miles west of Detroit. The claim was registered in Detroit in May, and the plat was filed three months later. The village, named for the wives of the founders, shortly afterwards acquired the name which remains to this day: Ann Arbor.

Charles Bresler and his family were among the first recorded permanent Jewish settlers in the county, residing in Ypsilanti some seven or eight miles east of Ann Arbor. Bresler, born in Cannstadt (near Wurtemberg, Germany) in 1816, arrived in Ypsilanti around 1837, where he worked in the horse and other farm stock trade as well as in the fur industry. He was shortly afterwards joined by his father, Leo, and two brothers Louis and Adolph. For a brief period, the Bresler home in Ypsilanti became the local synagogue; since services appear to have been held there on a regular basis, it would appear that at least six additional Jewish males lived in the area.

At the time of the 1850 census, the Ann Arbor Jewish community consisted of at least two dozen individuals; certainly the numbers were sufficient to establish what was the first known Jewish cemetery in Michigan. Most prominent was the Weil family. In his history of the Detroit Jewish community, Irving Katz (1955) names at least two dozen likely Jewish men living in the area: "Woodel, a Bohemian Jew; Leo, Charles, Adolph, and Louis Bresler; Charles, Henry, and Emanuel Lederer; Moses Rindskoff; Charles Fantle; Solomon Bendit; David Weidenfeld and brother, Adam Hersch; Isaac Altman; Simon Sloman; Fantes brothers; Alex and Martin Guiterman; Solomon Sondheim, Benjamin Goodkind, one Hayman, one Feder."

Denis and Fanny Hayman, with their five children, were farmers living in Superior Township in 1850. All were born in the United States, Denis in Vermont. Whether this is the Hayman to whom Katz refers, and if so, whether they were Jewish, is unknown. Indeed, the same question might be posed for others in Katz's list. As with the Bresler family, many of these men and their families later moved to Detroit.

# *One*

# First Half Century

The nucleus of the Weil family consisted of five brothers: Leopold (born in Ckyne, Bohemia, now the Czech Republic, in 1820), Solomon (1821), Moses (1824), Jacob (1827), and Marcus (1829). According to local historian Helen Aminoff, Weil family tradition suggested the Weils originated in Spain, where the family name was Levi, an anagram of Weil. Solomon was the first to settle in Ann Arbor, arriving around 1845. Some two years later, Solomon was joined by his wife Dory/Dora and their children. Leopold Weil and his wife Rachel/Rosa, as well as their two children, came to Ann Arbor shortly after Solomon. Judah Sittig, Rachel's brother and a Weil landsman, and Judah's wife Mary also arrived during this period. The other brothers likewise settled in Ann Arbor during these years.

Jacob Weil and his brothers established a tannery business, J. Weil and Brothers, near Huron and First Streets, ultimately employing over 100 persons. The tannery was one of four located along Allen's Creek west of the downtown. Solomon and Dora are listed in the 1860 census with six children and a family domestic; Leopold and Rachel with six children are present as well. Also included in the records are Jacob, his wife Deborah (née Fantle), and their one-month-old son, as well as Jacob's brothers Marcus, unmarried at the time, and Moses. It was Moses's wife Reila who died in 1858, and whose gravestone was discovered in 1980 at a fraternity in Ann Arbor. After the death of his first wife, Moses was remarried to Theresa (née Lederer), whose family had originated in Chicago. Moses ultimately supported six children from his two marriages. Marcus would marry Theresa's sister Bertha in 1860.

During the 1860s, the Weil families gradually moved to the larger cities of Chicago and Newark, New Jersey. The Weils continued to own real estate in Ann Arbor. Solomon's son Louis even continued in business, dealing in animal hides. The Fantle family, related to the Weils through the marriage of Deborah Fantle and Jacob Weil, continued to live in Ann Arbor until at least the 1880s. Although there likely remained some limited Jewish presence in the Ann Arbor area during these ensuing decades, the heart of the community left with the Weils.

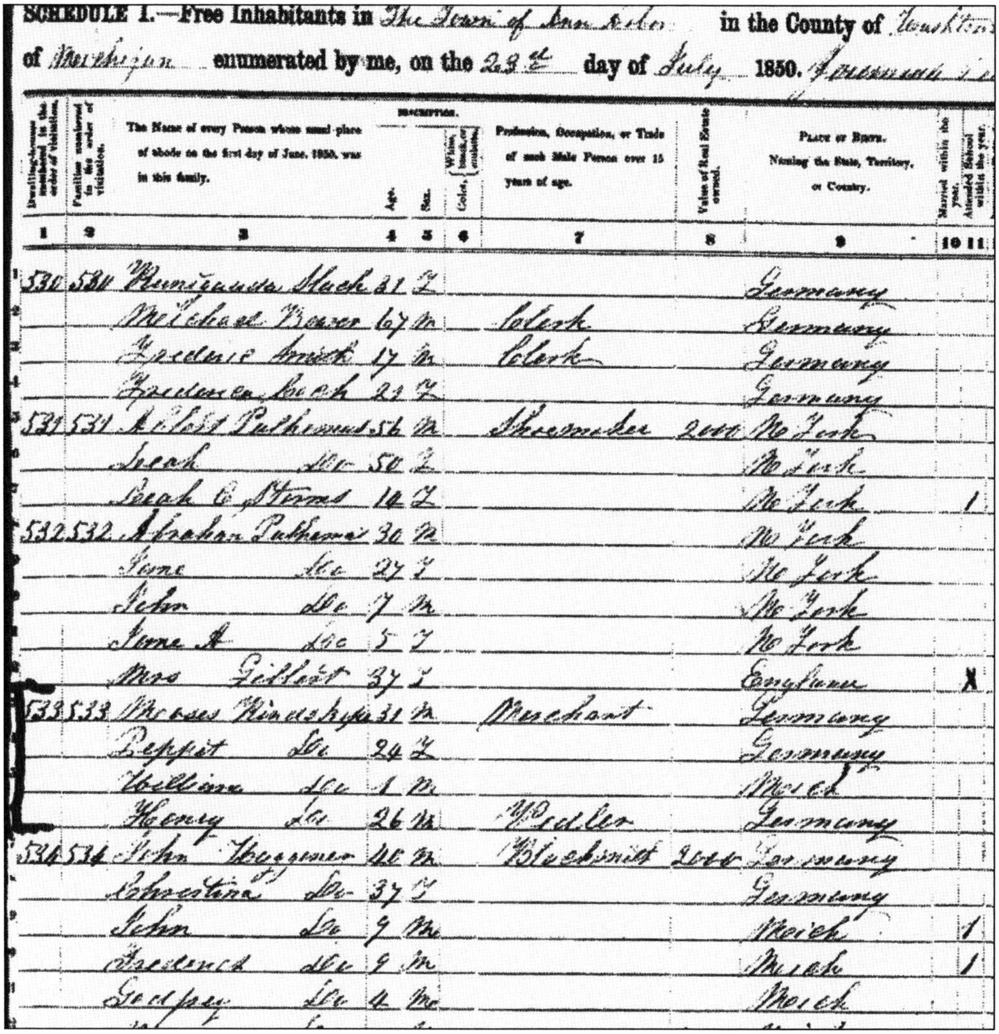

SCHEDULE 1.—Free Inhabitants in The Town of Ann Arbor in the County of Washtenaw of Michigan enumerated by me, on the 23d day of July 1850.

| Dwelling-houses numbered in the order of visitation | Families numbered in the order of visitation | The Name of every Person whose usual place of abode on the first day of June, 1850, was in this family | Age | Sex | Color | Profession, Occupation, or Trade of each Male Person over 15 years of age | Value of Real Estate owned | Place of Birth, Naming the State, Territory, or Country | Married within the year | Attended School within the year |
|---|---|---|---|---|---|---|---|---|---|---|
| 1 | 2 | 3 | 4 | 5 | 6 | 7 | 8 | 9 | 10 | 11 |
| 530 | 530 | Kunigunda Mack | 31 | F | | | | Germany | | |
| | | Michael Beaser | 67 | M | | Clerk | | Germany | | |
| | | Frederic Smith | 17 | M | | Clerk | | Germany | | |
| | | Frederica Koch | 23 | F | | | | Germany | | |
| 531 | 531 | Albert Pulhemus | 56 | M | | Shoemaker | 2000 | New York | | |
| | | Sarah Do | 50 | F | | | | New York | | |
| | | Sarah C. Storms | 14 | F | | | | New York | | 1 |
| 532 | 532 | Abraham Pulhemus | 30 | M | | | | New York | | |
| | | Jane Do | 27 | F | | | | New York | | |
| | | John Do | 7 | M | | | | New York | | |
| | | Jane A Do | 5 | F | | | | New York | | |
| | | Mrs Gilbert | 37 | F | | | | England | | X |
| 533 | 533 | Moses Rindskopf | 31 | M | | Merchant | | Germany | | |
| | | Peppet Do | 24 | F | | | | Germany | | |
| | | William Do | 1 | M | | | | Mich | | |
| | | Henry Do | 26 | M | | Peddler | | Germany | | |
| 534 | 534 | John Thummer | 40 | M | | Blacksmith | 2000 | Germany | | |
| | | Christina Do | 37 | F | | | | Germany | | |
| | | John Do | 9 | M | | | | Mich | | 1 |
| | | Frederick Do | 9 | M | | | | Mich | | 1 |
| | | Godfrey Do | 4 | M | | | | Mich | | |

**CENSUS RECORD FROM 1850.** Solomon Bendit and Moses Rindskopf/Rindskoff, "Ox head," were the earliest known Jewish settlers in the Ann Arbor area itself, although, like many of the Jews of Washtenaw County in the 1840s, they later moved to Detroit. Moses Rindskopf is listed as a 31-year-old merchant with a wife and child. A Henry Rindskopf, possibly a brother, was living in the same household and working as a peddler. In the 1860 census, Moses Rindskopf, now with five children, had moved west to Albion. Several other Jewish families are known to have settled in the Ypsilanti area, including those of the Charles Bresler, the Weil, and the Lederer families. Other than possibly Jewish surnames, there remains little beyond anecdotal evidence.

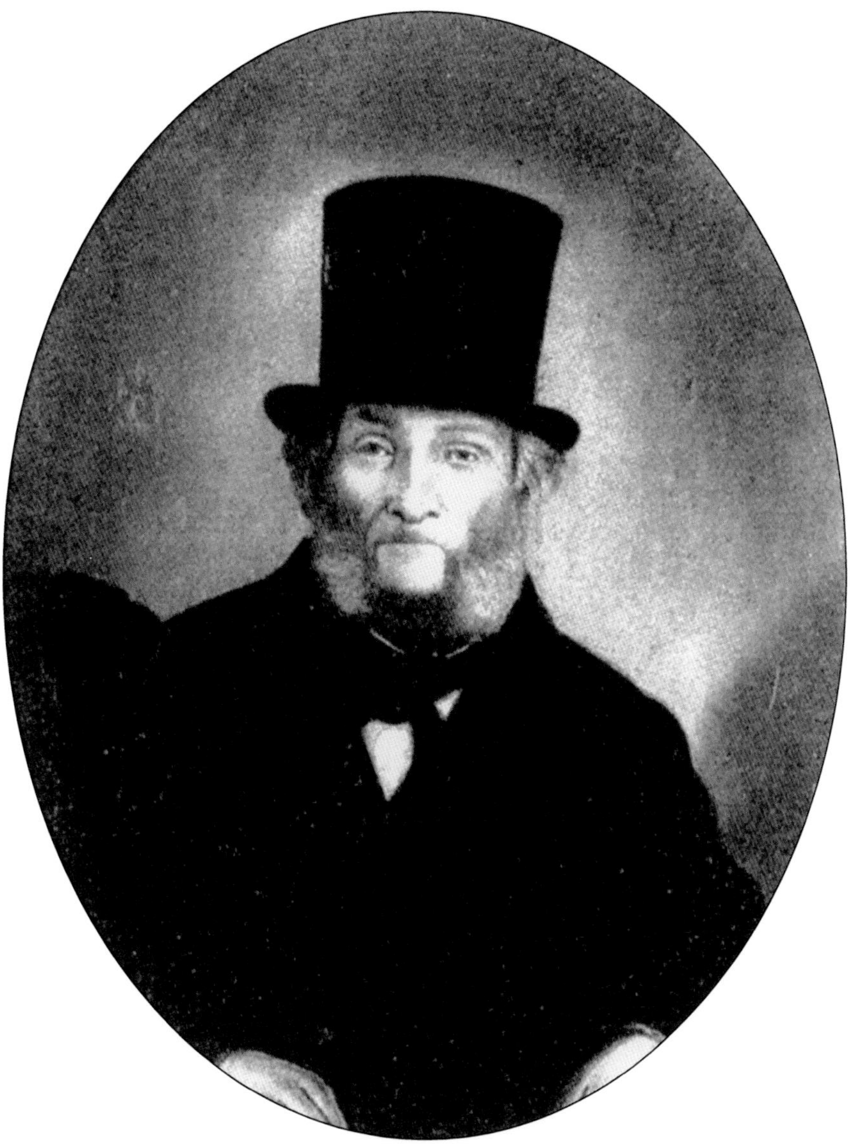

**JOSEPH WEIL (1777–1863).** Joseph Weil was the patriarch of the Weil family. Born in Bohemia in 1777, Joseph married Fannie Kauder in 1798. They had seven sons, two of whom died in infancy, while the rest migrated to the United States. Fannie died while still a young woman, and Joseph was shortly remarried to a woman from the same village, Sarah Stein. Joseph and Sarah emigrated to the United States in 1850 at the request of his sons, bringing with them a *Sefer Torah* Joseph purchased in Prague. The Weil home served as the first site for religious services, with Leopold, the oldest son, serving both as *hazzan* as well as the local *shohet,* "kosher butcher." Joseph was said to have been a "well preserved man," tall and spry even into his 80s. Apparently injured as the result of an accident, Joseph died in 1863. Sarah died shortly afterward. Each is buried in the Forest Hill Cemetery in Ann Arbor. (JHSM.)

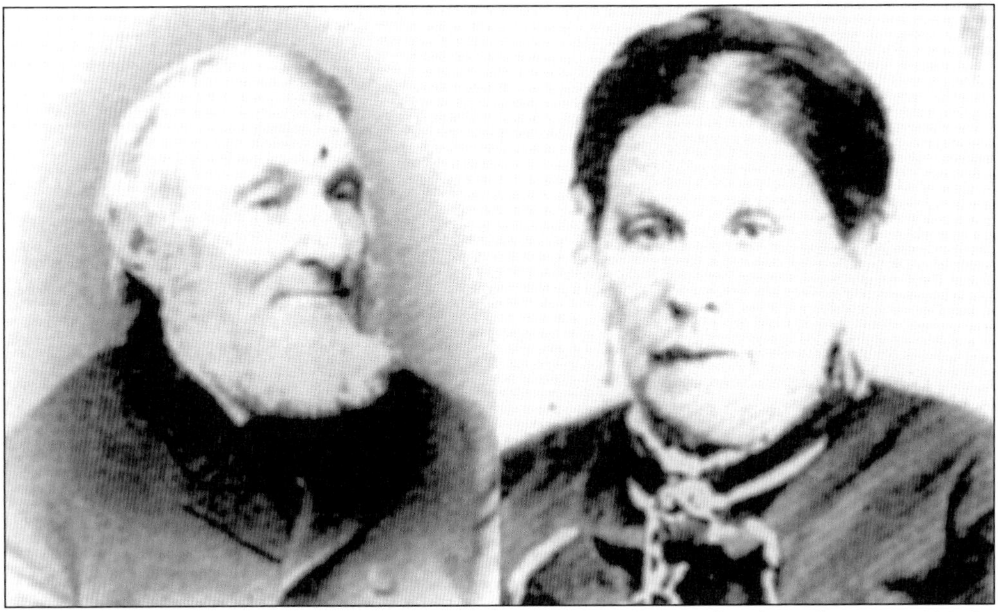

**LEOPOLD AND RACHEL WEIL.** Leopold was the oldest of the five brothers, born in 1820. In approximately 1841, he married Rachel/Rosa Sittig, an 18-year-old woman from Bohemia. They had two children, Edward and Aaron (Hiram), who came to Ann Arbor with them, five additional children were born later. Leopold served both as hazzan and shohet. The family moved to Chicago during the 1870s. Leopold died in 1894. (JHSM.)

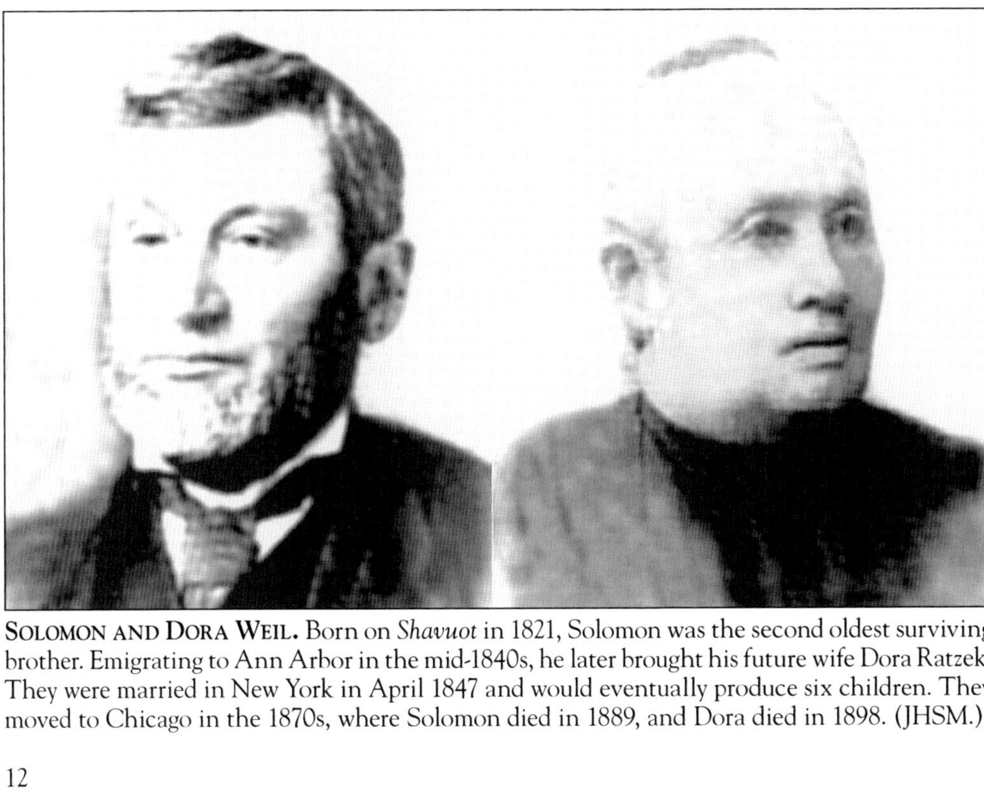

**SOLOMON AND DORA WEIL.** Born on *Shavuot* in 1821, Solomon was the second oldest surviving brother. Emigrating to Ann Arbor in the mid-1840s, he later brought his future wife Dora Ratzek. They were married in New York in April 1847 and would eventually produce six children. They moved to Chicago in the 1870s, where Solomon died in 1889, and Dora died in 1898. (JHSM.)

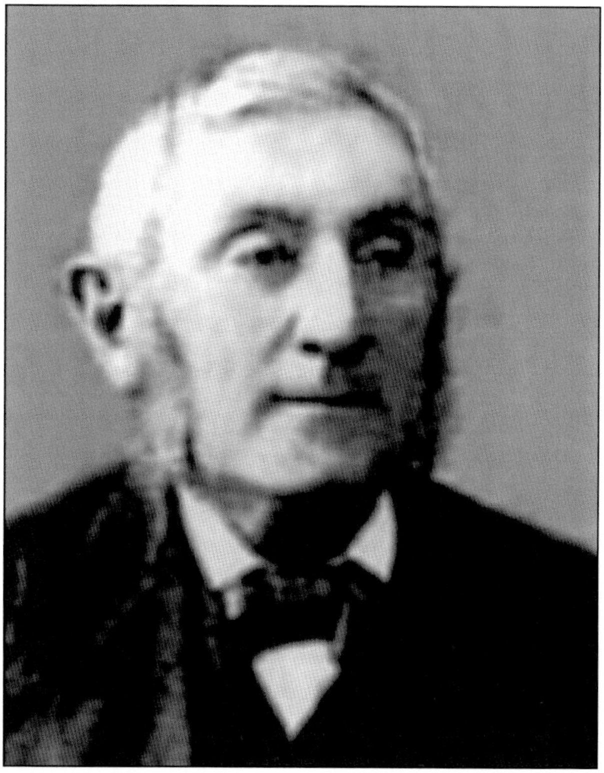

**Moses and Theresa Weil.** Moses, the third son, was born in 1824. At 19, he married Reila/Rosa Gans, a woman from Lintz, Austria. After living in Pontiac for a time, they moved to Ann Arbor with the rest of the family in 1857. On May 22, 1858, Reila died at the age of 24. In 1859, Moses was married a second time to Theresa Lederer, a woman he may have met during a business trip to Chicago. The Lederer family is known to have lived in Chicago, and her parents, Jacob and Josephine, were also from Bohemia. Sometime during the 1860s, Moses and Theresa moved to Chicago with their family, possibly rejoining Theresa's relatives, and where Moses maintained a number of businesses. He was apparently injured in the Chicago Fire of 1871 and remained in poor health until his death in 1880. (JHSM.)

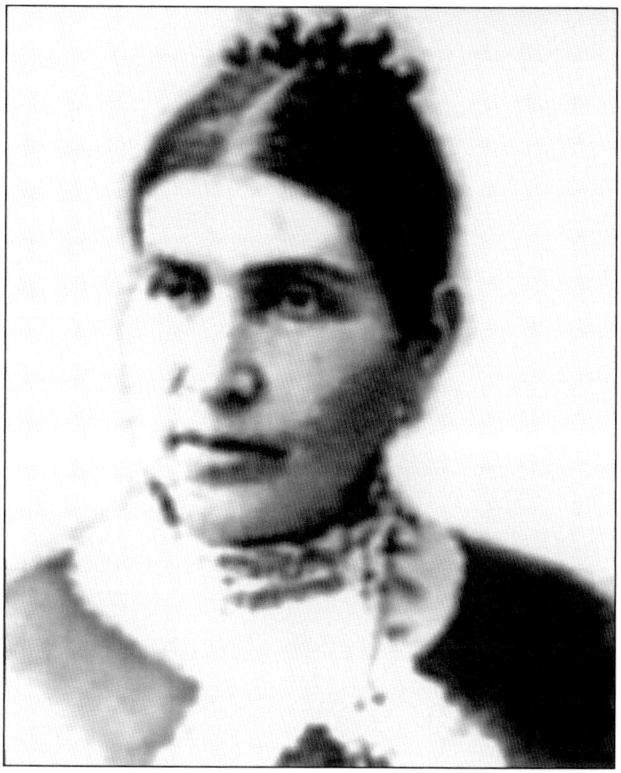

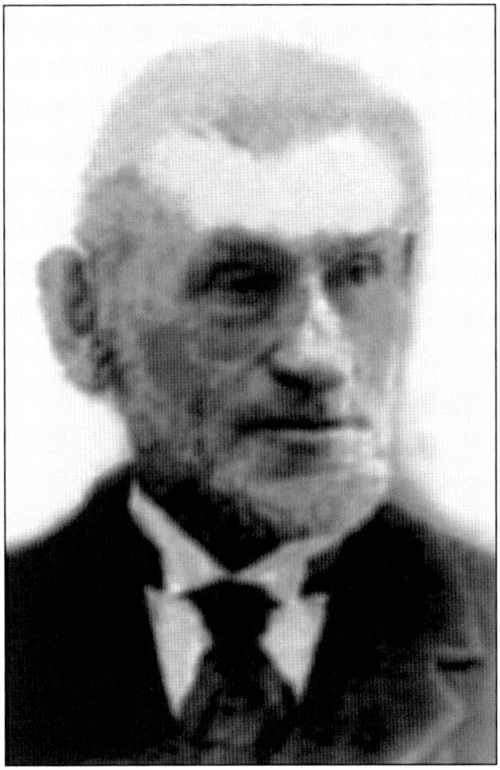

**JACOB AND DEBORAH WEIL.** Jacob Weil, the fourth son, was born in 1827. Jacob was the most educated of the brothers and had the reputation of being an outstanding speaker. Following bar mitzvah, he traveled to Prague for study in joining the rabbinate. In subsequent years, he spent time learning Talmud, before moving to Epirius and enrolling in the University of Hungary, where he graduated with honors. Jacob came to the United States, where he joined his brothers Marcus and Moses in Pontiac. There he worked as a bookkeeper and translator of French. The brothers moved together to Ann Arbor, forming the business of Weil and Brothers. In 1859, Jacob married Deborah Fantle. Since he was well educated, he may have been offered a position at the university for the teaching of languages, which he refused. Certainly Jacob's Judaism appeared to present no problems, since in 1859, he was elected alderman and was nominated for mayor. In the early 1860s, Jacob and Deborah moved to Newark, where he opened a branch of the family business. Jacob died in 1912. (JHSM.)

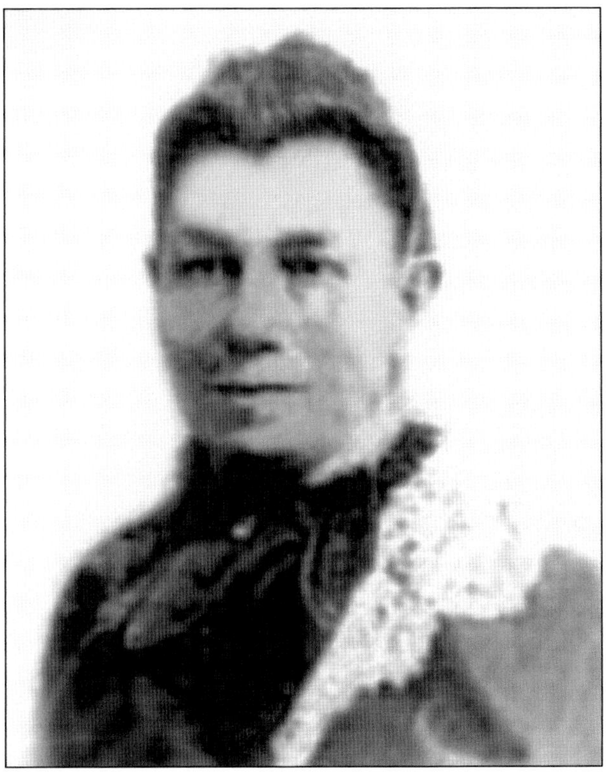

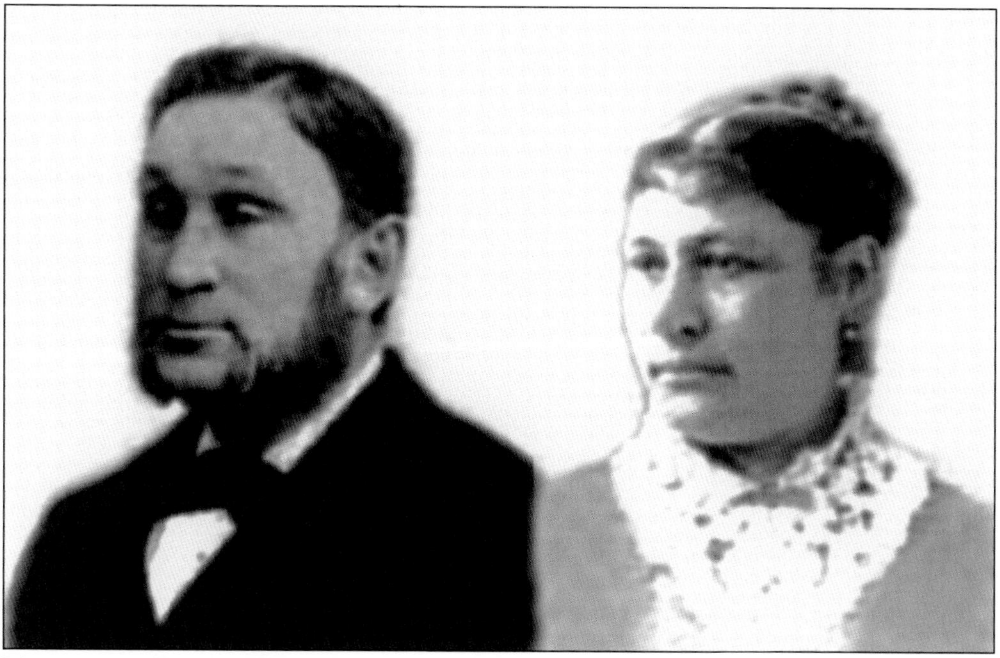

**Marcus and Bertha Weil.** Marcus, the youngest brother (born in 1829), was the last to marry. Probably introduced to Bertha Lederer by her sister Theresa, they were married in December 1860. As was the case with most of the brothers, Marcus moved to Chicago during the 1860s, where he spent the remainder of his life. (JHSM.)

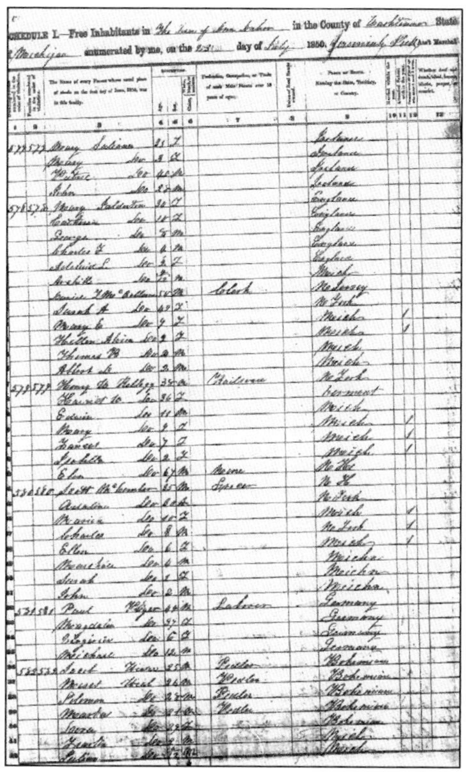

**1850 Census Record for the Weil Family.** Four of the brothers, Jacob (25), Moses (26), Solomon (28) and his wife Dora (29), and Marcus (21), are all living in the same household, along with two of the children. Each of the men's occupations is listed as that of a peddler. After peddling dry goods throughout much of southern Michigan, the Weil brothers established their business, first in Pontiac, then in Ann Arbor around 1849.

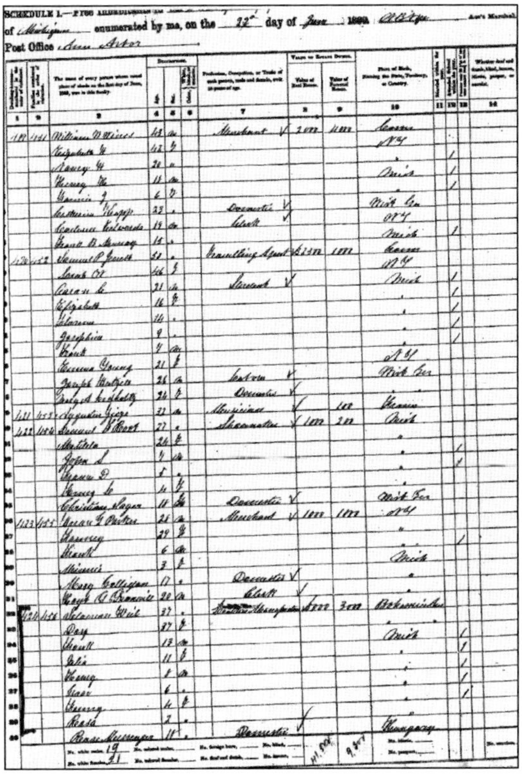

**CENSUS RECORD FROM 1860.** The census record lists Solomon Weil, his wife Dory, and their six children: Frank, Julia, Henry, Isaac, Fanny, and Reosa/Rosa. The family was wealthy enough to include an 18-year-old domestic, Reose Weisinger from Hungary. Solomon had been the first to emigrate to America, selling dry goods as did his brothers later. He settled in Ann Arbor around 1845.

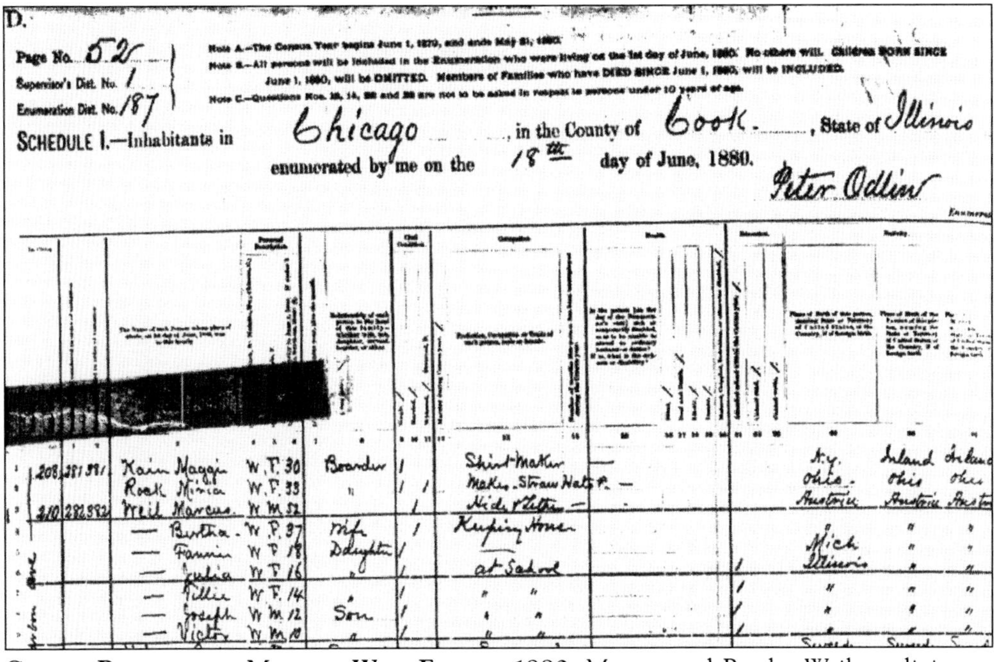

**CENSUS RECORD FOR MARCUS WEIL FAMILY, 1880.** Marcus and Bertha Weil are living at 210 Dearborn Street in Chicago with their children: Fannie, Julia, Tillie, Joseph, and Victor. Marcus's brother Moses had been the first to move to Chicago, and Marcus joined him around 1862. Marcus's profession continued to be that of a hide cutter.

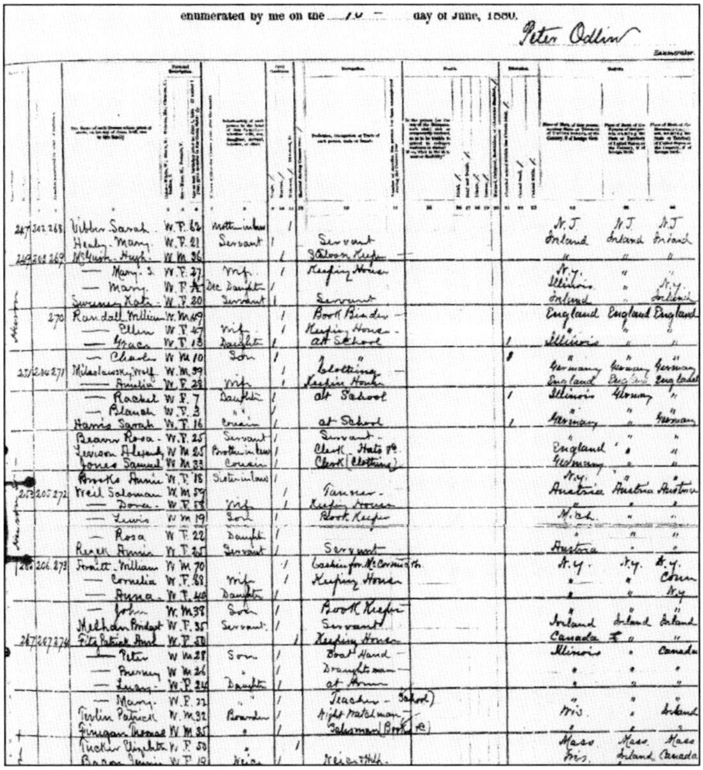
enumerated by me on the [illegible] day of June, 1880.

Peter Odlin

**CENSUS RECORD FOR SOLOMON WEIL FAMILY, 1880.** Solomon and Dora Weil and their children Lewis and Reosa/Rosa are listed as living at 253 Huron Street in Chicago. Solomon remained a tanner throughout his professional life. After living in Ann Arbor for 23 years, they moved to Chicago in 1870. Several of the Weil brothers, including Moses and Marcus, had previously moved to that city.

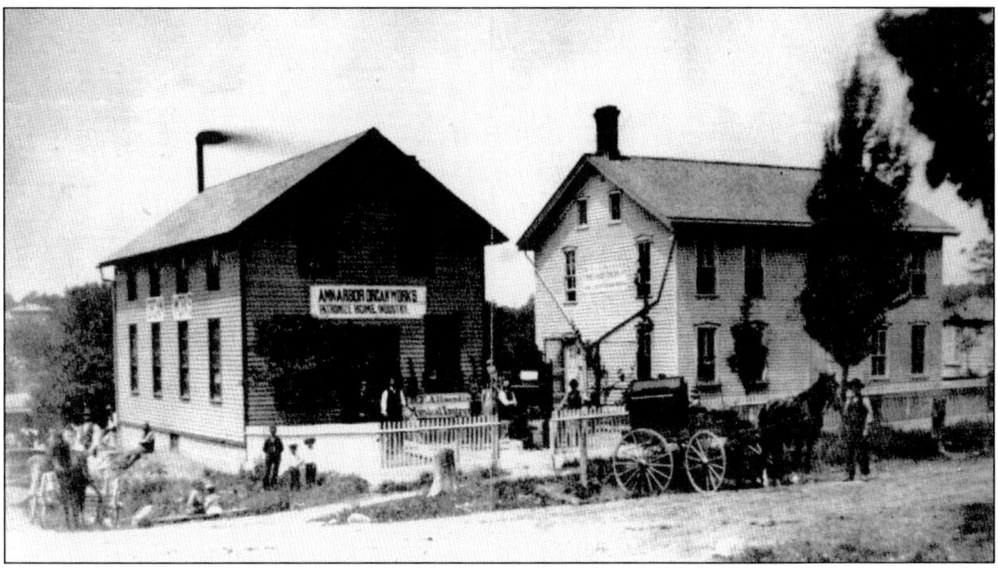


**ALLMENDINGER ORGAN WORKS, AROUND 1884.** The house on the right was originally that of the Weil family, located on First Street between Liberty and Washington Streets. The house was later purchased by the Allmendinger family and, with purchase of the factory on the left, it became part of the Ann Arbor Organ Works. The Weil households, located at various times along Washington and Huron Streets, were the sites at which religious services were held. This house near First and Washington Streets (300 West Washington Street) would arguably represent Ann Arbor's first synagogue. (BHL.)

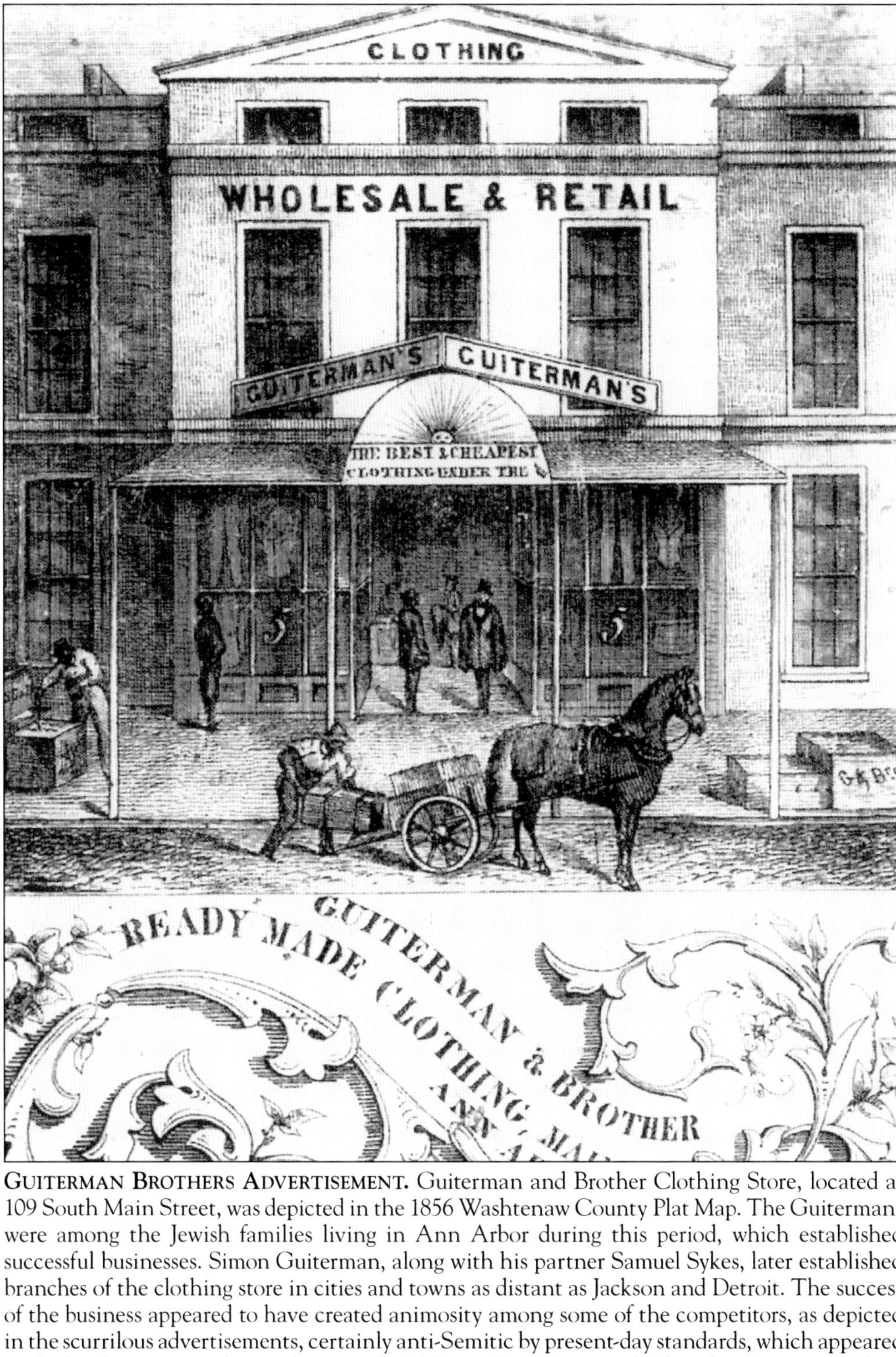


**GUITERMAN BROTHERS ADVERTISEMENT.** Guiterman and Brother Clothing Store, located at 109 South Main Street, was depicted in the 1856 Washtenaw County Plat Map. The Guitermans were among the Jewish families living in Ann Arbor during this period, which established successful businesses. Simon Guiterman, along with his partner Samuel Sykes, later established branches of the clothing store in cities and towns as distant as Jackson and Detroit. The success of the business appeared to have created animosity among some of the competitors, as depicted in the scurrilous advertisements, certainly anti-Semitic by present-day standards, which appeared in the local newspaper during this period. A Martin Guiterman is also listed in census records as living in Ann Arbor, although any relationship would only be speculative. (BHL.)

**MICHIGAN ARGUS ADVERTISEMENT.** During a period of several months in 1851 and 1852, advertisements were placed in the *Michigan Argus* warning customers not to shop at Jewish-owned businesses. Such advertisements were primarily directed at businesses owned by Samuel Sykes and the Guiterman brothers. While not typical, the advertisements depict the anti-Semitism found in portions of the population.

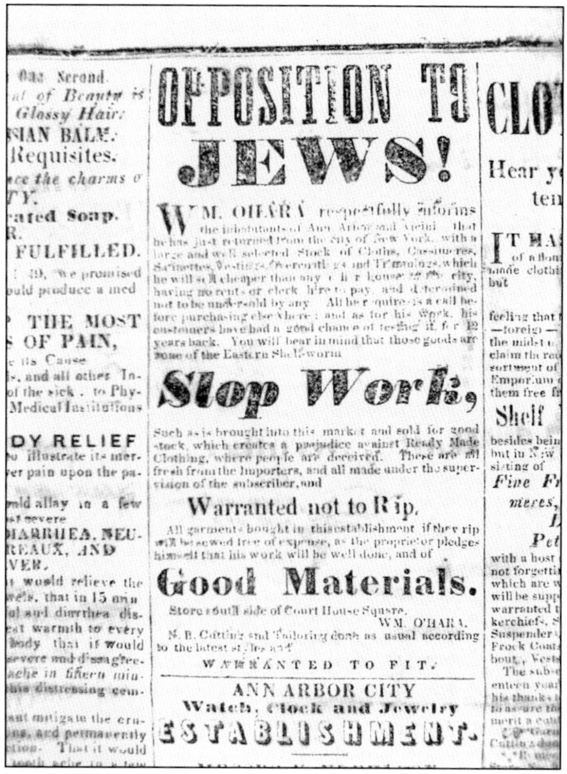

OPPOSITION TO JEWS!

WM. OHARA respectfully informs the inhabitants of Ann Arbor and vicinity that he has just returned from the city of New York, with a large and well selected Stock of Cloths, Cassimeres, Satinettes, Vestings, Overcoatings and Trimmings, which he will sell cheaper than any other house in the city, having no rents or clerk hire to pay, and determined not to be undersold by any. All he requires is a call before purchasing elsewhere; and as for his work, his customers have had a good chance of testing it, for 12 years back. You will bear in mind that those goods are none of the Eastern Shelf-worm

Slop Work,

Such as is brought into this market and sold for good stock, which creates a prejudice against Ready Made Clothing, where people are deceived. These are all fresh from the Importers, and all made under the supervision of the subscriber, and

Warranted not to Rip,

All garments bought in this establishment if they rip will be sewed free of expense, as the proprietor pledges himself that his work will be well done, and of

Good Materials.

Store south side of Court House Square.

WM. O'HARA.

N. B. Cutting and Tailoring done as usual according to the latest styles and

WARRANTED TO FIT.

ANN ARBOR CITY
Watch, Clock and Jewelry
ESTABLISHMENT.

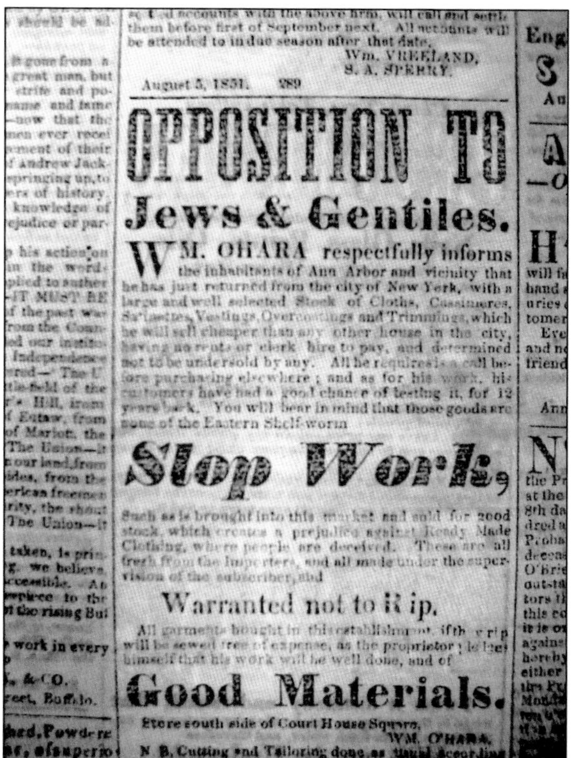

...all accounts with the above firm, will call and settle them before first of September next. All accounts will be attended to in due season after that date.

Wm. VREELAND,
S. A. SPERRY.

August 5, 1851. 289

OPPOSITION TO Jews & Gentiles.

WM. OHARA respectfully informs the inhabitants of Ann Arbor and vicinity that he has just returned from the city of New York, with a large and well selected Stock of Cloths, Cassimeres, Satinettes, Vestings, Overcoatings and Trimmings, which he will sell cheaper than any other house in the city, having no rents or clerk hire to pay, and determined not to be undersold by any. All he requires is a call before purchasing elsewhere; and as for his work, his customers have had a good chance of testing it, for 12 years back. You will bear in mind that those goods are none of the Eastern Shelf-worm

Slop Work,

Such as is brought into this market and sold for good stock, which creates a prejudice against Ready Made Clothing, where people are deceived. These are all fresh from the Importers, and all made under the supervision of the subscriber, and

Warranted not to Rip.

All garments bought in this establishment if they rip will be sewed free of expense, as the proprietor pledges himself that his work will be well done, and of

Good Materials.

Store south side of Court House Square.

WM. O'HARA.

N. B. Cutting and Tailoring done as usual according to the latest styles and

**ADVERTISEMENT IN MICHIGAN ARGUS.** Advertisements were not necessarily directed solely against Jewish merchants, as in this particular example, which ran over several months in the 1852 issues of the *Michigan Argus*. That resentment did not exist among much of the population is attested by the general acceptance of Jewish citizens, as well as the election of Jacob Weil to alderman by the Ann Arbor citizenry.

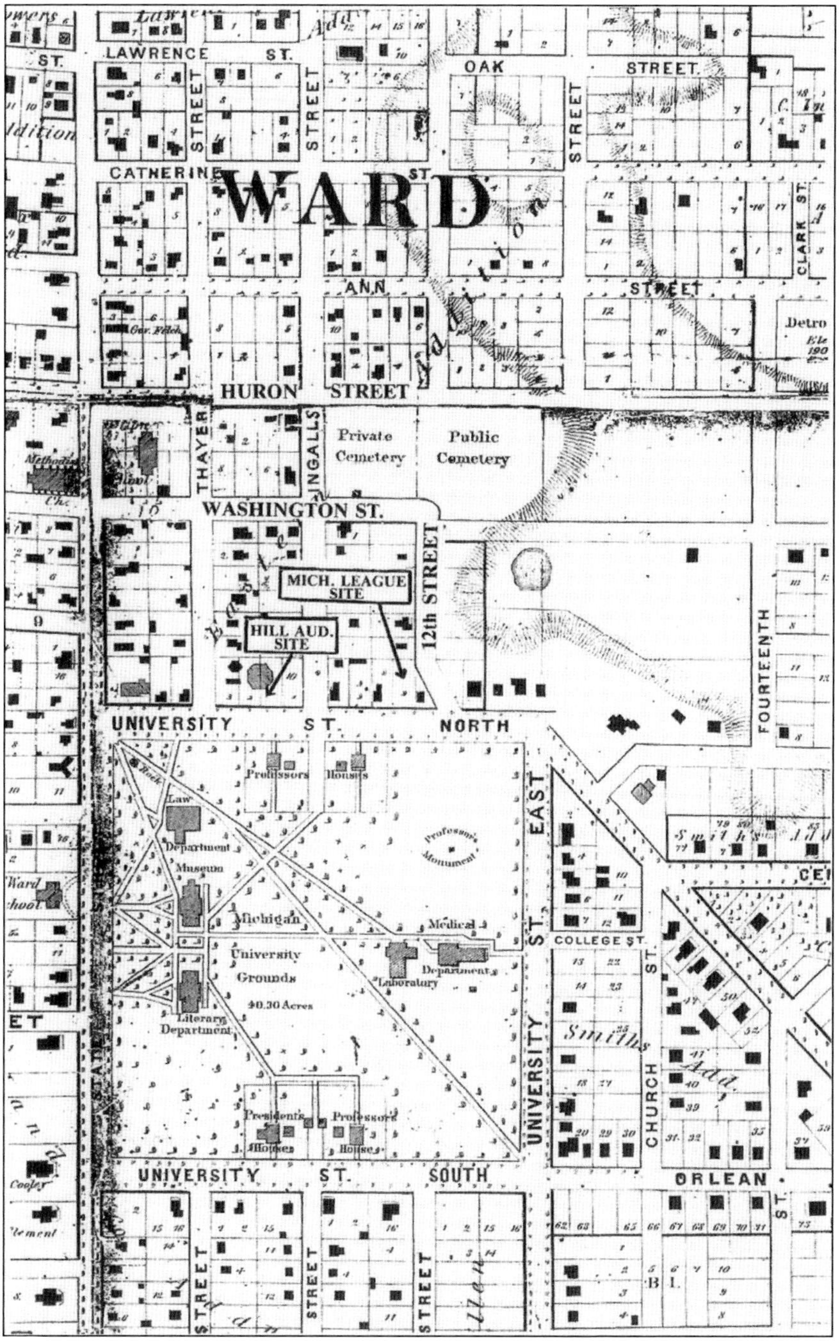


**Map of Ann Arbor, 1870.** The "Private Cemetery" indicates the site of the Jewish cemetery. Fletcher Street now divides what had been two cemeteries on the same plot of land. The Power Center for Performing Arts is now located on the site of the Public Cemetery, Horace H. Rackham Building is currently located on the west side of the Private Cemetery. Confusion later existed as to whether the Jewish cemetery was actually owned by the Weil family or was open to the Jewish community. When a Jewish cemetery in Detroit was honored as the "first" of its kind in Michigan, it was the result of this confusion. (JHSM.)

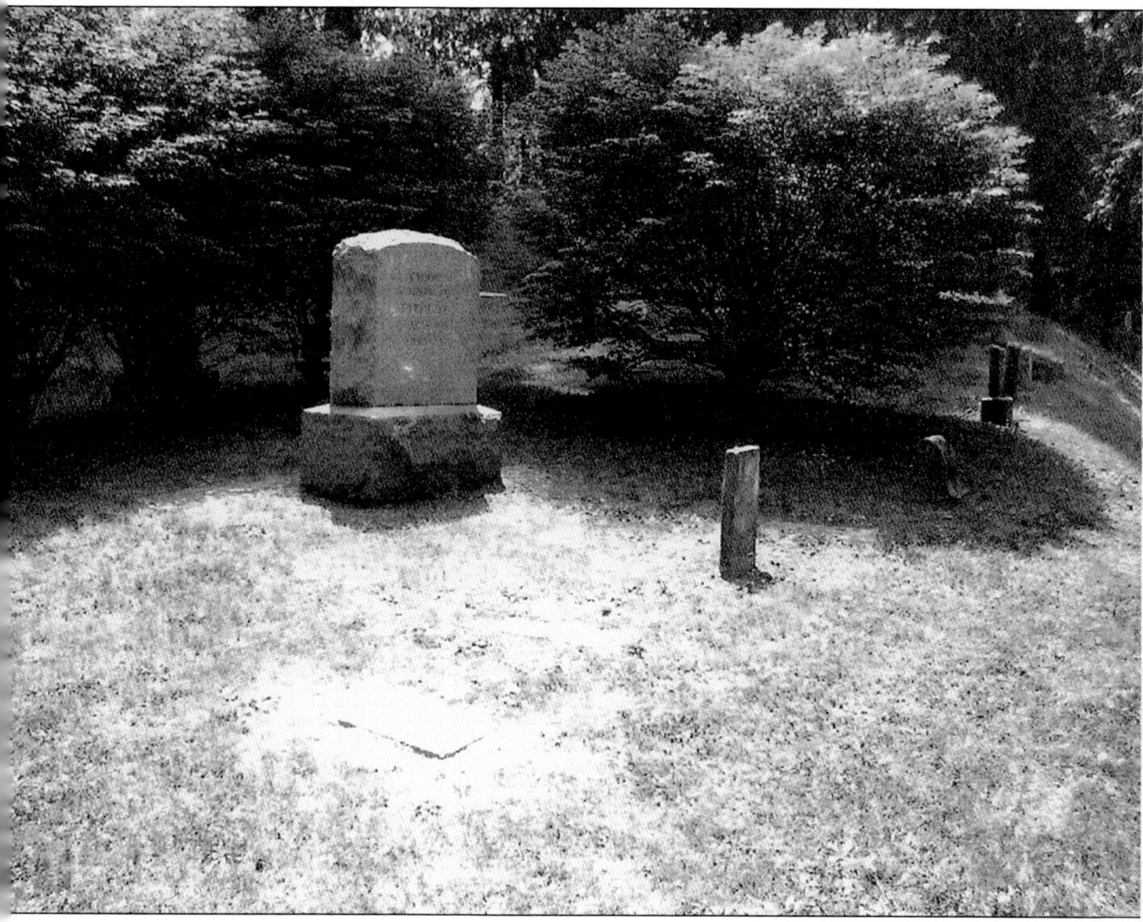

**WEIL PLOT, FOREST HILL CEMETERY, ANN ARBOR.** During the 1880s, the city of Ann Arbor claimed the land that had been the site of the Jewish and Public cemeteries for recreational facilities, necessitating eventual movement of the graves. The contract signed in May 1900 authorizing the reinterment of the bodies from the Rackham site indicated 10 lots had been purchased, only six burials were recorded. The cost of the transaction was $1. The large gravestone lists six Weil family members: Joseph (deceased 1863), his wives Fannie (buried in Europe) and Sarah (deceased 1868), and Leopold and Rachel's children: Edward (deceased 1853) and Frances (deceased 1853). Other headstones at the site include those for Jacob's son Samuel (deceased 1881), Minnie Weidenfeld (deceased 1861), and Max Guiterman (deceased 1857), members of local Jewish families. The question of why only six reinterments took place in the 10 lots has not been answered. (Authors.)

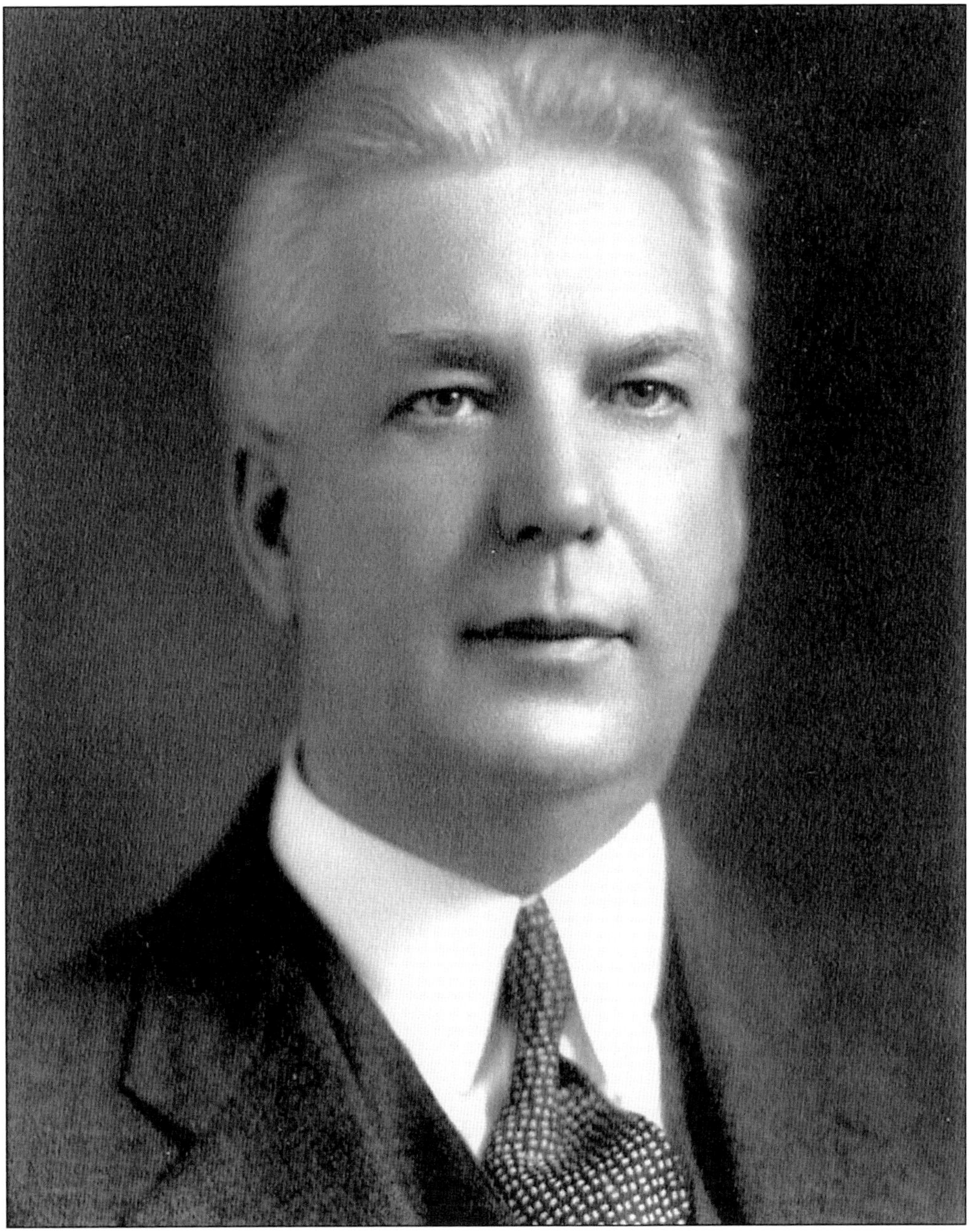

**Max Winkler.** The presence of Jewish faculty at most American universities was uncommon in the 19th century, and the University of Michigan was certainly no exception. However, during the last decades of the century, at least three Jewish scholars joined the faculty; each would play a significant role in the development of the institution in the new century. Max Winkler (1866–1930) was the first. Winkler was initially hired as an instructor in German in 1890, while still working on the doctorate he received two years later. In 1895, he was appointed assistant professor of German and promoted to full professor in 1902 as well as department chair, a position he held until his death. His former home at 1520 Cambridge Road still stands and is listed in the Washtenaw-Hill historic district. (BHL.)

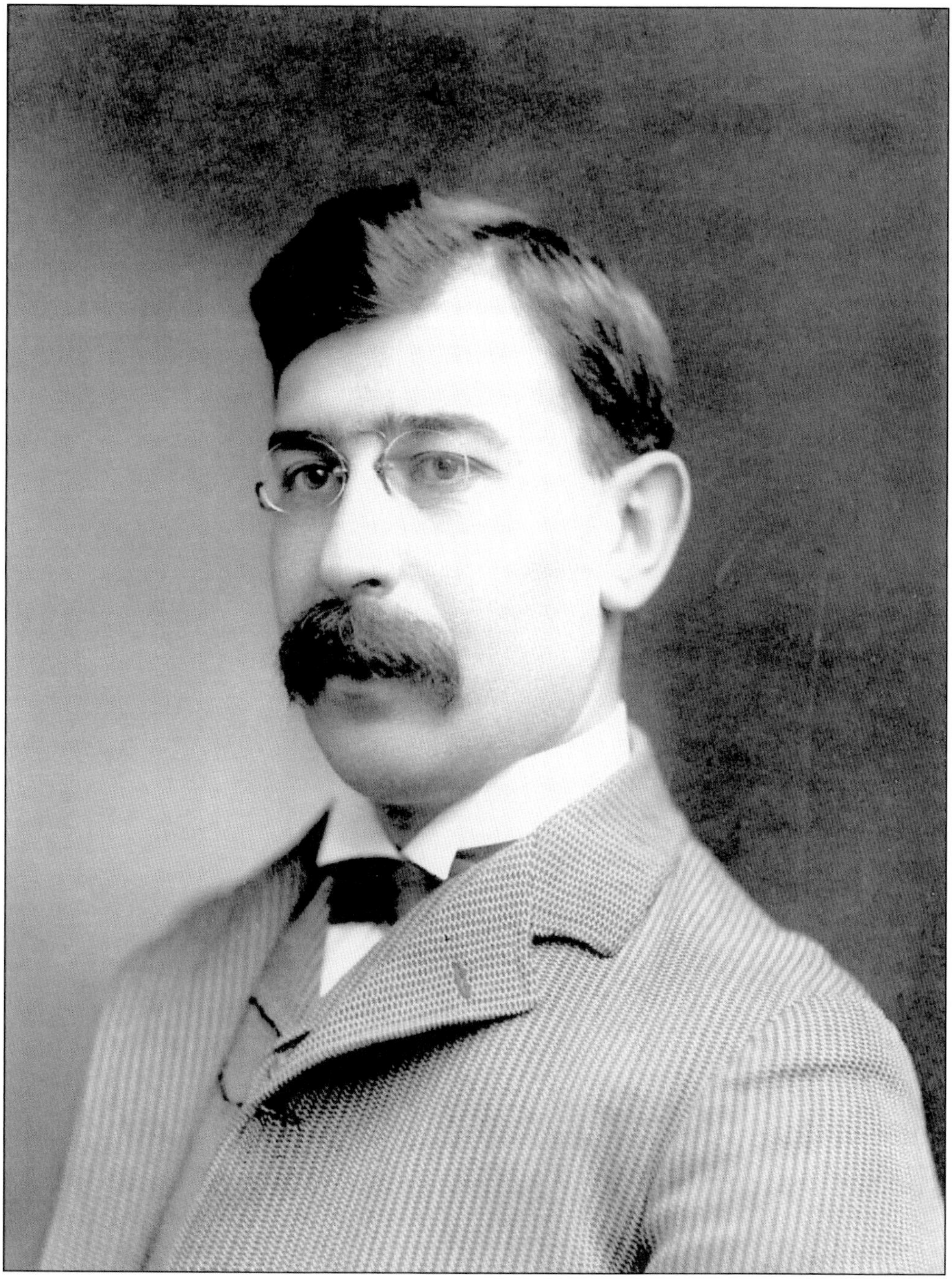

**MORITZ LEVI (1857–1942).** Moritz Levi joined the university faculty in 1890 as an instructor in French. By the time he retired in 1923, Levi had earned the title of professor emeritus of French. In addition to authoring several books, Levi had a connection with students that earned him significant admiration. As one of the first Jewish professors at the university, his reception was not always easy. To quote Martha McKay, one of his first students, "I was in Moritz Levi's class the first day he ever met a class at Michigan, and saw him triumph by sheer strength of will over a bunch who thought they would drive out the strange young Jew." (BHL.)

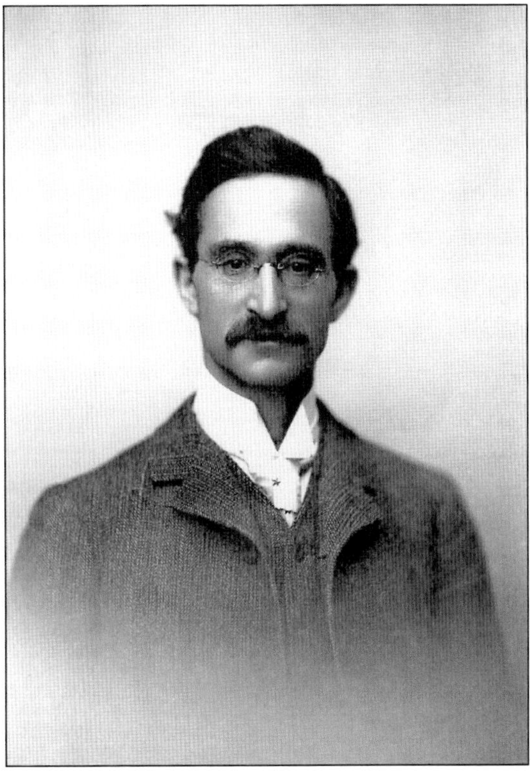

**MOSES GOMBERG (1866–1947).** Gomberg was born in Elizabetgrad, Russia, and graduated from the University of Michigan in 1890 with a degree in chemistry. He earned his doctorate from the university in 1894. After a brief sojourn in Germany, Gomberg returned to Ann Arbor, where he spent the rest of his career. In 1904, Gomberg reached the rank of full professor. While his research encompassed a wide area of organic chemistry, he was most noted for his work on free radicals, laying the groundwork in linking these molecules to cell damage and aging. (BHL.)

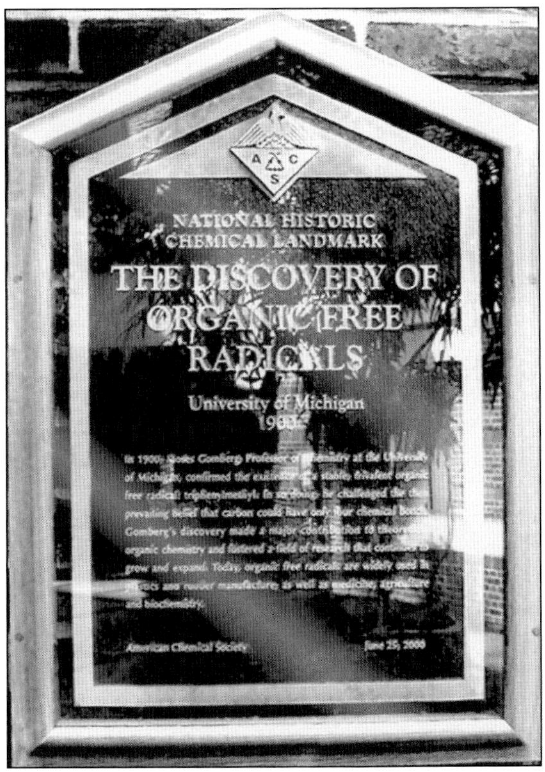


**CENTENNIAL COMMEMORATION PLAQUE.** To commemorate the centennial of Professor Gomberg's discovery of triphenylmethyl, the first demonstration that such free radical chemicals exist in nature, a symposium was held at the university in June 2000. At that time, a plaque that acknowledged Gomberg's work was presented. The plaque hangs in the lobby of the Chemistry Building, near the campus Diag. (Authors.)

# *Two*

# Osias Zwerdling and the Formation of Beth Israel Congregation

For over a half century, Osias Zwerdling was synonymous with Beth Israel Congregation. One could argue that without Zwerdling's drive and influence, there would have been no Beth Israel; certainly, it would have been significantly different without him.

In the decades following the loss of the Weils, the Jewish community of Ann Arbor was effectively dormant. With the absence of any members, the synagogue on Washington Street reverted to other uses. There were a few Jewish faculty, none of whom appeared to be particularly observant, and even the occasional Jewish student. The first all Jewish sorority on campus, Alpha Epsilon Phi, was not established until 1921, while the first Jewish fraternity on campus, Sigma Alpha Mu, was only established in 1923. For celebrations or commemorations of life cycle events, or even for attending services during High Holy Days, it was often necessary to travel to Detroit.

In 1902, the arrival in Ann Arbor of Osias Zwerdling and Philip Lansky marked the true beginnings of what would be a lasting community. Working as a peddler while driving a horse and wagon, Lansky was able to save enough money to found his own scrap metal and junk business. Zwerdling arrived in Ann Arbor about the same time. Lansky and Zwerdling became the primary individuals around whom the congregation developed. Other Jewish families eventually arrived, including Abraham and Jenny Levy, who established a shoe making business.

Life cycle events were routinely held in the homes of local Jewish families during this first decade. In 1907, for example, *Yahrzeit* "memorial" services as well as other events were carried out in the Lansky home. Formal organization of the congregation would take place in 1916, in part the result of fortuitous events. Rabbi Joseph Slomon and his son, both from Jerusalem, were in the United States to solicit funds for Jewish institutions. While traveling to Detroit on the interurban railway, he survived an accident that killed his son and forced the rabbi to be hospitalized in Ann Arbor. Unable to speak English, Rabbi Slomon had difficulty communicating. Osias Zwerdling was asked to serve as a go-between for University Hospital and the local rabbi as well as for hospital staff. Sufficiently recovered by the month of Elul to at least temporarily leave the hospital, Rabbi Slomon insisted against the physician's wishes that he be allowed to travel to Detroit for the High Holy Days. As a compromise, he was allowed to attend services in the Zwerdling home. Following the Yom Kippur fast, members of the community met to discuss the formal establishment of a Jewish congregation.

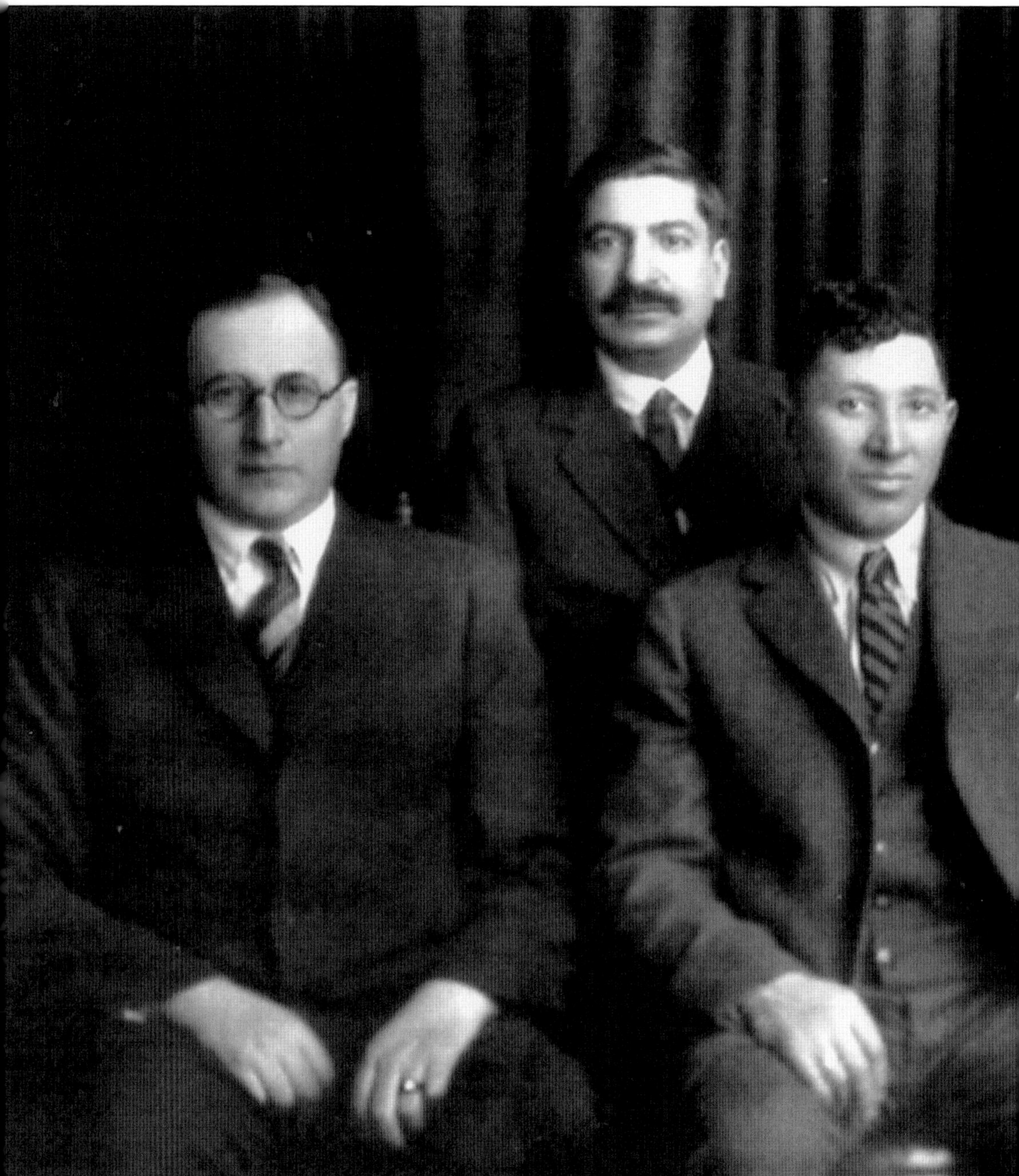

**FOUNDING MEMBERS OF BETH ISRAEL CONGREGATION, 1916.** Pictured from left to right are (first row) David Friedman, Philip Lansky, Osias Zwerdling, and William Bittker; (second row) David Mordsky and Israel Friedman. In 1918, Zwerdling was elected president. Israel Friedman became vice president, William Bittker was the first secretary/treasurer, and David Friedman, Phil Lansky, and David Mordsky were elected as trustees. Lansky and his wife Eva owned a successful scrap metal business on Beakes Street, later moving to North Main Street, where the

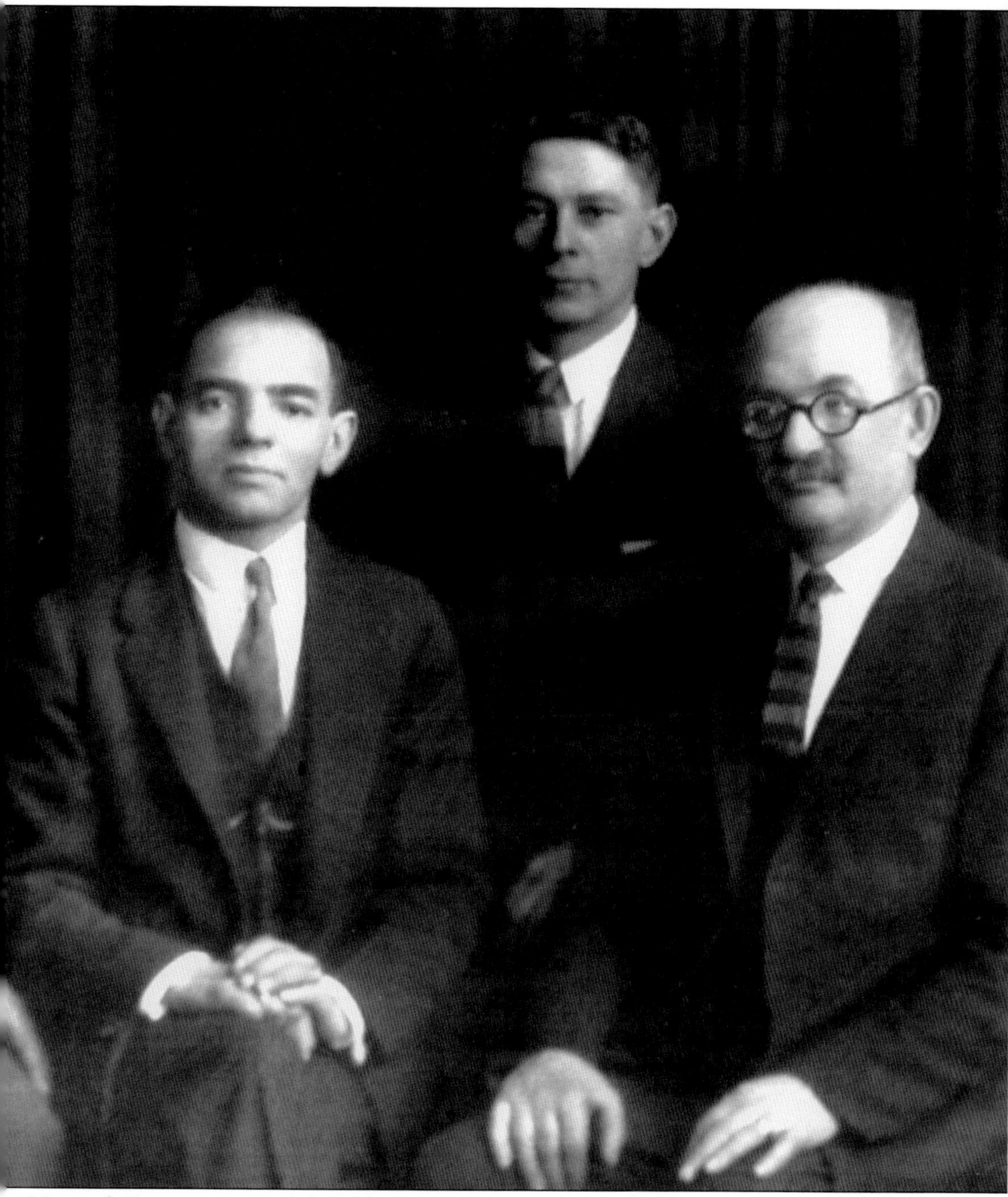

Nonprofit Enterprise at Work (NEW) Center is now located. In 1921, the Zwerdlings' son Morris became the congregation's first bar mitzvah. David Friedman and his wife Sadie ran a junk business on Canal Street near Broadway, living at 418 Main Street. Israel and Rose Friedman, living at 513 Division Street, had a junk business as well. David and Fannie Mordsky ran a tailor shop. William Bittker sold men's clothing. (BIC.)

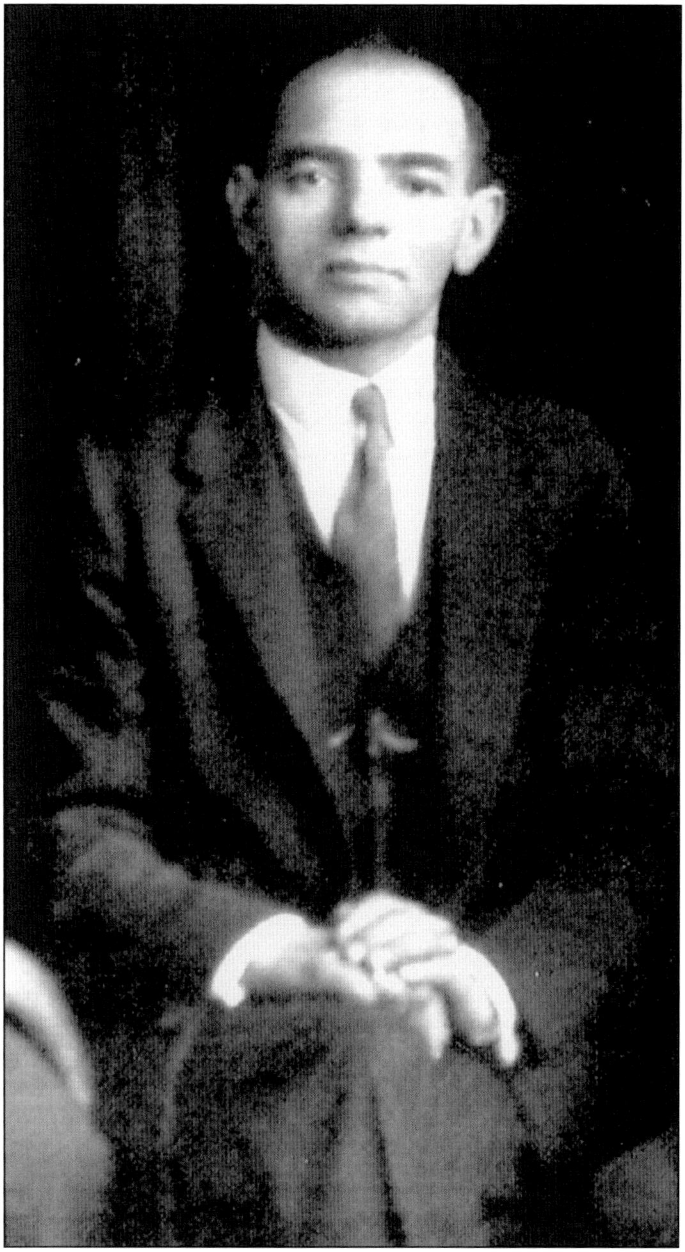

**OSIAS ZWERDLING (1878–1974).** In the period after the Weils had departed, the Ann Arbor area had no significant Jewish population, and for services or life cycle events it was necessary to travel to Detroit. Osias Zwerdling had arrived in Ann Arbor in 1902, about the same time as Phil Lansky. The first High Holy Day service held in Ann Arbor during the new century occurred in 1913, when Osias and Hannah Zwerdling, married in 1907, opened their home to the community. Although the congregation was not yet formally organized, 1913 can be marked as the year in which the seeds of Beth Israel were started. In subsequent years, High Holy Day services were held at various sites around the city. Ceil Pear, for example, later reminisced that the congregation also occasionally met at the Zwerdling home on Baldwin Street to conduct services. (BIC.)

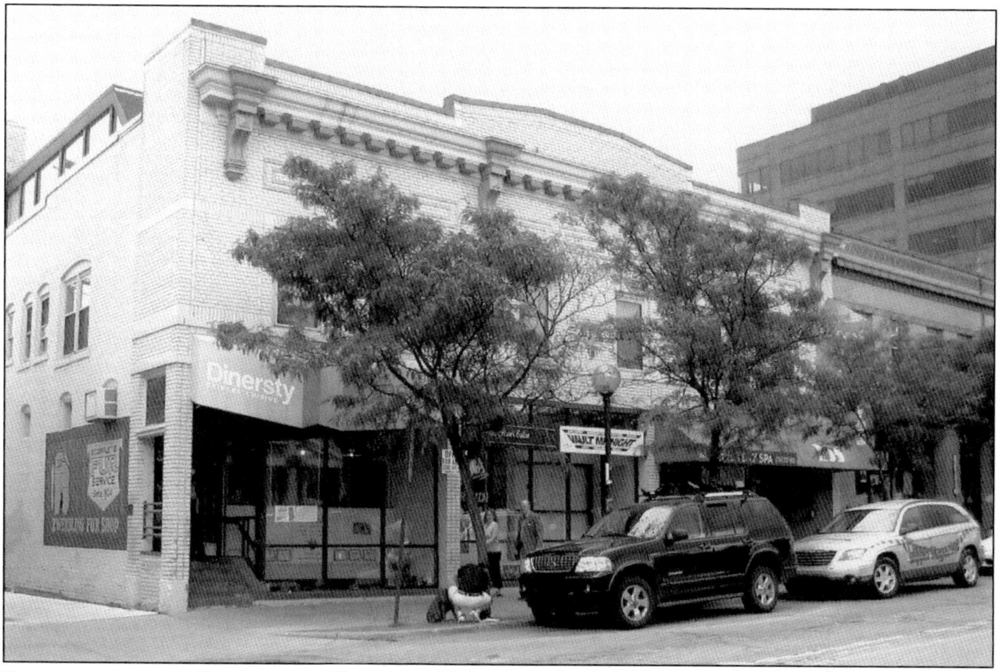

PORTION OF THE ZWERDLING-DARLING BLOCK, 241 EAST LIBERTY. The Zwerdling portion of the building was built in 1915 and served as both the Zwerdling business, after a move from 333 South Main Street, as well as the Zwerdling home, located on the upper floor. The business, furrier and tailor, would be successful for decades. (Authors.)

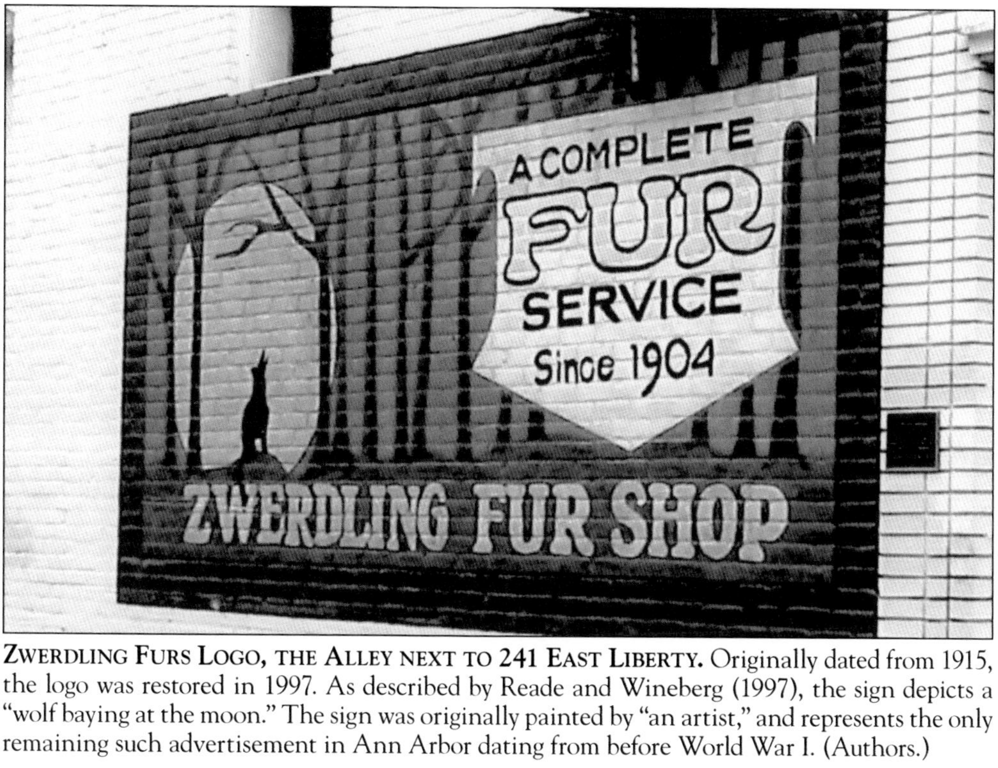


ZWERDLING FURS LOGO, THE ALLEY NEXT TO 241 EAST LIBERTY. Originally dated from 1915, the logo was restored in 1997. As described by Reade and Wineberg (1997), the sign depicts a "wolf baying at the moon." The sign was originally painted by "an artist," and represents the only remaining such advertisement in Ann Arbor dating from before World War I. (Authors.)

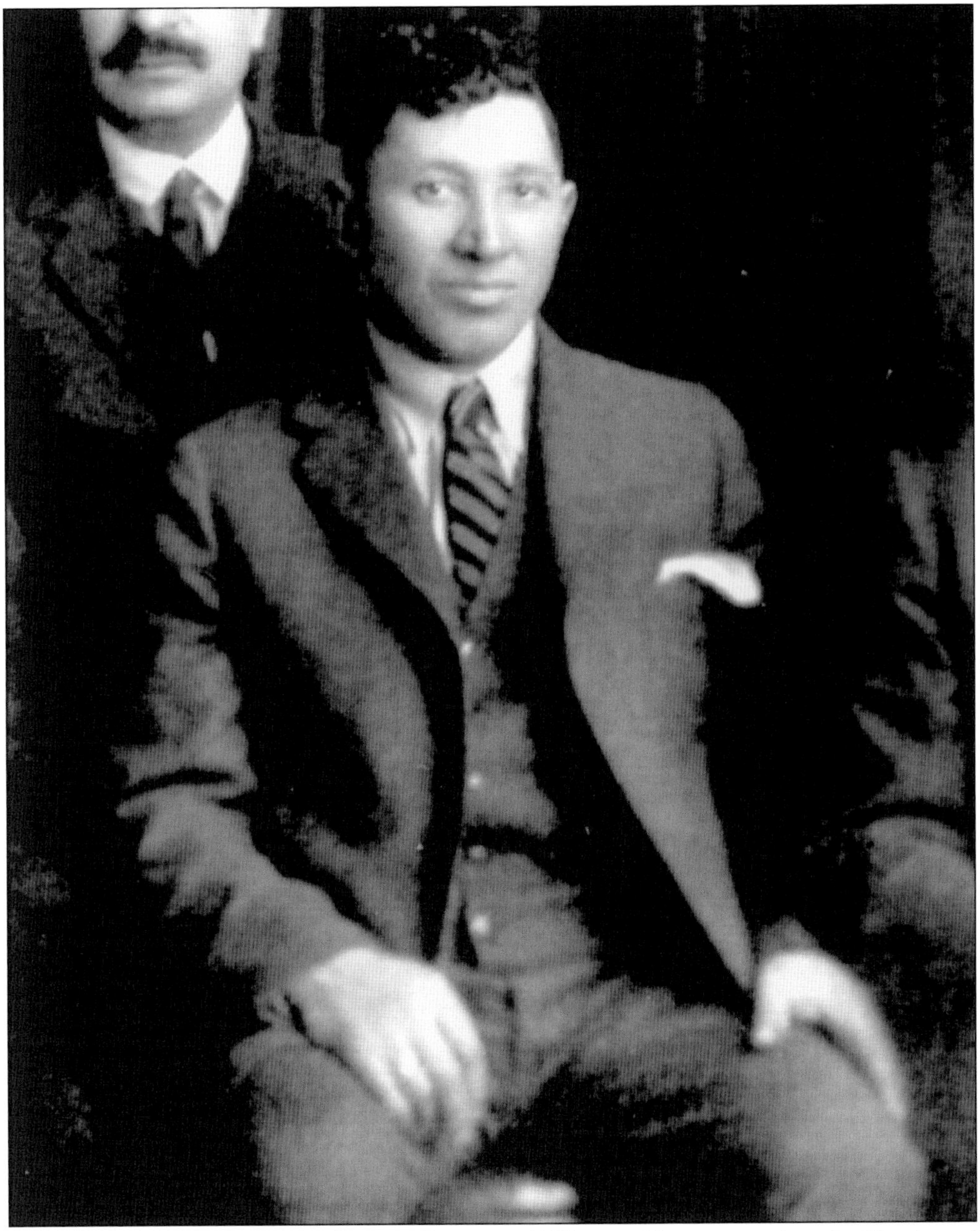

**Philip Lansky.** Philip Lansky, born in Russia in 1887, joined his aunt and uncle, Hattie and William Lansky, who owned a grocery store at 24 Broadway at the time. William Lansky had come to North America in 1882, first through Canada and then Ohio. The family eventually settled in Ann Arbor in 1895 because they had heard "it was a wonderful place to live" and because they felt it was important to develop a Jewish community in the area. Living at first on Maiden Lane, William and Hattie later moved to a house at 334 Beakes Street, where they established a scrap metal business, dealing in "rags, rubber and all kinds of metals" (328–348 Beakes Street). Memorial services were initially held at the William Lansky home prior to Philip's arrival. Other than a synagogue on Washington Street in the 1880s, no formal Jewish presence was known until the arrival of Phil Lansky and Osias Zwerdling. (BIC.)

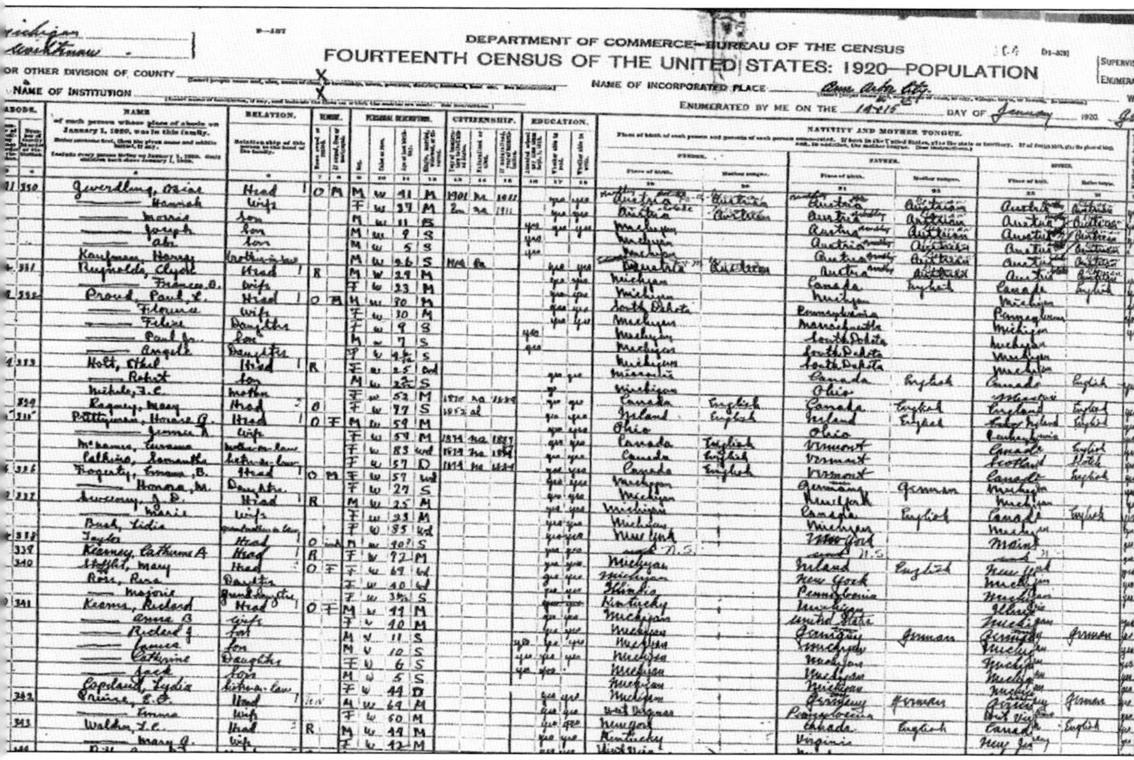
DEPARTMENT OF COMMERCE—BUREAU OF THE CENSUS

FOURTEENTH CENSUS OF THE UNITED STATES: 1920—POPULATION

NAME OF INCORPORATED PLACE Ann Arbor City

ENUMERATED BY ME ON THE 14 & 15 DAY OF January 1920.

**CENSUS RECORD, 1920.** According to these and earlier records, the Zwerdling family: Osias; Hannah; their three children, Morris, Joseph, and Abraham; as well as Hannah's brother, Harry Kaufman, then lived at 618 Lawrence Street. Osias arrived in the United States in 1901, Hannah some years later, both were naturalized in 1911. Morris Zwerdling became the first bar mitzvah in the Ann Arbor community. The Zwerdlings would later move to Baldwin Street, where occasionally services would still be held.

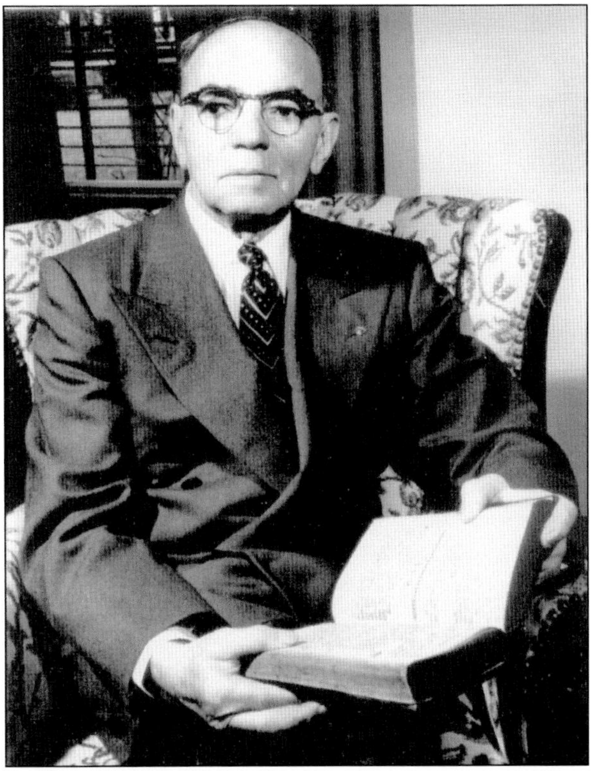

**OSIAS ZWERDLING.** A special commemoration was held for Osias Zwerdling on the occasion of his 75th birthday. Zwerdling would live for 96 years, his mind still active at the end. When Zwerdling died, the eulogy presented by Rabbi Allan D. Kensky described the man as "A prince of Israel . . . a patriarch of a family and community, a lover of humanity, a leader for all ages. We have lost a man of Biblical dimensions." (BIC.)

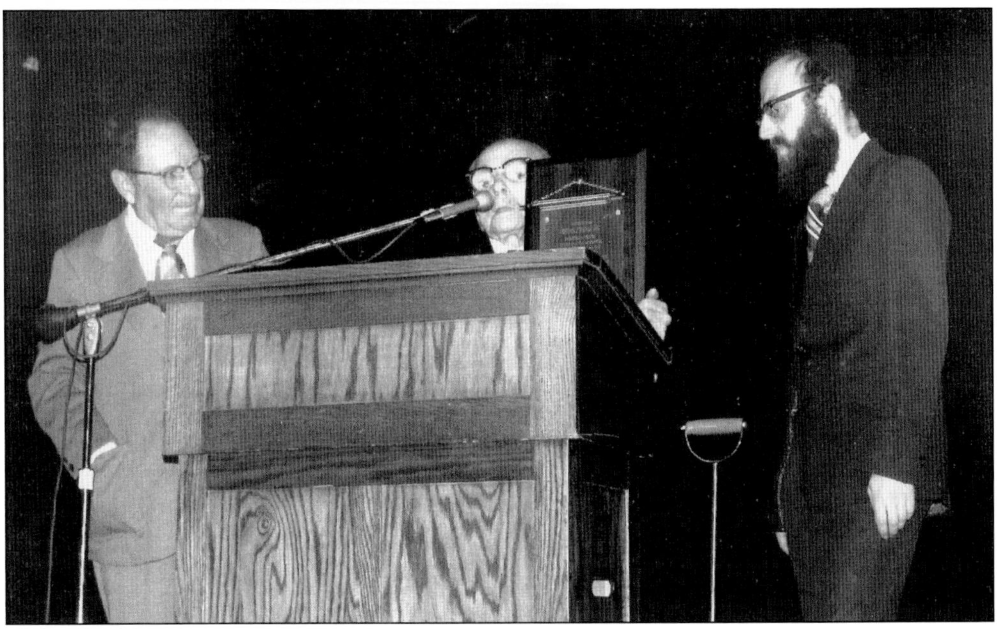

**NINETY-SIX-YEAR-OLD OSIAS ZWERDLING.** On the right is Rabbi Yitschak Meir Kagan, associate director of the Chabad-Lubavitch Foundation of Michigan. In 2001, at the age of 59, Rabbi Kagan was killed in an automobile accident while returning from a pilgrimage to the grave of Rabbi Menachem Schneerson, in New York. On the left is Dr. William Haber. The award was for Zwerdling's decades of service. (BIC.)

# *Three*

# Spiritual Guidance and a First Home

The first decades of the 20th century represented a period of unprecedented growth in immigration from Eastern European countries. A significant portion of these immigrants were Jewish, producing an entirely new demographic from the earlier Jewish immigrants who came primarily from central Europe. While most of these Jews settled in the larger cities in the east, many moved on, creating Jewish centers where none had previously existed. As noted by Lee Shai Weissbach, "of the 197 U.S. cities with communities of 1,000 or more Jews in 1927, 37 percent had no identifiable Jews" a generation earlier. Ann Arbor was barely a point on the same demographic map. In a population of some 19,500 persons, according to the 1920 census, approximately 300 were identifiably Jewish. Even these numbers dropped by half during the 1920s; it would not be until the 1950s that the Jewish population would again reach 300.

Such small populations were rarely sufficient to import and support a rabbi. Fortunately, there were usually sufficient individuals trained in *Halacha*, "Jewish law," that laypersons could conduct services and carry out life cycle events as capably as any rabbi. Although not ordained, such persons could still be provided with the honorary title of reverend. The same individual might work as the local shohet, kosher butcher, and serve as both a *melamid*, "teacher," and hazzan, cantor. In 1918, the small Beth Israel Congregation of approximately 30 families hired Rev. Pincos Grobstein to carry out these duties. (The spelling is that listed in the Ann Arbor city directory.) He was paid $18 per week (*chai*) and provided with a house at 414 North Main Street, the current site of the Greek Orthodox Church. Grobstein lived in Ann Arbor with his wife Ethel until at least 1924, after which time the community had no official resident spiritual leader. During this period, the site of formal worship would migrate from year to year. For a time, High Holy Day services were held at the Lansky home on Beakes Street or in the Zwerdling home. As the numbers of participants increased, rooms were rented around the downtown area. Finally, in 1927, the congregation purchased the property at 538 North Division Street, and the house became the first permanent synagogue in the community.

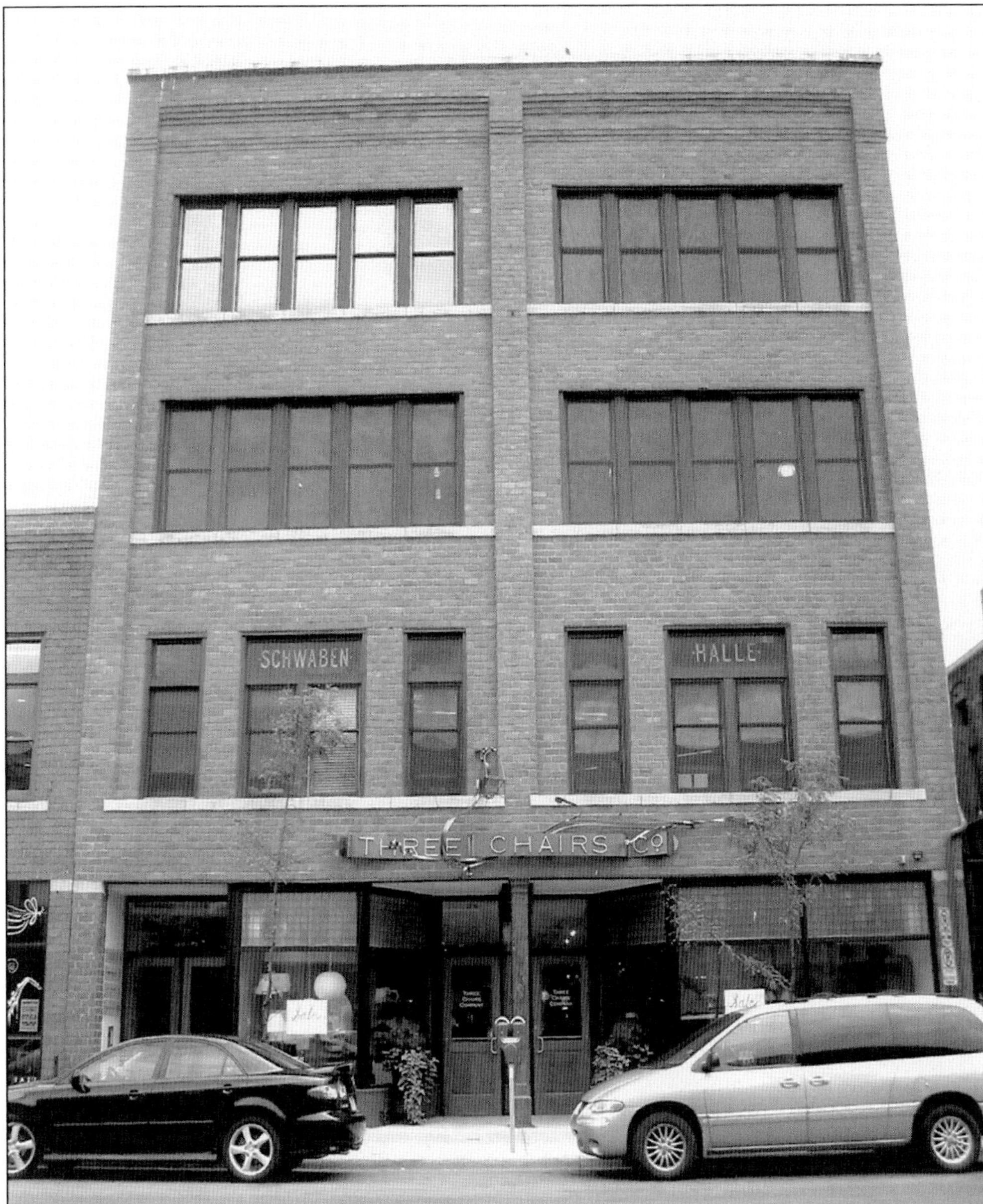


**SCHWABEN HALLE, 215 SOUTH ASHLEY STREET.** For several decades after the beginning of the new century, services were held in private homes. As the number of congregants grew during the 1920s, various rooms or buildings were rented as meeting areas. The Salvation Army headquarters in the rooms above the chamber of commerce office at East Ann Street and Fourth Avenue was utilized for two years. Schwaben Halle, now the rooms above the Three Chairs Company on Ashley Street, was utilized for one year, as well as the library building owned by the Ladies Library Association on East Huron Street. The library building was demolished in 1925 when the Bell Telephone Company erected its first building on the site. The building has undergone several renovations since then, and as the current home of SBC/Ameritech, shows no resemblance to its original uses. Only Schwaben Halle retains a semblance of the original image of the synagogue sites. (Authors.)

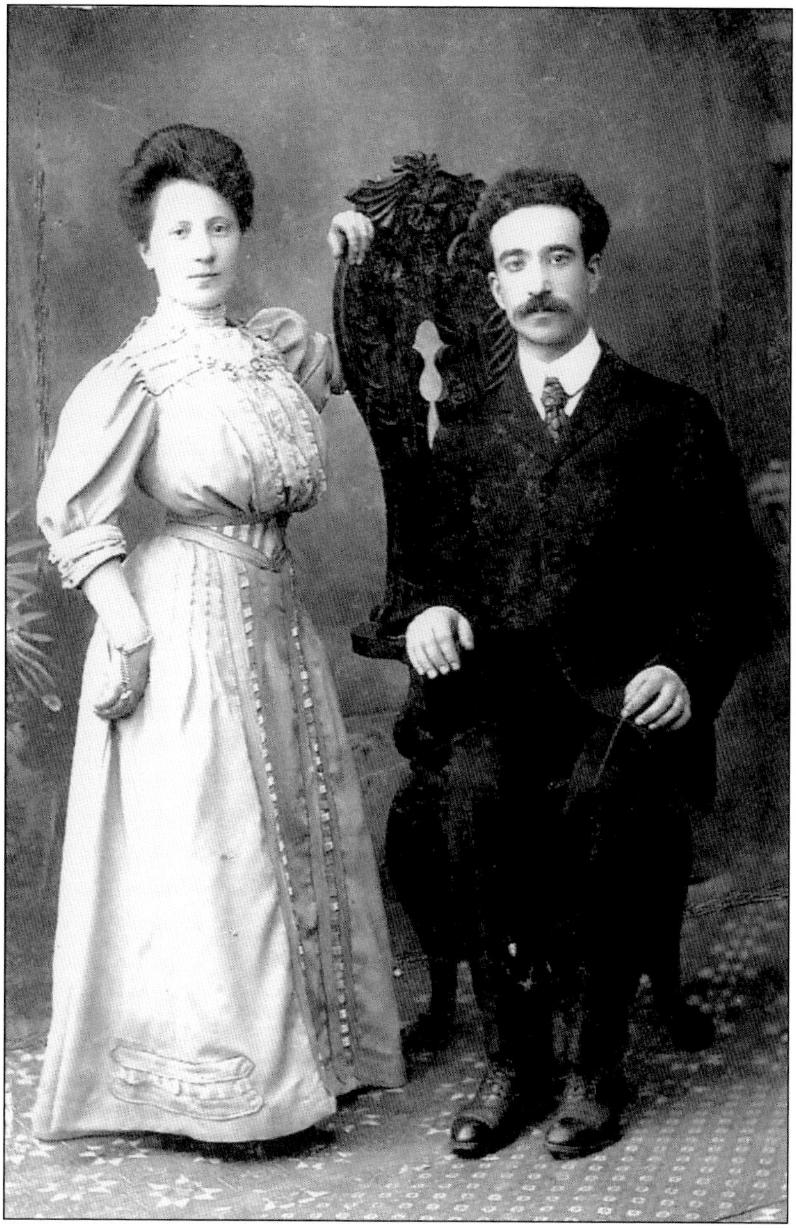

**THE REVEREND JACOB KAMENETZKY, WITH WIFE CELIA.** Born in Russia around 1882, Jacob Kamenetzky came to the United States in 1904. According to census records, Celia was born in approximately 1884 and had arrived in the United States several years earlier than her future husband. Jacob and Celia married in 1909 and for a time settled in Detroit. While he did serve as a spiritual leader at several congregations, Jacob was never formally ordained; however, he still maintained the title of reverend and was trained in halacha, Jewish law. Following the departure of Rev. Pincos Grobstein sometime during the early 1920s, the congregation was briefly without a formal spiritual leader. In 1924, Kamenetzky was hired, serving also as hazzan, shohet, and melamid, teacher. Celia died in 1959, and Jacob died five years later. (Phoebe Amante.)

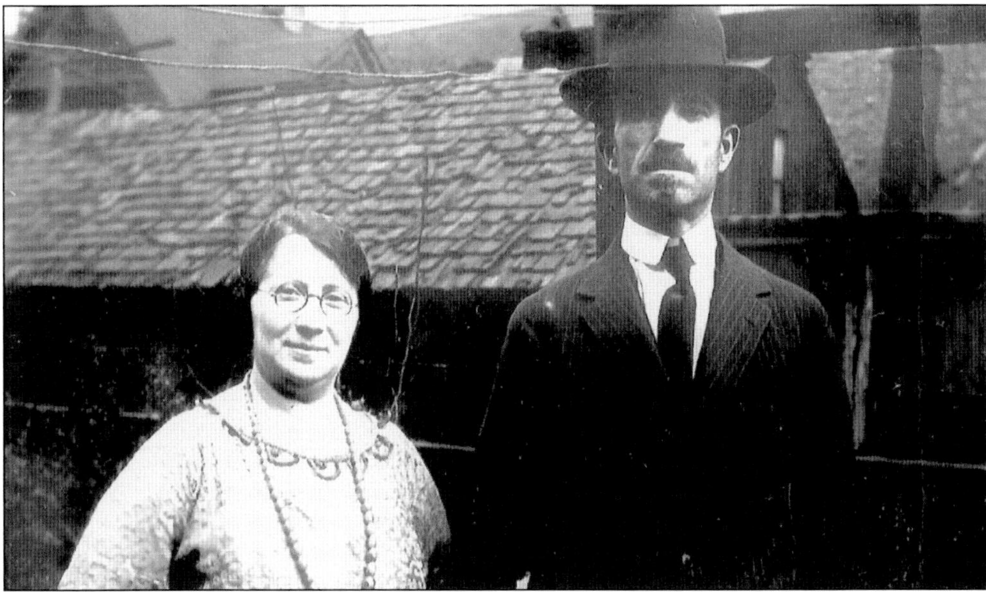

**THE KAMENETZKY FAMILY.** In 1924, the Reverend Jacob Kamenetzky, his wife, and daughters Mollie and Naomi joined the Ann Arbor community to carry out spiritual and other duties much as his predecessors had. For several years, the family lived in the house on North Main Street that the congregation owned. Following the purchase of a house on North Division Street in 1927, the family moved into more elaborate quarters. The Kamenetzkys would remain in Ann Arbor until moving to Detroit in 1932. (Phoebe Amante.)

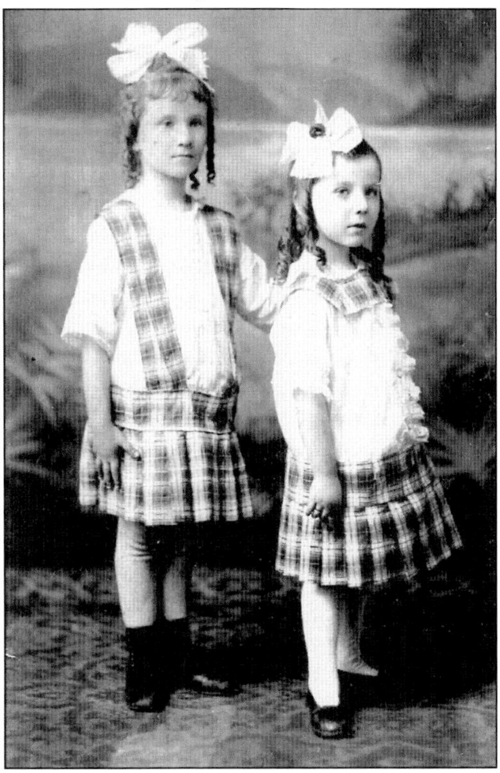

**MOLLIE (LEFT) AND NAOMI KAMENETZKY.** Naomi Kamenetzky would later become a member of the Lansky family with her marriage to Philip's son Samuel. Naomi and Samuel Lansky would have two daughters, Kay and Phoebe. In this manner, two prominent families in Ann Arbor's Jewish history merged. (Phoebe Amante.)

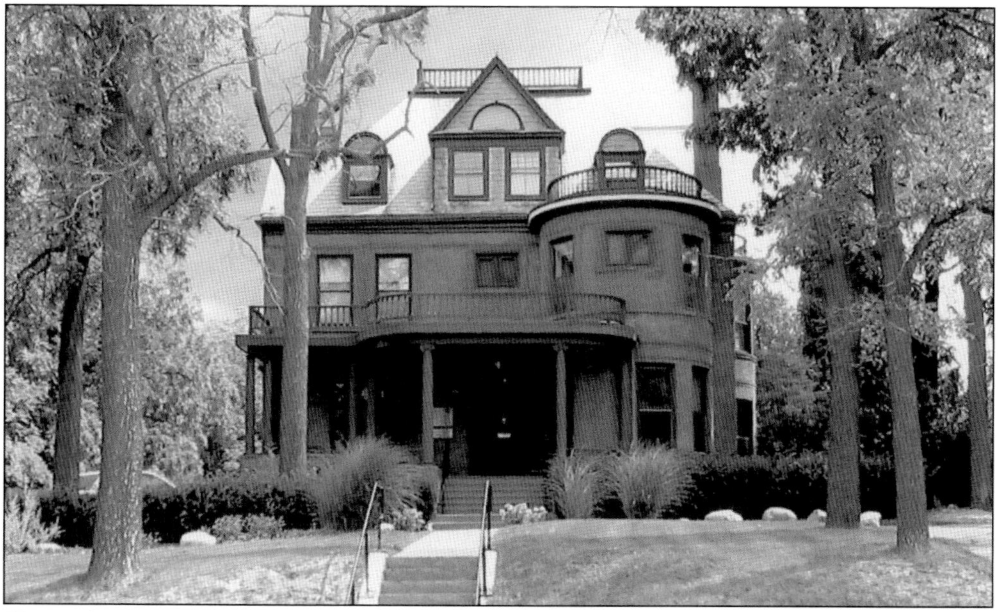

**HENRY CORNWELL HOUSE.** In April 1927, the congregation purchased the vacant Cornwell home at 538 North Division Street for use both as a synagogue and as a home (rabbinate) for the Kamenetzky family. The structure was built in 1894 by Henry Cornwell, who, with his brother Harvey, became wealthy from the local lumber industry. The home remained in the Cornwell family until after World War I. The building is currently the office for several local attorneys. (Authors.)

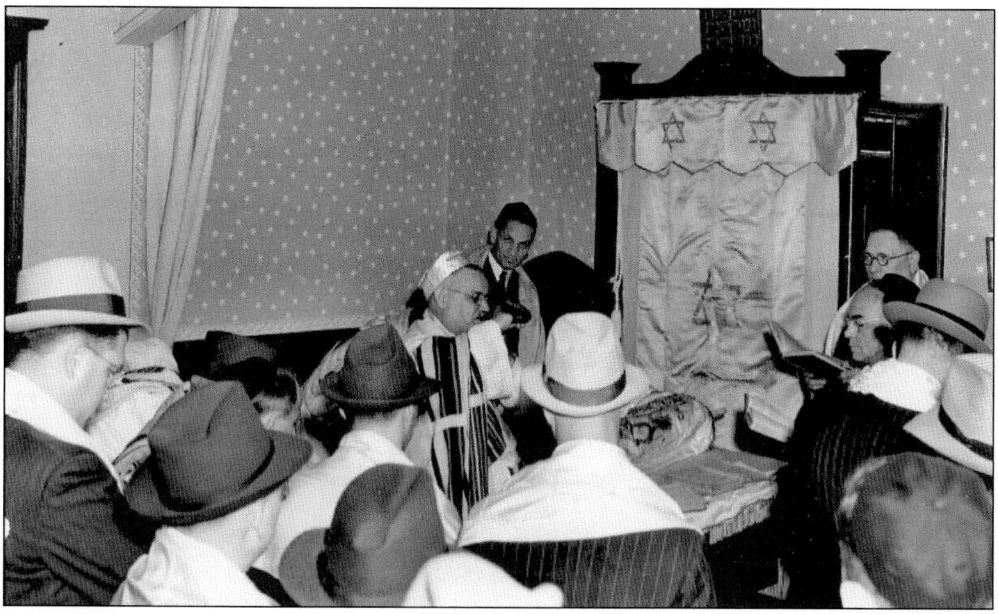

**ROSH HASHANAH CELEBRATION, 1940.** The North Division Street property served as the synagogue for two decades until its sale in 1946. In addition to services, the house was also the rabbinate during these years. At least two individuals can be identified in the photograph taken during the new year celebration: Phil Lansky (right with glasses) and Osias Zwerdling (in front of Lansky). It has been suggested, the Reverend Isaak Goldman (center) is leading the service, but with the absence of known images of him, this cannot be confirmed. (BIC.)

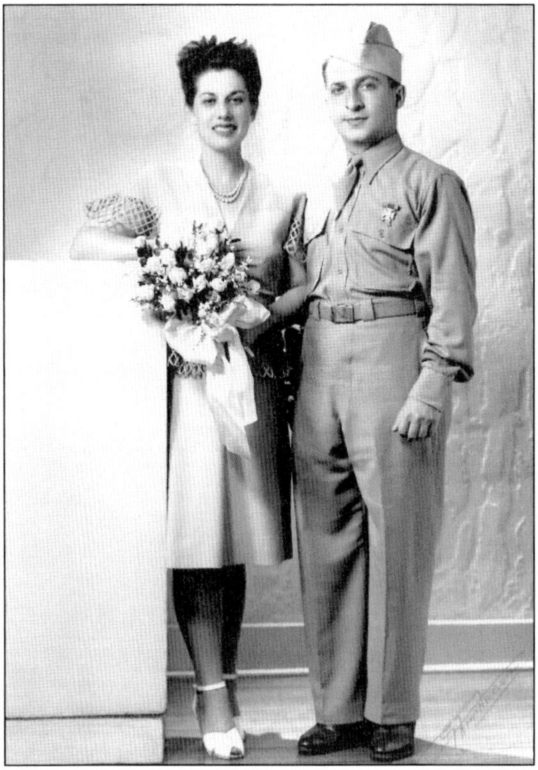

**MARRIAGE OF PHILIP SEYMOUR AND CLARA PORTNOFF.** The North Division Street rabbinate hosted numerous life cycle functions, as well as services, during the years in which it was owned by the congregation. Among these affairs was the July 4, 1944, wedding of the Seymours, presided over by the Reverend Isaak Goldman. It is believed this may represent the only wedding held at the North Division Street site. (Clara Seymour.)

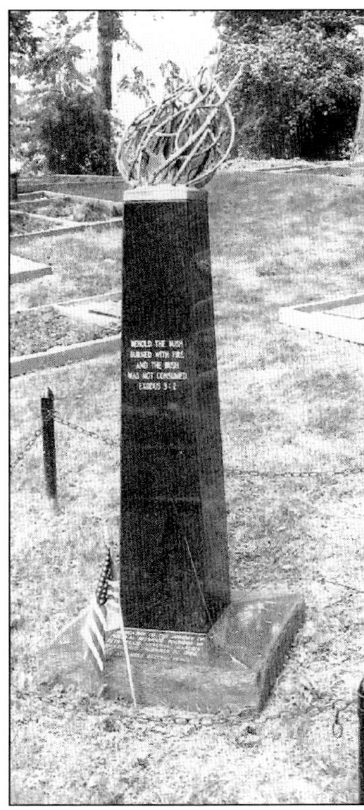

**MEMORIAL AT THE SEYMOUR GRAVE SITE.** Phil Seymour was a major figure in the congregation for the many years prior to his death in 1985. Most members of the congregation were unaware of his extensive philanthropy due to his desire to remain anonymous while extending generosity to others. Among his contributions was his role in establishing Beth Israel Memorial Gardens, located near the southeastern entrance to Arborcrest Cemetery on Glazier Way. The Gardens were incorporated in 1955. (Authors.)

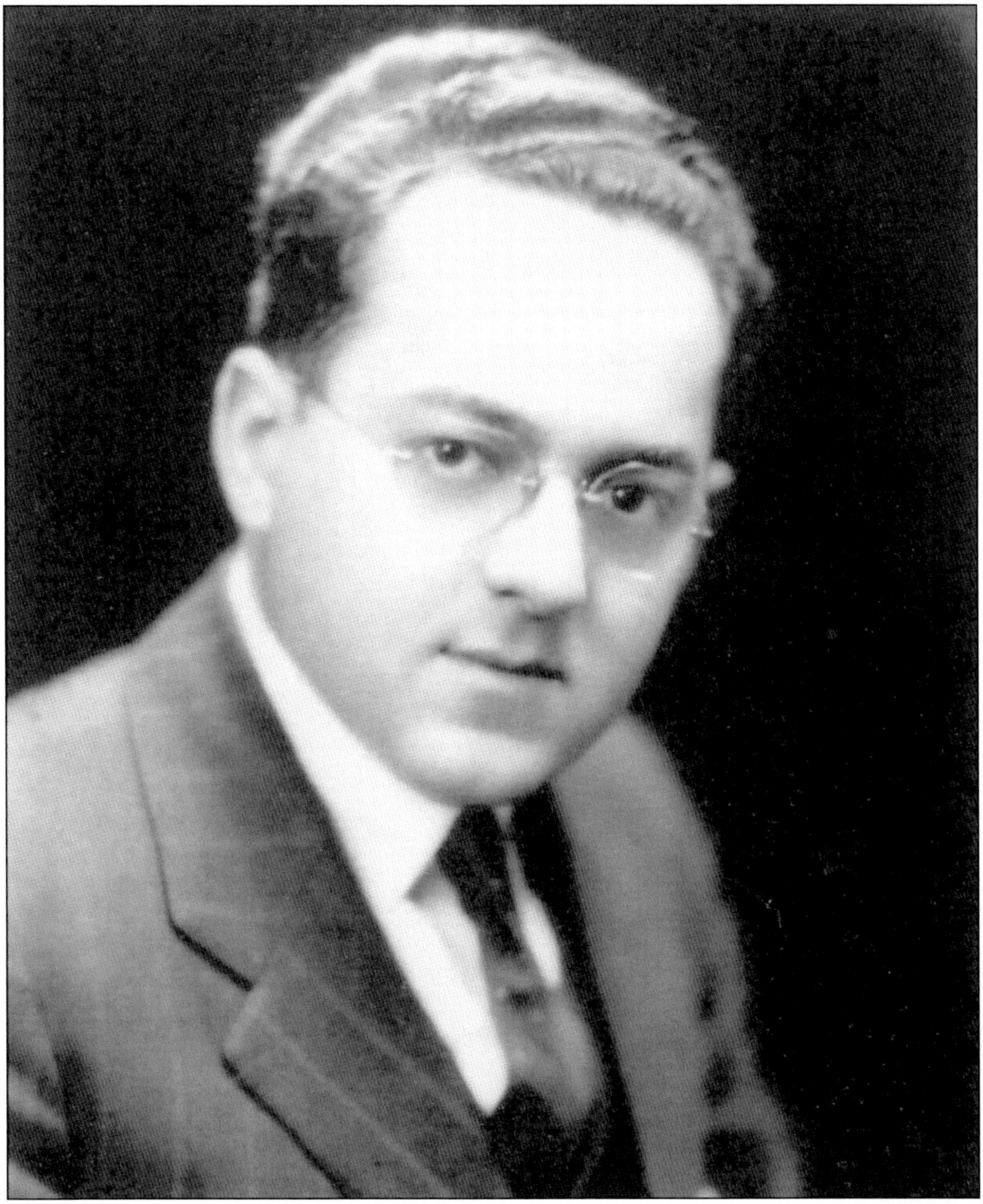

**JOSHUA SPERKA (AROUND 1905–1982).** Rabbi Joshua Sperka was the first ordained rabbi hired to serve the Beth Israel Congregation, earning approximately $20 per month. Rabbi Sperka was born in what is now Poland into a family with a Hasidic background. At 17, he arrived in the United States, where he attended the Hebrew Theological Seminary in Chicago. During the 1930s, he joined a congregation in Mount Clemens, Michigan, and then entered the University of Michigan, earning a master of science degree in mid-eastern studies. While attending school in Ann Arbor, he served the Beth Israel Congregation (1932–1934). During this period, his home was above the synagogue, located on North Division Street. After completing his degree program, Rabbi Sperka and his family moved to Detroit, where he served Congregation B'nai David until 1953. During these years, he also served as the first Jewish chaplain in the Michigan prison system. (Shlomo and Deanna Sperka.)

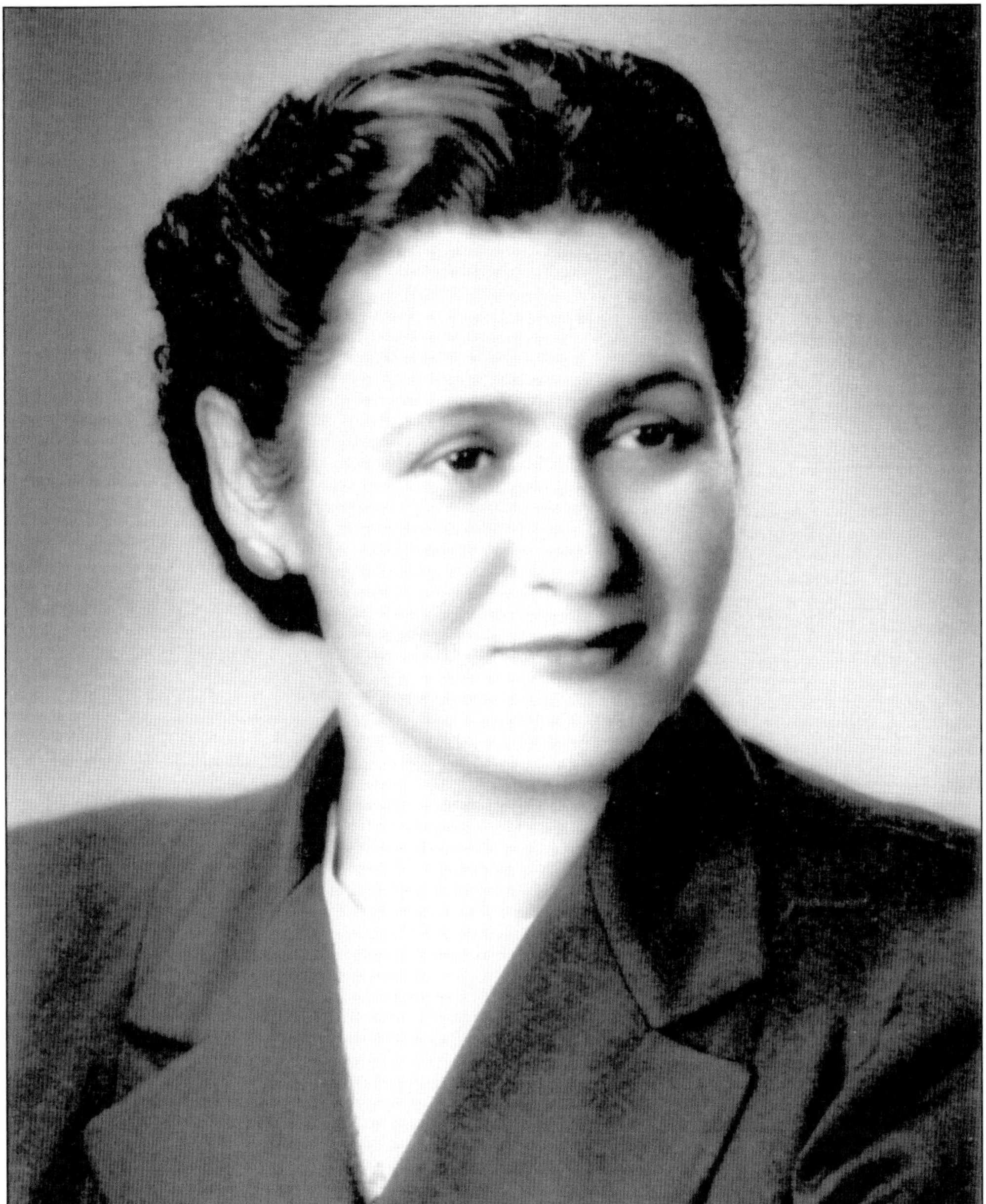

**YETTA PEIMAN SPERKA.** Born in Toronto, Yetta Peiman moved to Detroit, where she met her future husband in an intercollegiate debate. Peiman began a speaking career when her Yiddish-speaking father took her to political clubs in pre-Great War Toronto to recite patriotic English poetry. It should be kept in mind that in the context of the time, a young outspoken Jewish woman would stand out in the community. She remained active throughout the Jewish community even after her marriage, as both a speaker and a local playwright. Married in 1931, and mother of four children, Yetta Peiman Sperka relished the irony that a young Jewish woman who had not finished college was a member of the University of Michigan faculty wives, a privilege open to her given the professional position of her husband. She died in 1984. (Shlomo and Deanna Sperka.)

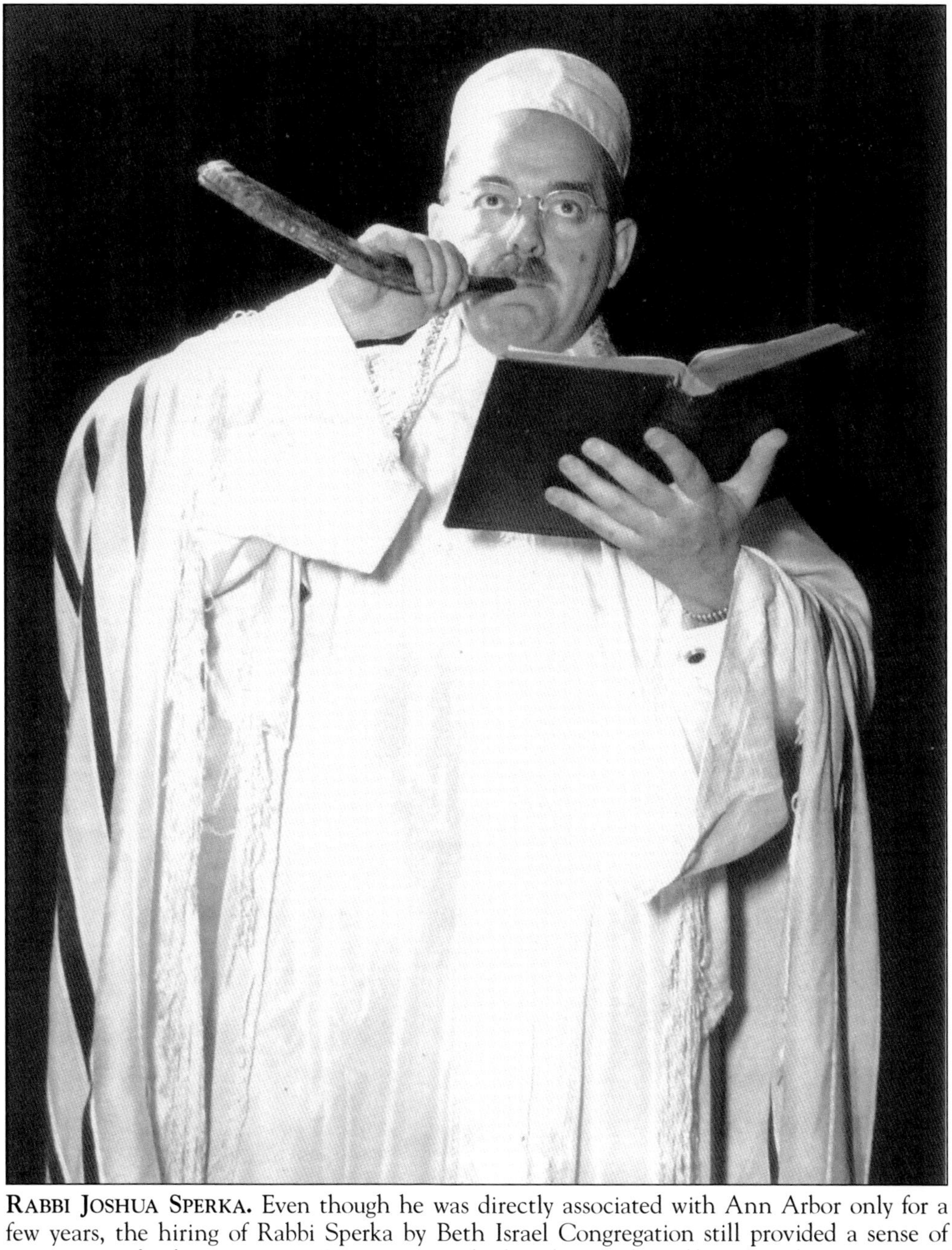

**RABBI JOSHUA SPERKA.** Even though he was directly associated with Ann Arbor only for a few years, the hiring of Rabbi Sperka by Beth Israel Congregation still provided a sense of permanence for the community. Prior ministers had not been ordained but carried out a variety of religious duties. Their presence in Ann Arbor had been mostly incidental to other factors. After retirement and living elsewhere in the Detroit area with his family, Rabbi Sperka continued his professional work in a variety of endeavors, including the authoring of several books containing commentaries on the Biblical Wisdom Literature (Job, Proverbs, Ecclesiastes). He also served as a representative of the Jewish National Fund, as a chaplain in Jewish nursing homes, and as a volunteer rabbi for Young Israel. (Shlomo and Deanna Sperka.)

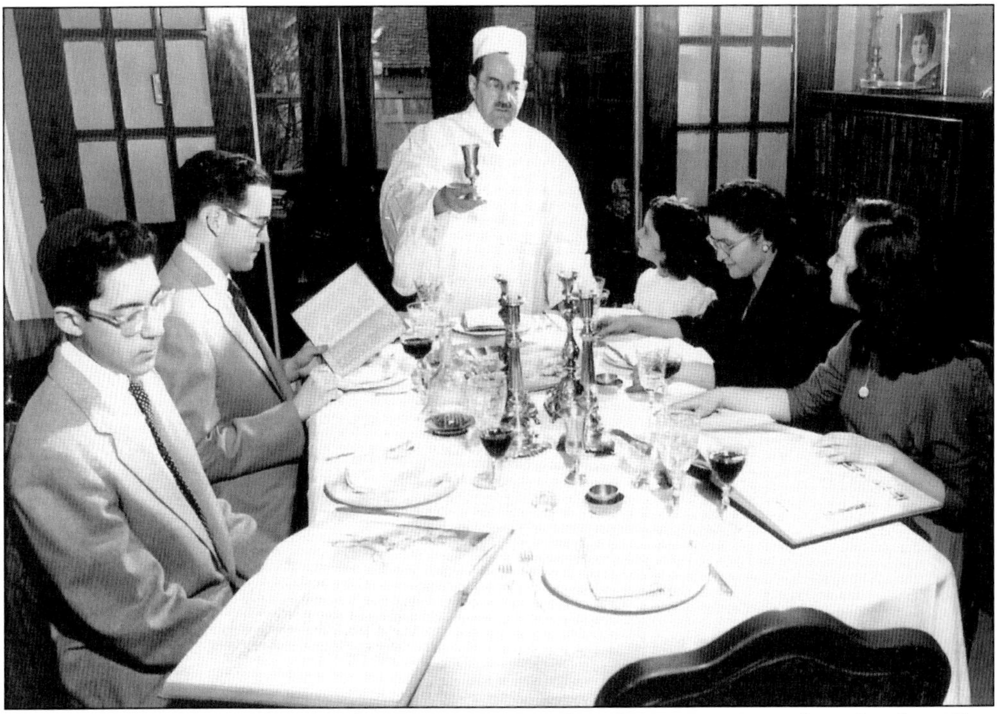

**Seder at the Sperka Home.** The Sperkas remained in the area, as have their families. This particular photograph was taken at their Detroit area home to which they moved upon leaving Ann Arbor. (Shlomo and Deanna Sperka.)

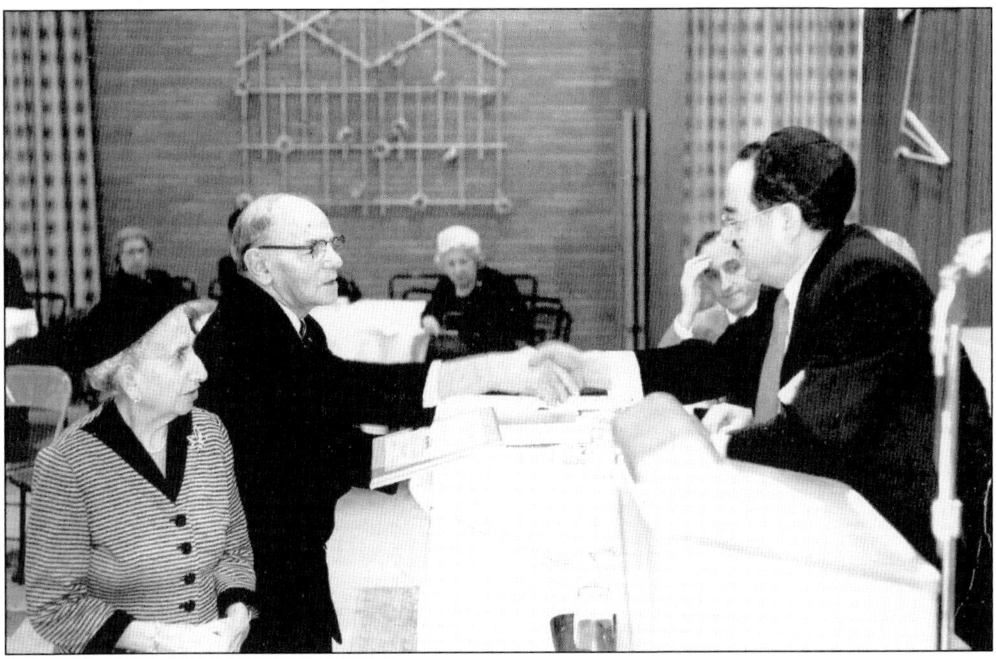

**Rabbi Joshua Sperka at Jewish National Fund Ceremony.** Rabbi Sperka remained active in Jewish affairs throughout his life. He is shown here presenting the Jewish National Fund award to Osias and Hannah Zwerdling in the early 1970s. (BIC.)

# *Four*

# Growth and Diversity in the 1950s

With the departure of Rabbi Sperka, Beth Israel was without a formal ordained rabbi for over a decade. Isaak Goldman and his wife Sara joined the congregation in 1934, and Goldman served much in the way as had the Reverend Kamenetzky earlier, as melamed, shohet, and hazzan. The Reverend Goldman left Ann Arbor in 1944, and the position remained vacant for two years. By 1946, Beth Israel Congregation had reached a crisis. The number of Jewish faculty associated with the university, as well as other Jewish townsfolk, had begun to increase in the decades since the congregation was formed, with the result that the Ann Arbor Jewish community in total now encompassed some 200 persons, not including students. Membership in Beth Israel Congregation consisted of approximately 40 families.

After construction on the second building at 1429 Hill Street was completed, both Hillel and Beth Israel moved to the site, with the congregation leasing space in the new building. The Sunday school was located there as well. Rabbi Gershon Rosenstock, a student rabbi from Chicago, had briefly served as a part-time resident rabbi (1947), but for most of the period until 1952, no ordained rabbi was hired by the congregation. Herschel Lymon, rabbi and director at Hillel, was shared between Hillel and Beth Israel and would generally carry out any duties requiring a rabbi until his departure in 1953. In recognition of the arrangement established between the congregation and Hillel, the name was modified first to Beth Israel Center and then to the Beth Israel Community Center in December 1951.

In June 1952, Julius Weinberg, director of the cultural commission and internal relations committee for the Detroit Jewish Community Council, became the spiritual leader at Beth Israel, the first ordained rabbi hired for that purpose since Rabbi Sperka two decades earlier. In some sense, the 1950s represented a new beginning for the congregation. In 1950, it was estimated that the Jewish population of Ann Arbor and the surrounding area consisted of a minimum of 240 persons. This was certainly an underestimate, since it did not include university numbers in the figure, as well as the likelihood that there existed at least 75 Jewish families in the congregation. Regardless, the numbers resembled those from the early 1920s. By 1960, the number of Jews in the area exceeded 1,000 and continued to increase throughout the decade.

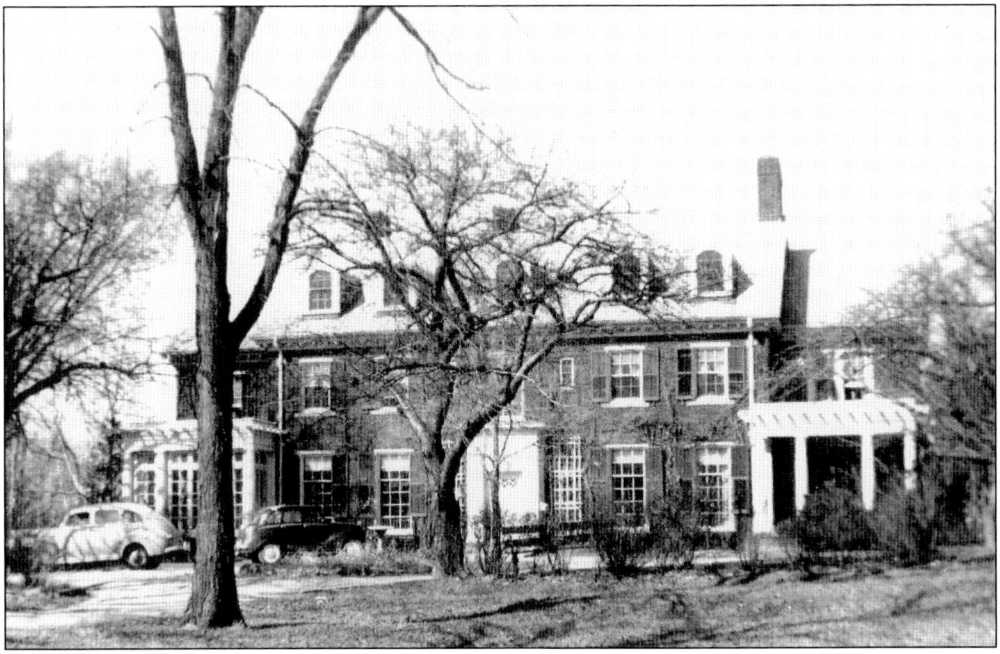

PATTERSON HOUSE, 2101 HILL STREET. In 1948, Beth Israel moved, as did the Hillel Foundation from its Hazen Street location, to the Patterson home at 2101 Hill Street, which the two organizations shared. Beth Israel remained in these quarters for three years, until the new Hillel building at 1429 Hill Street was completed and dedicated in 1951. (BIC.)

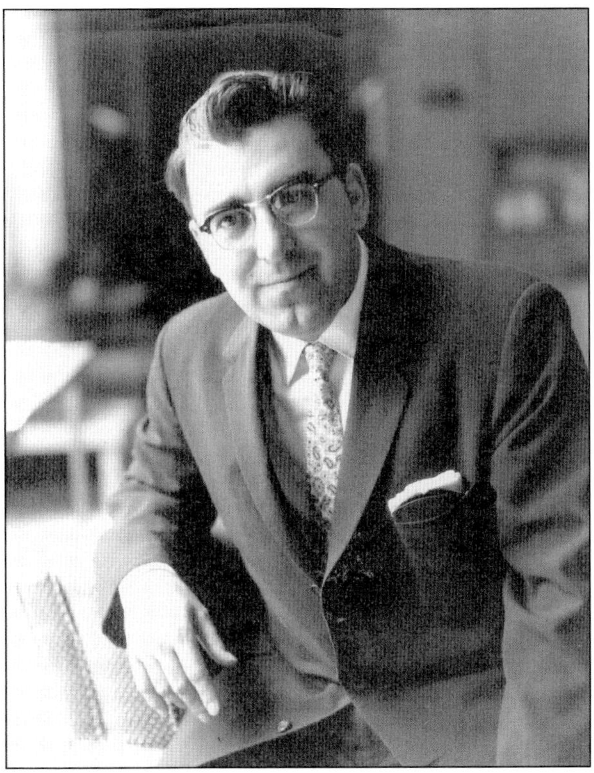

RABBI JULIUS WEINBERG (1922–1984). Rabbi Weinberg served the congregation for nine years, leaving in 1962 with Alezah, his wife, to return to academia at Wayne State University in Detroit. During his tenure, membership grew to include approximately 200 families. Rabbi Weinberg also fostered an adult education program, established specific requirements for becoming a bar mitzvah, and instituted a weekly Sabbath service. (BIC.)

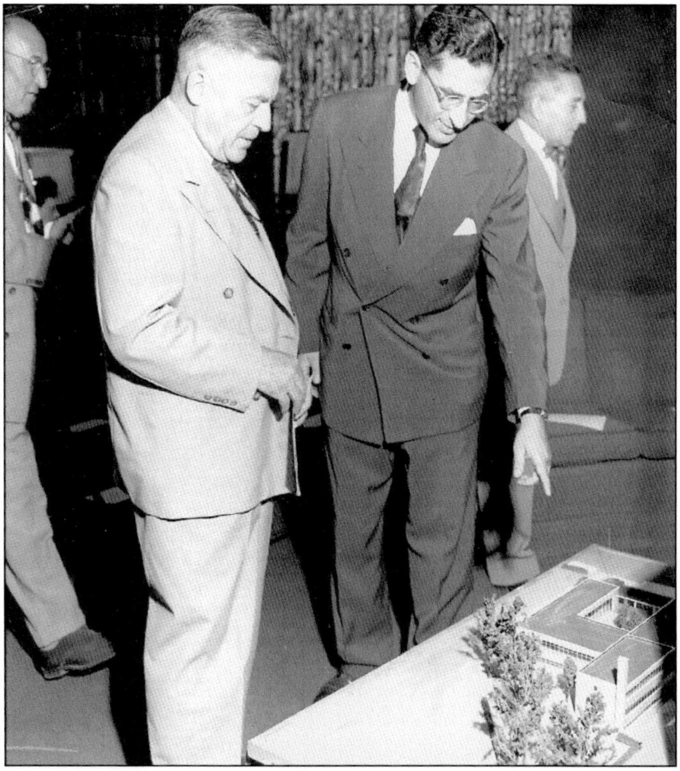

**UNIVERSITY PRESIDENT ALEXANDER RUTHVEN AND RABBI HERSCHEL LYMON.** By 1951, plans had been completed for a new community center, which would house both Hillel and Beth Israel. President Ruthven (left) and Rabbi Lymon are shown observing a model of the new structure. Board member Ben Paul Brasley is in the background on the right. (BIC.)

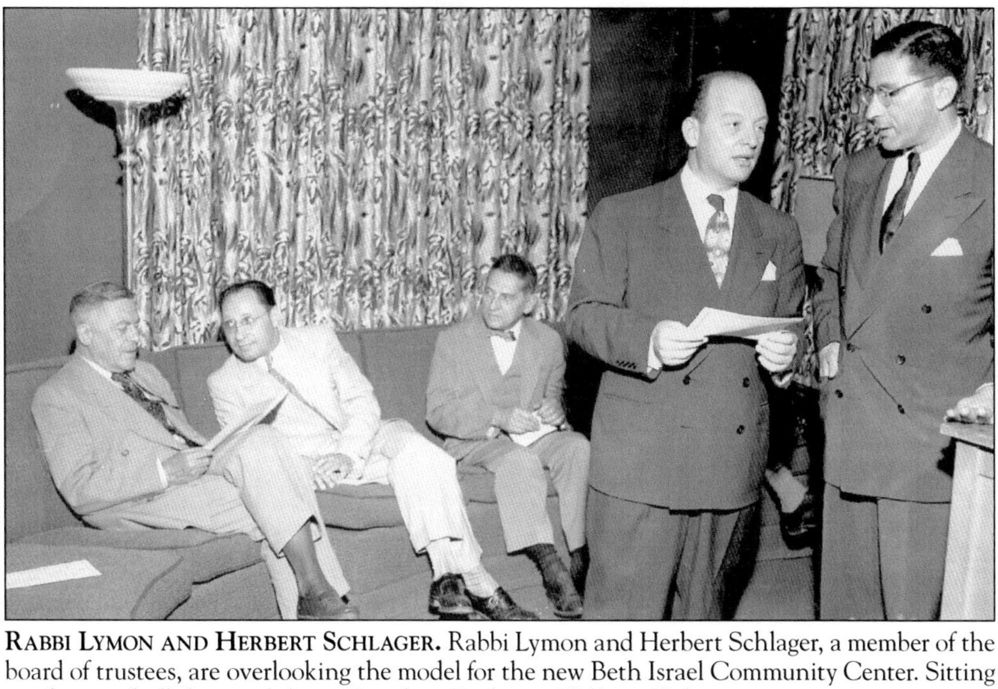

**RABBI LYMON AND HERBERT SCHLAGER.** Rabbi Lymon and Herbert Schlager, a member of the board of trustees, are overlooking the model for the new Beth Israel Community Center. Sitting on the couch (left to right) are President Ruthven; William Haber, university economist and major proponent for the erection of a more formal Jewish center; and Ben Paul Brasley. Brasley, a University of Michigan Law School graduate, contributed $100,000 to the project. (BIC.)

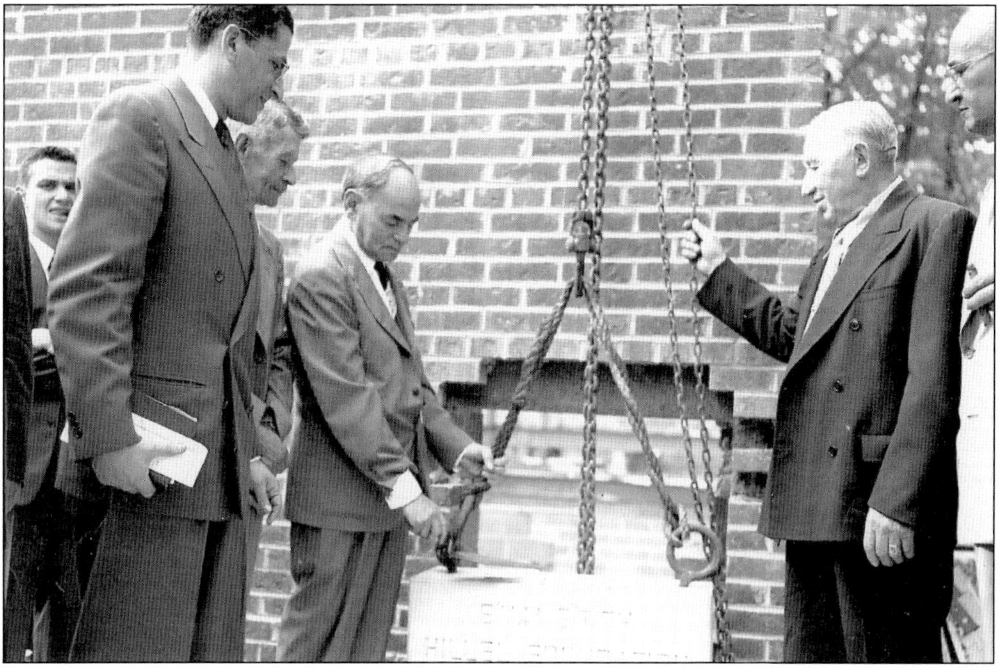

**LAYING OF THE HILLEL FOUNDATION/BETH ISRAEL CENTER CORNERSTONE, 1951.** From left to right are Rabbi Lymon, director of the Hillel Foundation; Israel Friedman, vice president of Beth Israel Congregation; Osias Zwerdling, president of Beth Israel Congregation; and Phil Lansky. Friedman, Zwerdling, and Lansky were the three surviving founders of the congregation established in 1916. (BIC.)

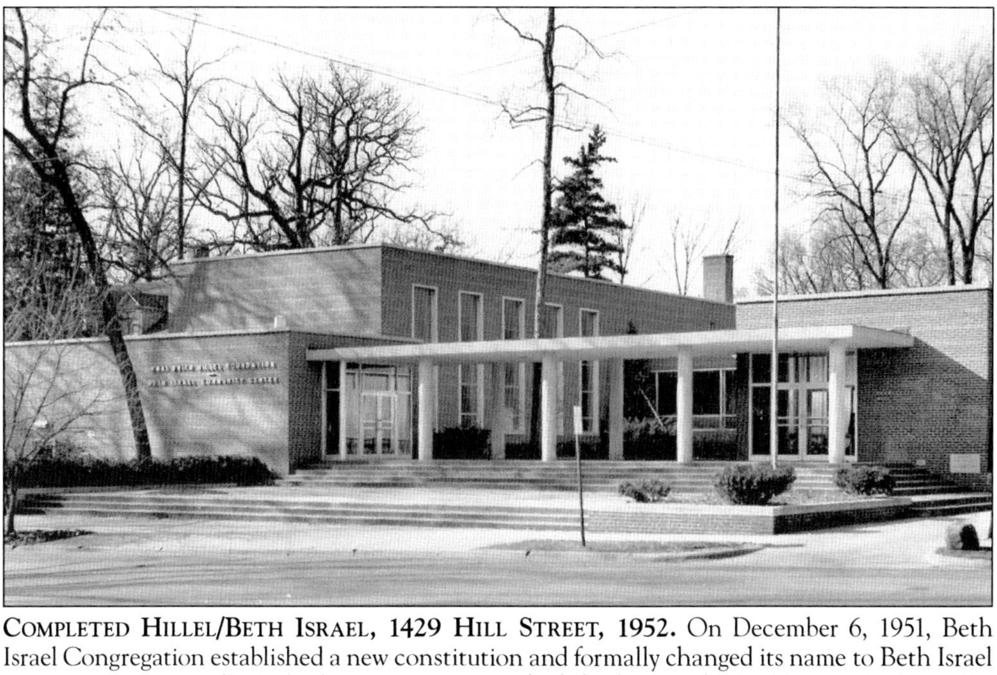

**COMPLETED HILLEL/BETH ISRAEL, 1429 HILL STREET, 1952.** On December 6, 1951, Beth Israel Congregation established a new constitution and formally changed its name to Beth Israel Community Center (BICC), the name it retained while sharing the building with the Hillel Foundation. Beth Israel utilized the left section of the building. (BIC.)

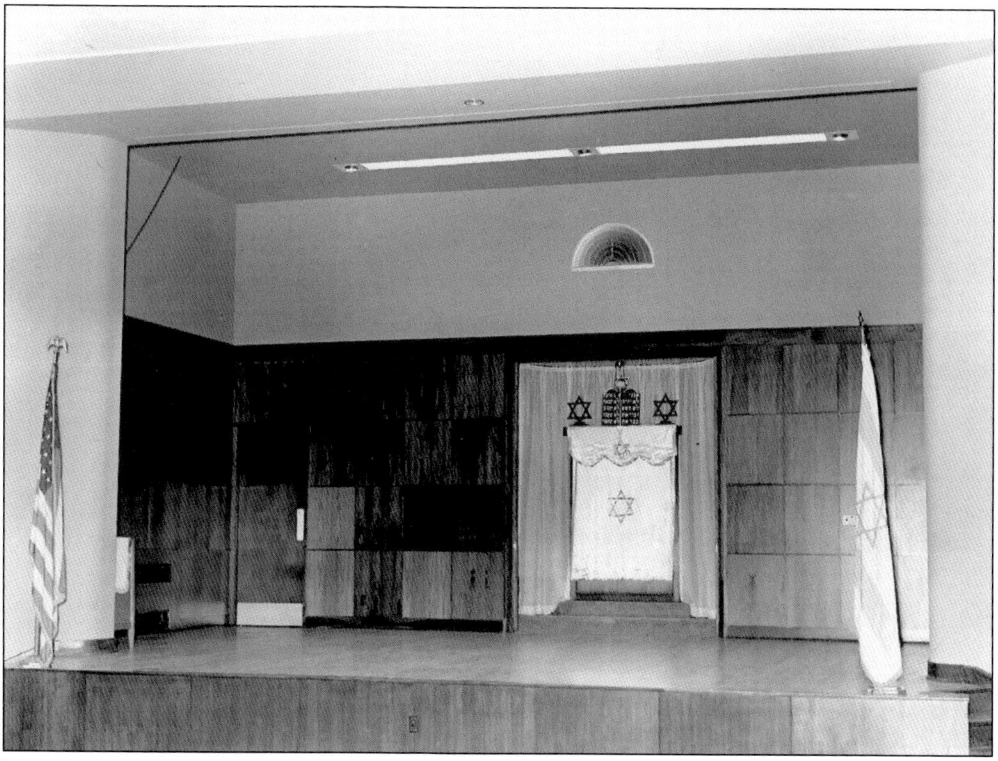

**MAIN CHAPEL IN THE BICC.** The new building served both the student organization Hillel, as well as the Jewish community at large. Services for the High Holy Days were held in this room. The changes proved successful, as there occurred a significant increase in membership, and the size of the Sunday school doubled. (BIC.)

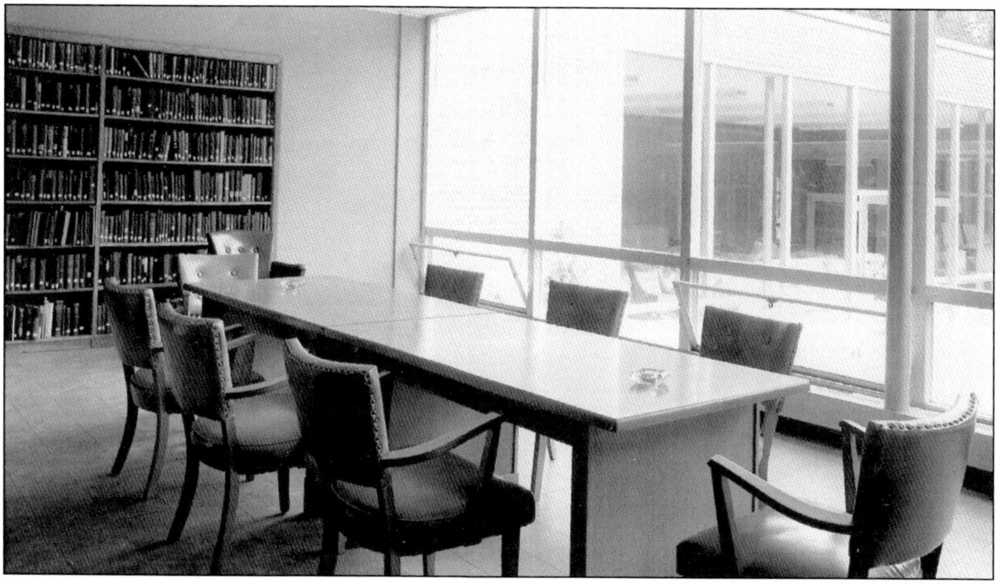

**HILLEL LIBRARY.** The library provided both a site for contemplation as well as a quiet area of study for Jewish students and members. The library also served as the future nucleus for a larger library facility later built in the 1970s as part of a newer synagogue. (BIC.)

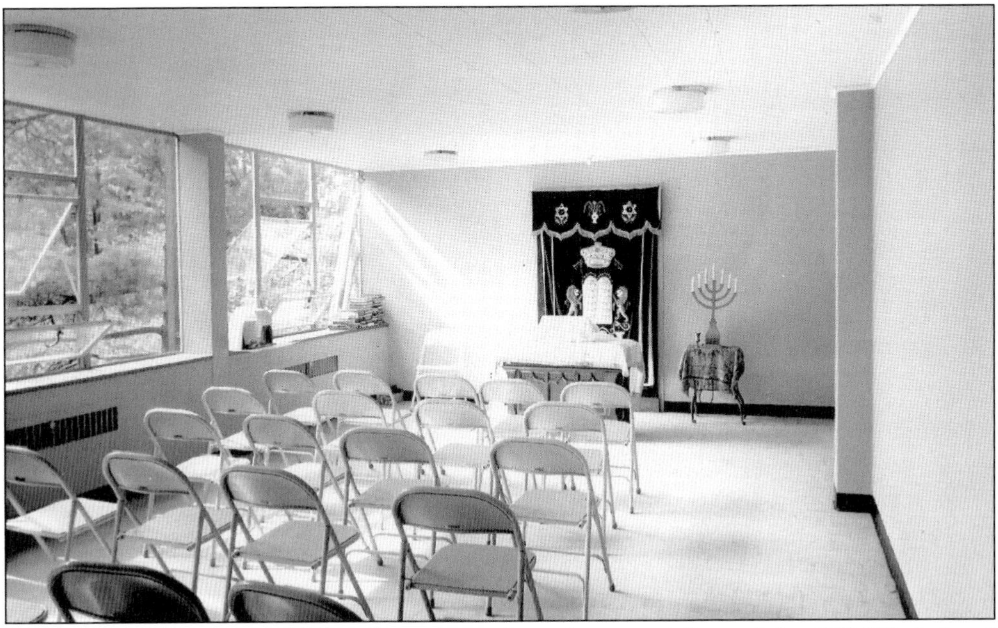

**HILLEL CHAPEL.** This small chapel was located on the second floor of the Hillel/Beth Israel Community Center and served for daily services or life cycle events when held or events requiring only limited space. (BIC.)

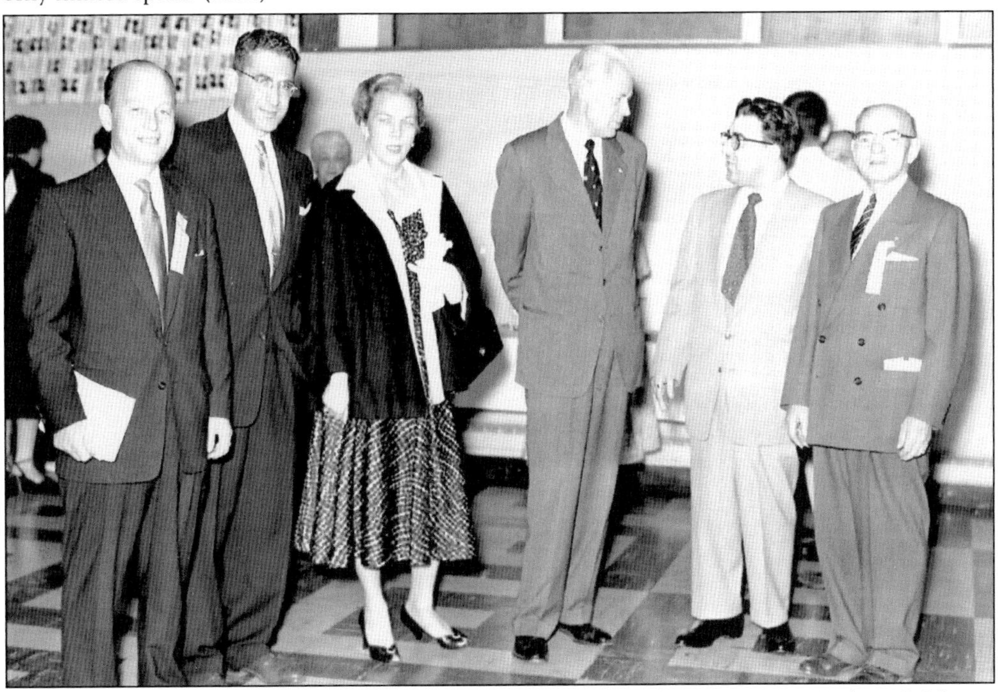

**HILLEL/BICC OPEN HOUSE, MAY 27, 1953.** From left to right are trustee Herbert Schlager, Rabbi Lymon, Anne Hatcher, university president Harlan Hatcher, Rabbi Weinberg, and Osias Zwerdling. The open house was for the purpose of fostering social relationships with the larger Ann Arbor community, as well as for providing an overview of Jewish traditions and organizations. The program was simultaneously broadcast on local radio station WPAG. (BIC.)

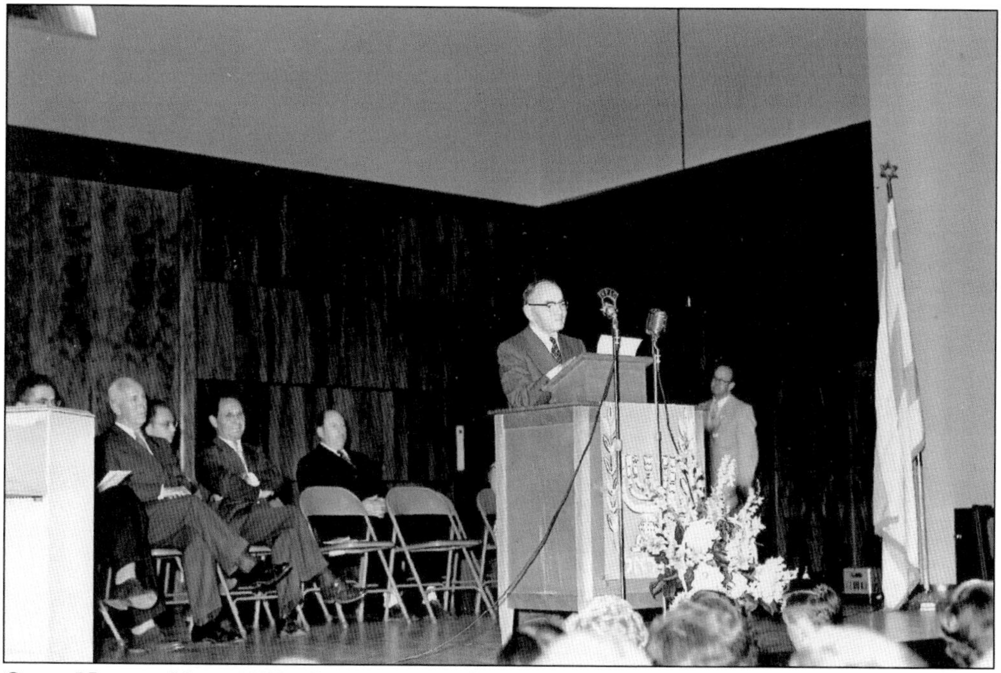

**Open House, May 1953.** Opening remarks were made by Osias Zwerdling. Zwerdling, as president and cofounder of the congregation, was honored with the privilege of helping dedicate the new center. (BIC.)

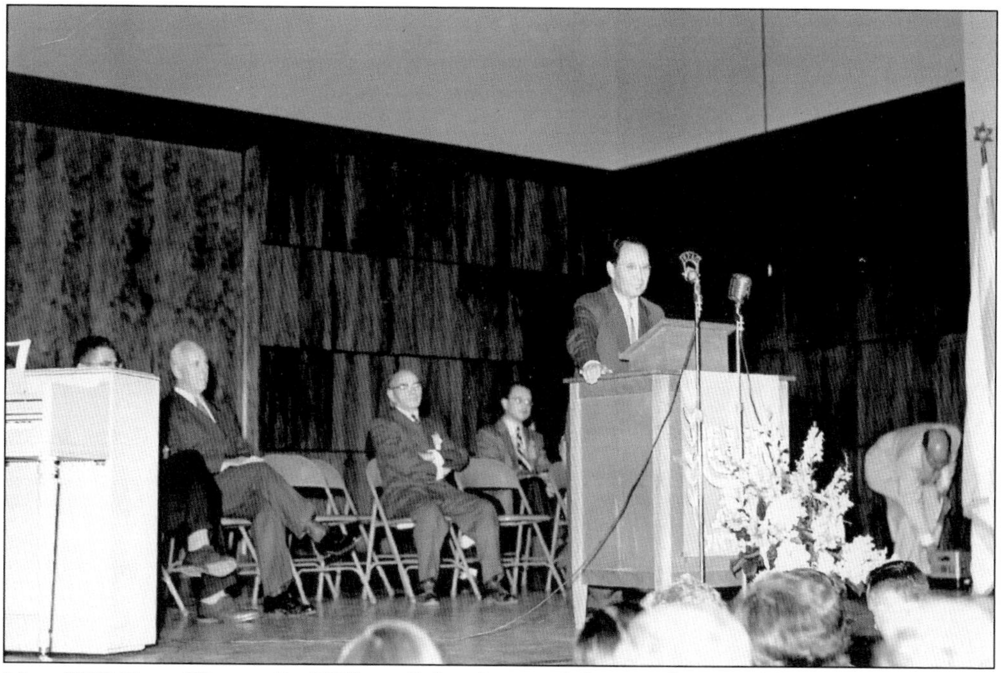

**May 1953 Open House.** Dr. William Haber discussed the significance of the new center. Haber was a professor of economics at the university. He had been involved in facilitating the moves of the organizations, first to the Patterson site, and subsequently to the newer site at 1429 Hill Street. He also played a significant role in developing plans for the new building. (BIC.)

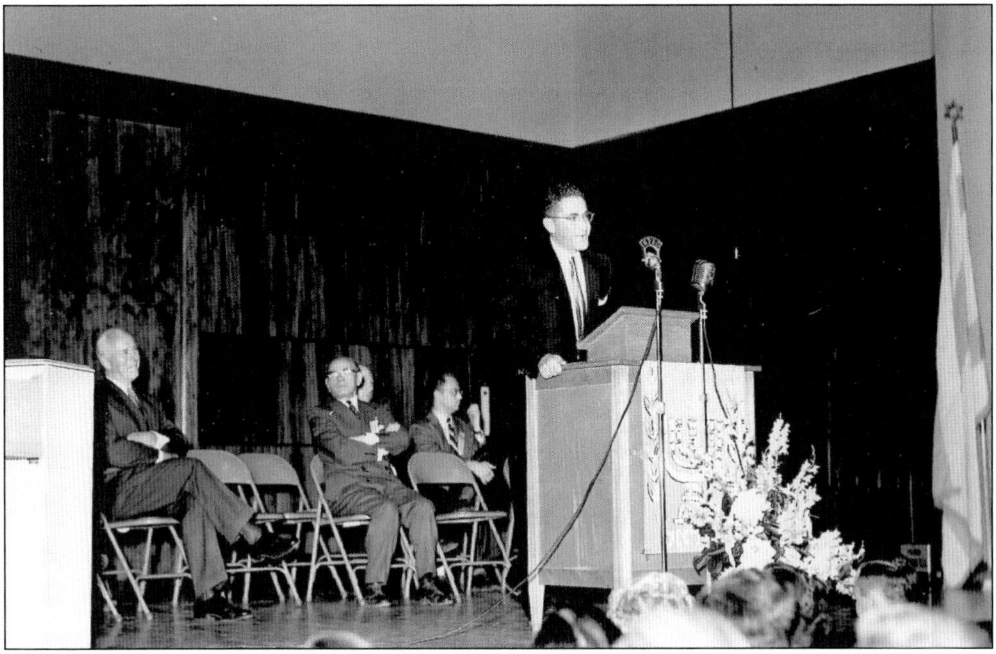

**OPEN HOUSE.** Rabbi Herschel Lymon, Hillel director, presented remarks welcoming the Ann Arbor community as well as discussing the concept of a more open community. Lymon was a conservative rabbi from Chicago, who came to Ann Arbor in the late 1940s to attend graduate school. (BIC.)

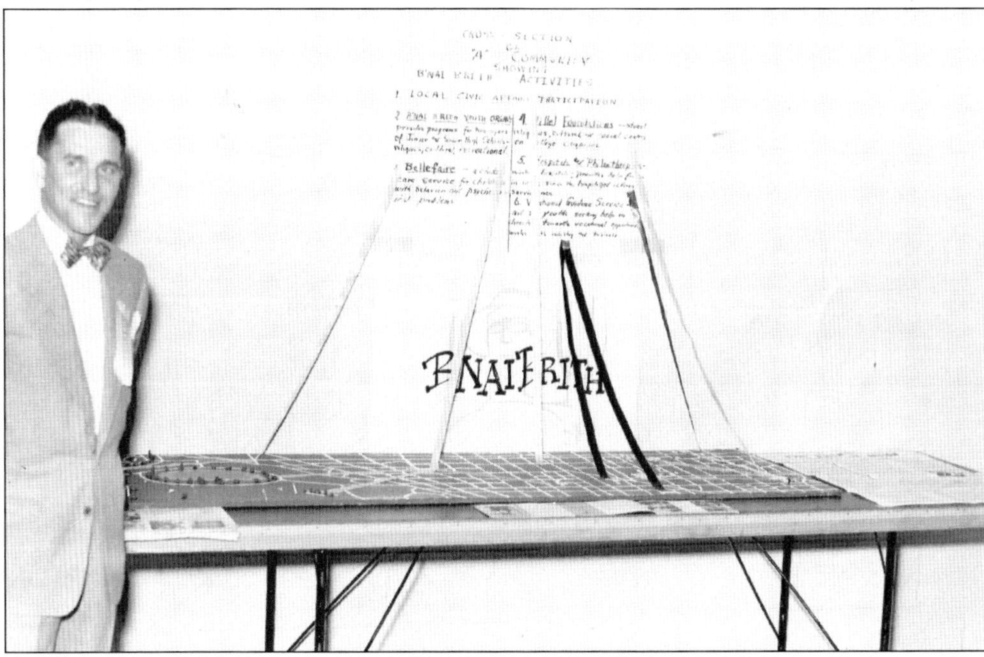

**RABBI LYMON.** For this exhibit, Rabbi Lymon provided explanations of B'nai Brith and its role as an umbrella organization for philanthropic and youth activities. Rabbi Lymon functioned as Hillel director as well as the spiritual leader for the Jewish community at large until his departure in 1953, about the same period during which Rabbi Julius Weinberg joined the congregation. (BIC.)

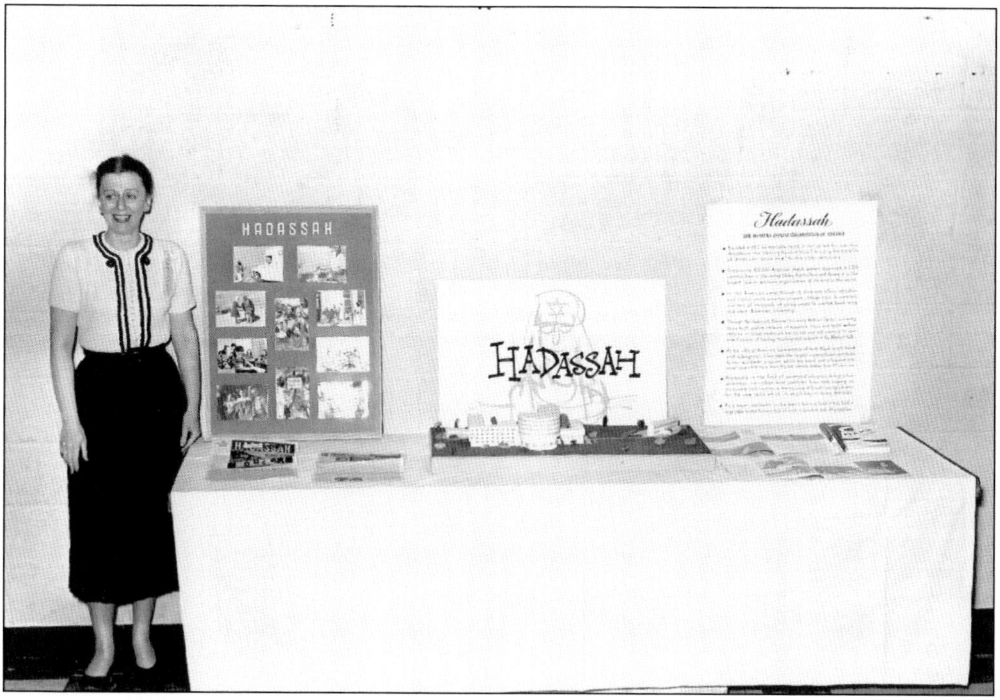


**PASSOVER DISPLAY.** The women's organization, *Hadassah,* was among those displaying information about Jewish holidays. Among items of interest were the roles of foods specific for the holiday. (BIC.)

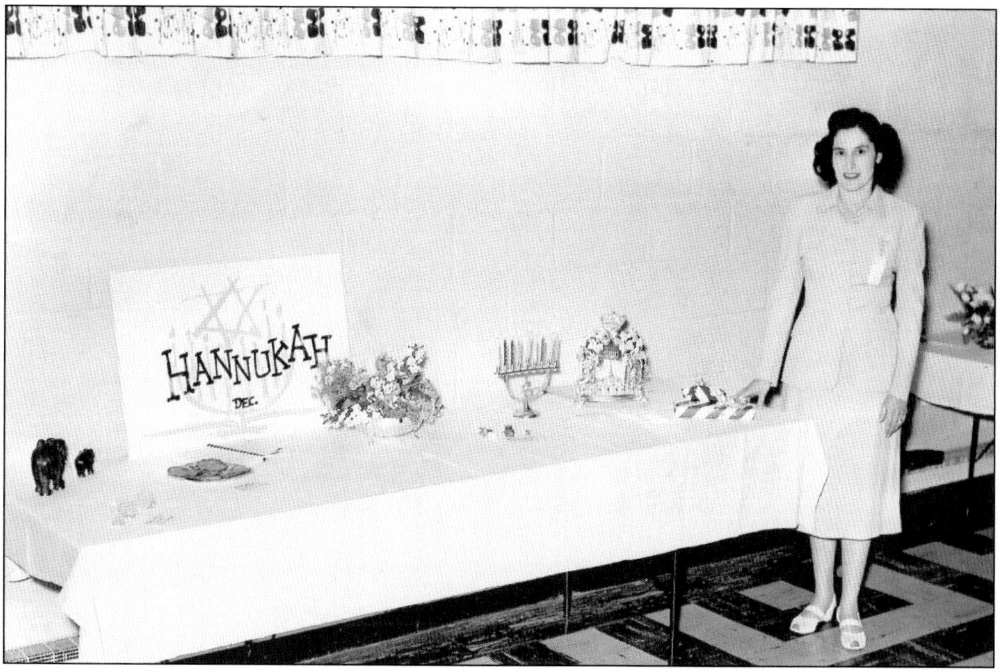


**HANUKKAH DISPLAY.** Similar displays for major Jewish holidays allowed the community at large to learn about Judaism and helped bridge the gap between "town and gown." Hanukkah was often of interest to non-Jewish individuals because its timing often coincided with Christmas. (BIC.)

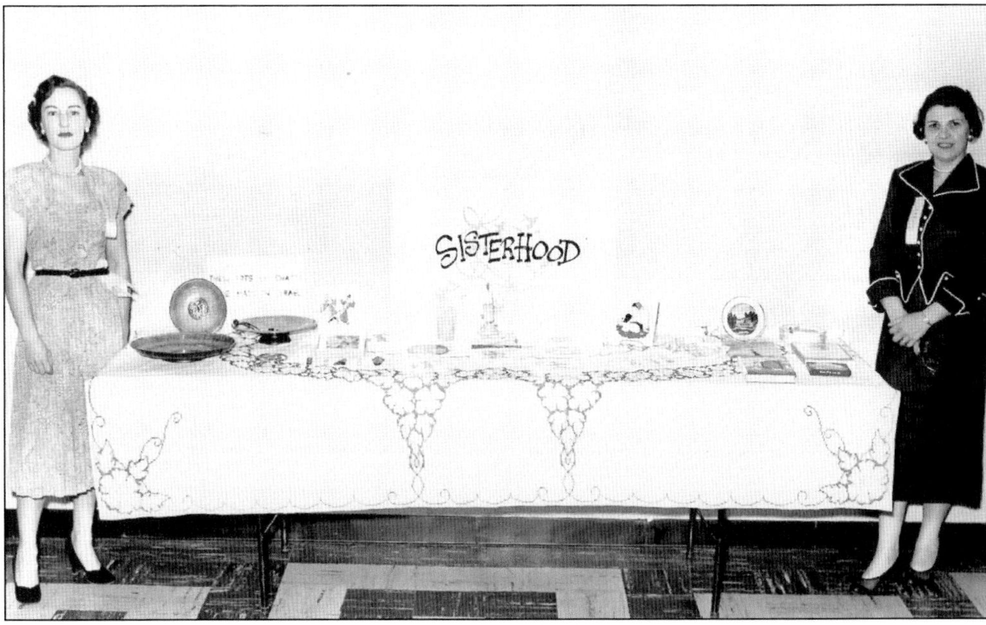


**BETH ISRAEL SISTERHOOD DISPLAY.** The Beth Israel Sisterhood had its origins in 1918, when Eva Lansky organized a Ladies Auxiliary for the Jewish community. Among later sisterhood presidents were Lillian Scott, Ruth Friedman, Mollie Ingber, Clara Seymour, and currently, Judy Cohen (Beth Israel) and Andy Ludwig and Debra Linkner (Beth Emeth). Ruth Friedman and Barbara Saltinger were available to answer questions for the open house. (BIC.)

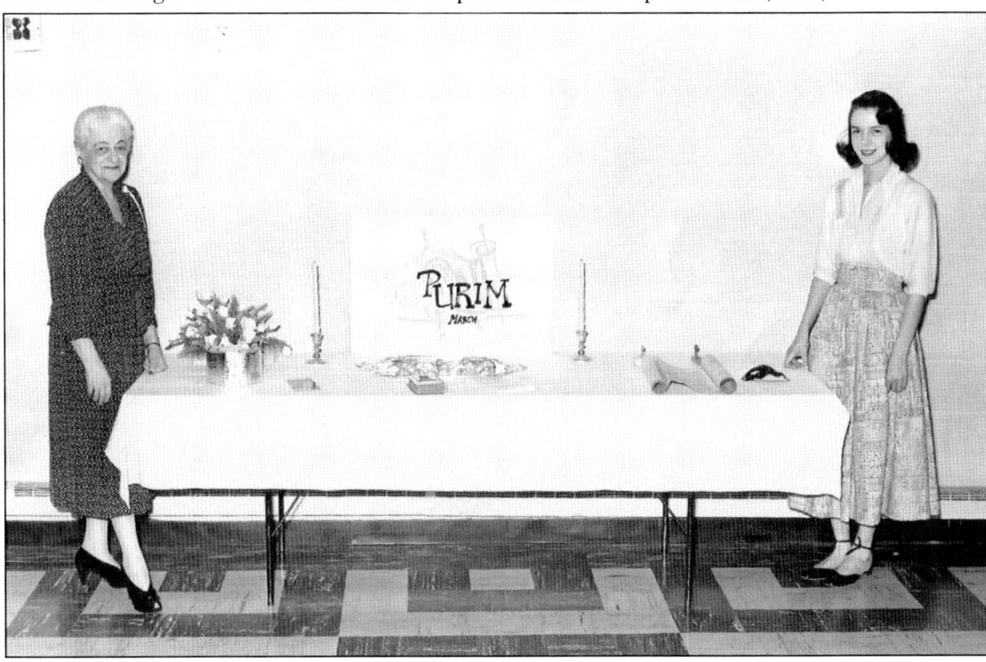


**PURIM DISPLAY.** Eva Benjamin (left) (1906–1989) was well known for her work both in Hadassah and particularly with the Beth Israel Sisterhood. Purim is one of the more festive holidays on the Jewish calendar, commemorating the role of Queen Esther and her cousin Mordechai in saving Persian Jews some 2,500 years ago. (BIC.)

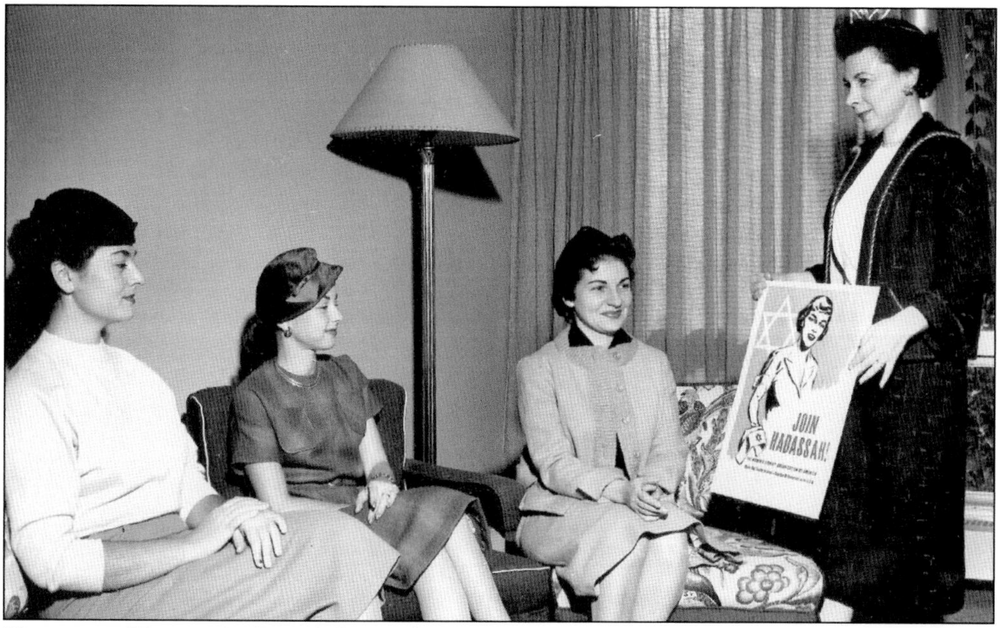


**HADASSAH TEA, 1957.** From left to right are Marilyn Krim, Audrey Levy, Ruth Bass, and Faye Woronoff. Hadassah and the sisterhood represent the primary women's Jewish organizations. Hadassah, "myrtle," was founded in 1912 by Henrietta Szold to meet medical needs in Palestine. It is now the largest Jewish women's organization in America and is respected for its charitable work. (BIC.)

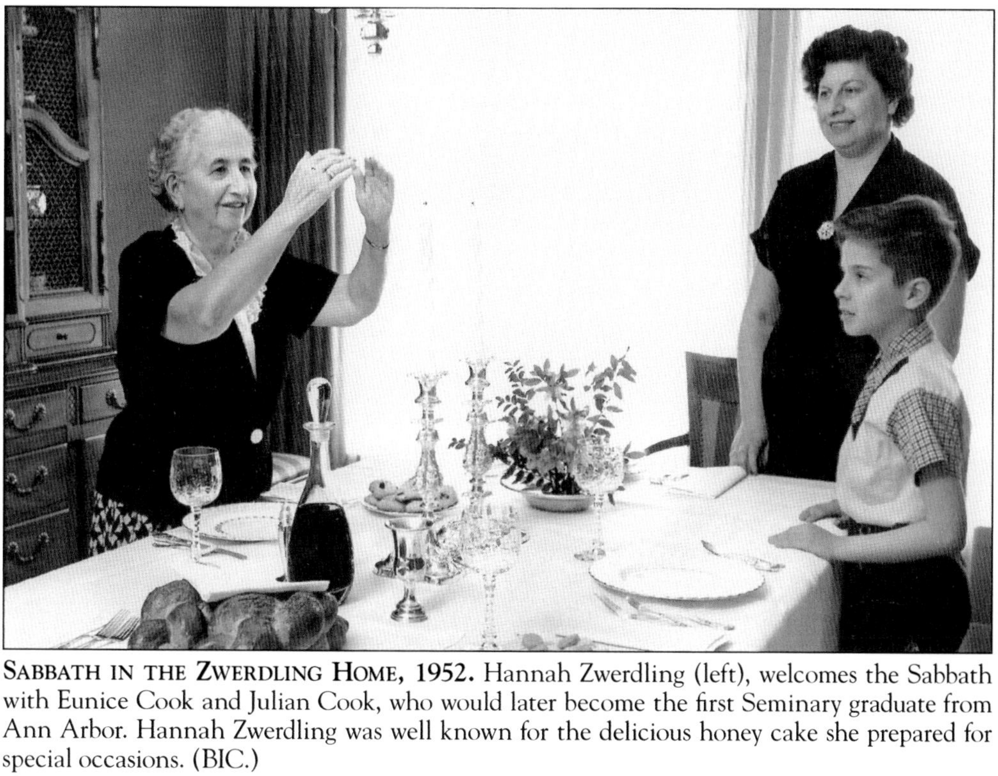

**SABBATH IN THE ZWERDLING HOME, 1952.** Hannah Zwerdling (left), welcomes the Sabbath with Eunice Cook and Julian Cook, who would later become the first Seminary graduate from Ann Arbor. Hannah Zwerdling was well known for the delicious honey cake she prepared for special occasions. (BIC.)

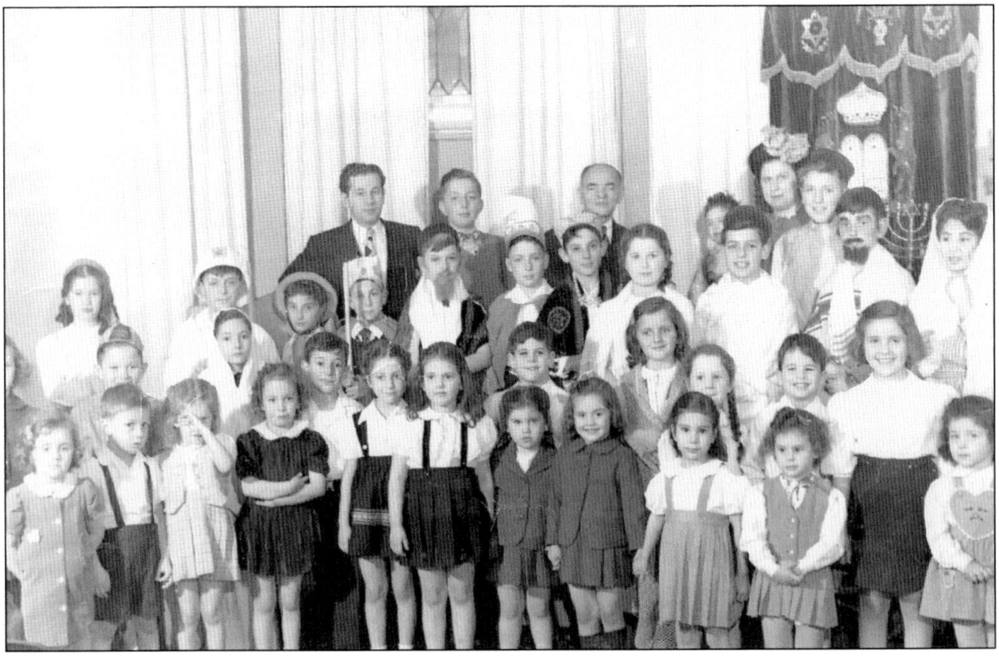

**PURIM CELEBRATION, AROUND 1955.** Jack Fagan (back, left), Osias Zwerdling, and Eunice Cook are the adults in the rear. In celebrating Purim, children dress in costumes depicting characters and events from the time of Queen Esther. The *Megillah* (scroll) of Esther is read in the service. (BIC.)

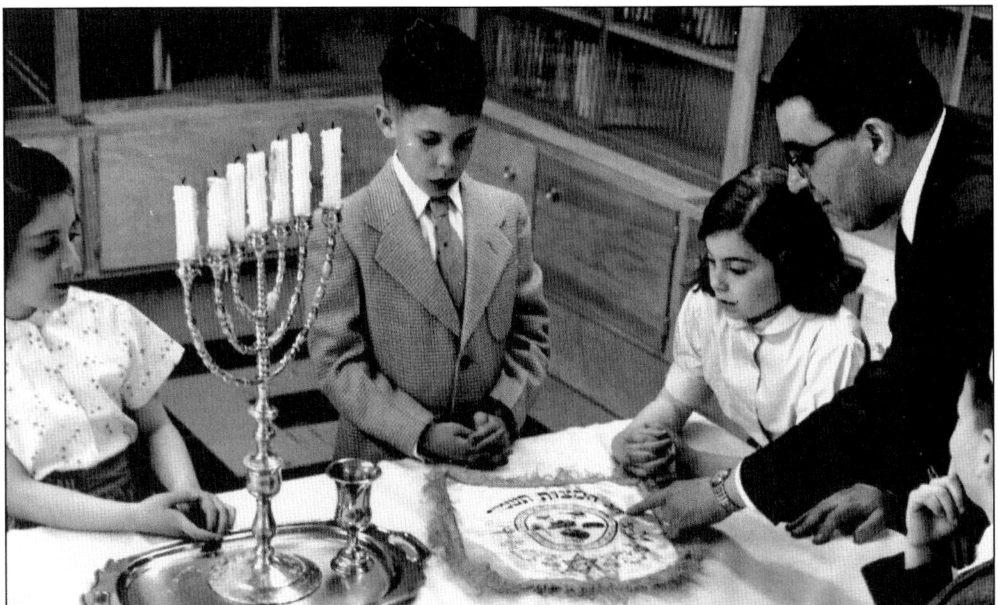

**RABBI WEINBERG, 1956.** The rabbi is explaining rituals of Judaism. Interactions with children represented a major goal of Rabbi Weinberg, the first ordained rabbi at the center in two decades. Among the changes instituted during his nine-year tenure was the establishment of specific guidelines and requirements for bar mitzvah. The Hebrew School grew from a single teacher with four pupils in 1952 to 50 children by 1962. (BIC.)

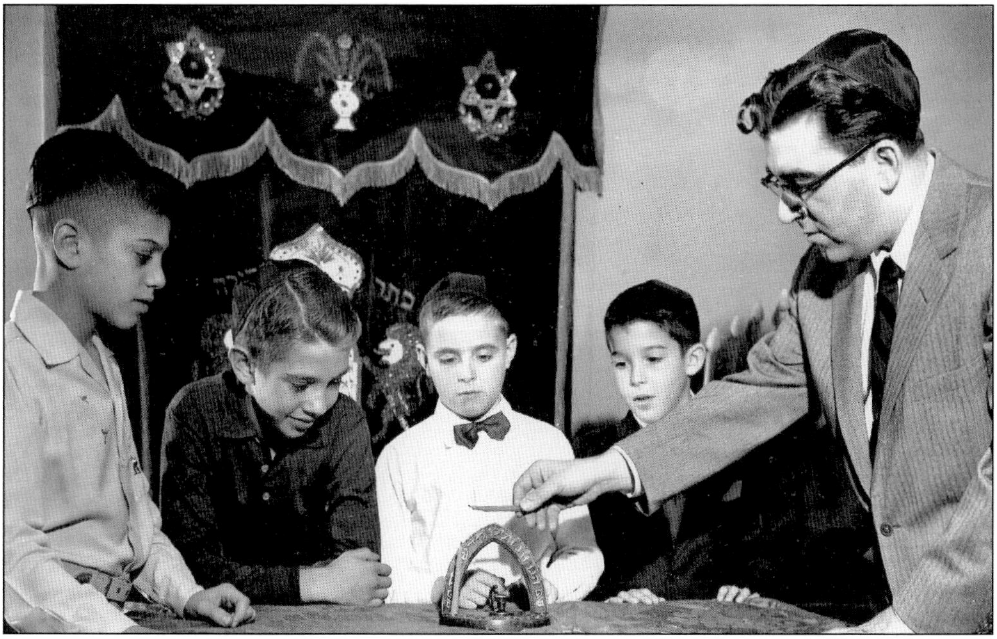

**RABBI WEINBERG, 1958.** While the picture does not depict anything specific to any holiday, Rabbi Weinberg is explaining various rituals. After completing his doctorate work in history at the University of Michigan, he joined the faculty at Wayne State University (1962–1964) and never returned to a synagogue pulpit as rabbi. In September 1965, Rabbi Weinberg joined the Department of History at Cleveland State University, where he remained as professor of history until his death. (BIC.)

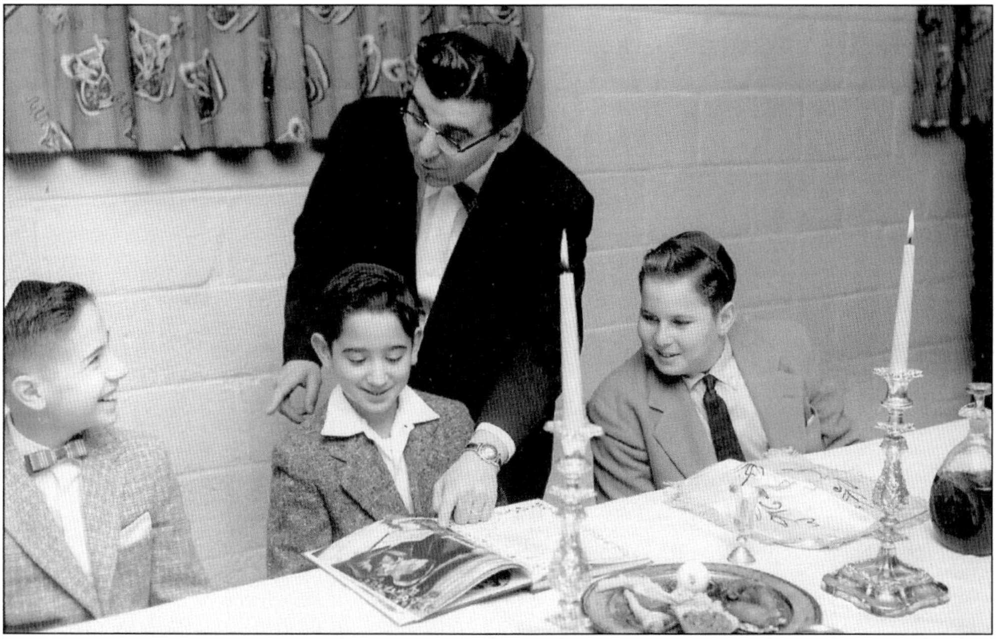

**RABBI WEINBERG, PASSOVER 1958.** The rabbi is explaining the Passover rituals to Jeffrey Ingber and Harvey Lansky (right). On the table are foods particular for the holiday, most notably the plate of matzoth. The formal dress was standard for such celebrations at the center, even for practice. (BIC.)

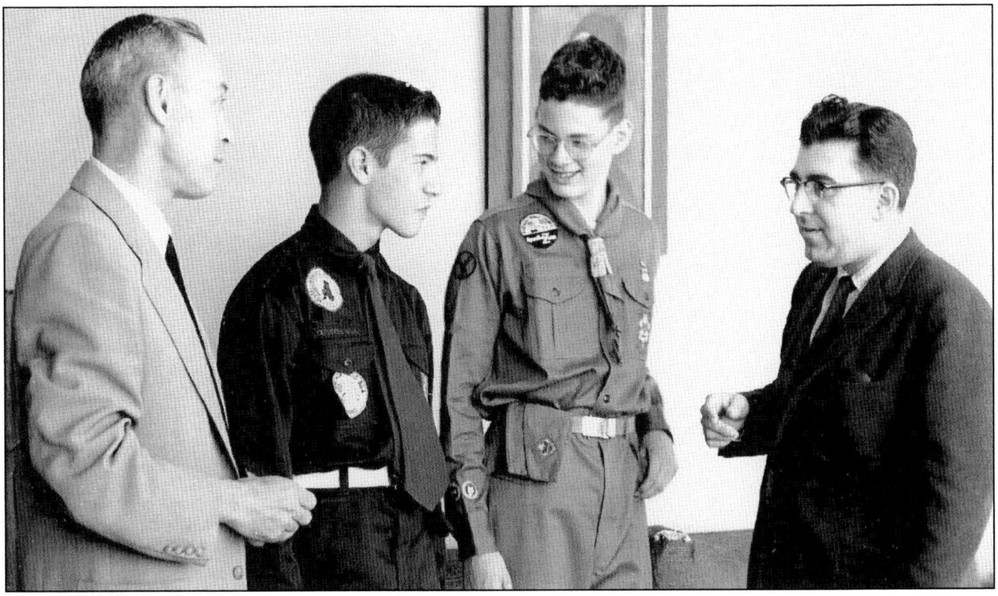

**RABBI WEINBERG WITH BOY SCOUTS.** As early as the 1920s, Beth Israel sponsored Cub Scout and Boy Scout troops, an activity carried out for several decades. Some of the boys whose families were members of Ann Arbor synagogues eventually became Eagle Scouts in ceremonies held at the center, and later, at the synagogue on Washtenaw, the three Feigelson sons, Daniel, Aaron, and Josh, and Steve Adler being examples. Likely there were others whose names were not found. The scout on the right with Rabbi Weinberg is Matthew Lampe. (BIC.)

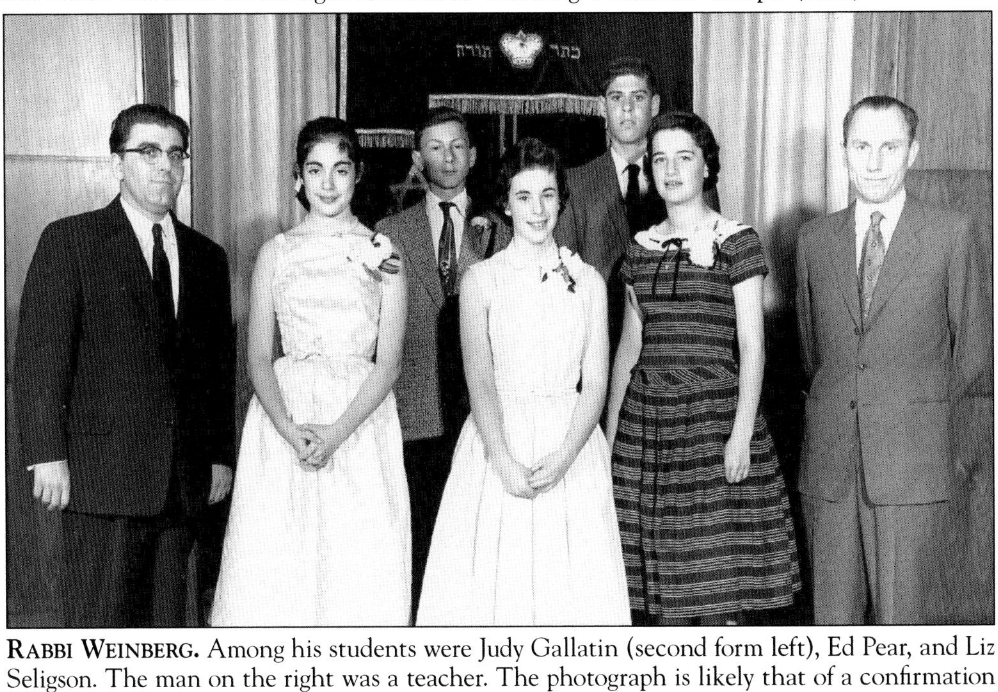

**RABBI WEINBERG.** Among his students were Judy Gallatin (second form left), Ed Pear, and Liz Seligson. The man on the right was a teacher. The photograph is likely that of a confirmation or graduation class from the community center. Adult education was also a component of Rabbi Weinberg's work, a monthly Yiddish reading group was also instituted. The program lasted over 20 years, long after Rabbi Weinberg had departed. (BIC.)

# *Five*

# Decades of Change

Rabbi Harold White, then completing a one-year tenure in Ireland, succeeded Rabbi Weinberg. Rabbi White's decision to relocate to Ann Arbor in large part was based upon the strong academic atmosphere in the Ann Arbor community, a significant number of members of the Jewish community were employed by the university.

The 1960s were characterized as a time of turmoil in the country, and Ann Arbor was certainly no exception. The participation of the Ann Arbor Jewish community in addressing the evil of racism had a long precedent. In the 1974 book *Hail to the Victors*, author John Behee describes plans for a protest against Michigan football coach Fielding H. Yost's decision to remove an African American player from a game against the Georgia Institute of Technology. Yost apologized to the southern coach, noting "the agitation [protest] was developed by a committee of five Jewish sophomore students." Rabbi White continued this tradition of fighting racism.

The 1960s represented a continuation of the serious growth of the congregation. When Rabbi White left for a position at American University in Washington in 1968, approximately 375 persons were members of Beth Israel, this despite the division of the congregation with formation of the reform temple, Beth Emeth. It might also be noted that the name of the organization also underwent a change, reverting back to the original Beth Israel Congregation in June 1963.

After three years of transition under Rabbis Joseph Krickstein and Mervin Tomsky, Rabbi Allan D. Kensky, a 1971 graduate from the Jewish Theological Seminary, joined the congregation. Rabbi Kensky presided over some of the most significant changes, both philosophical as well as physical, to the congregation in its history. One of the first was the granting of the privilege, on special occasions, of *aliyot* to women, the right to participate in the blessings over the Torah during religious services. What is today arguably a nonissue in most conservative congregations was at the time extremely controversial, and Rabbi Kensky's ability to shepherd the change was indicative of his growing rapport with the congregation.

Other changes during the decade beginning with the mid-1960s were even more dramatic. In 1966, a number of congregants separated from Beth Israel to form the first reform congregation in Ann Arbor: Temple Beth Emeth. Reasons for the separation were complex and were based upon both philosophical differences in the practice of Judaism as well as concern with the significant increase in costs that would result from the building of a new synagogue.

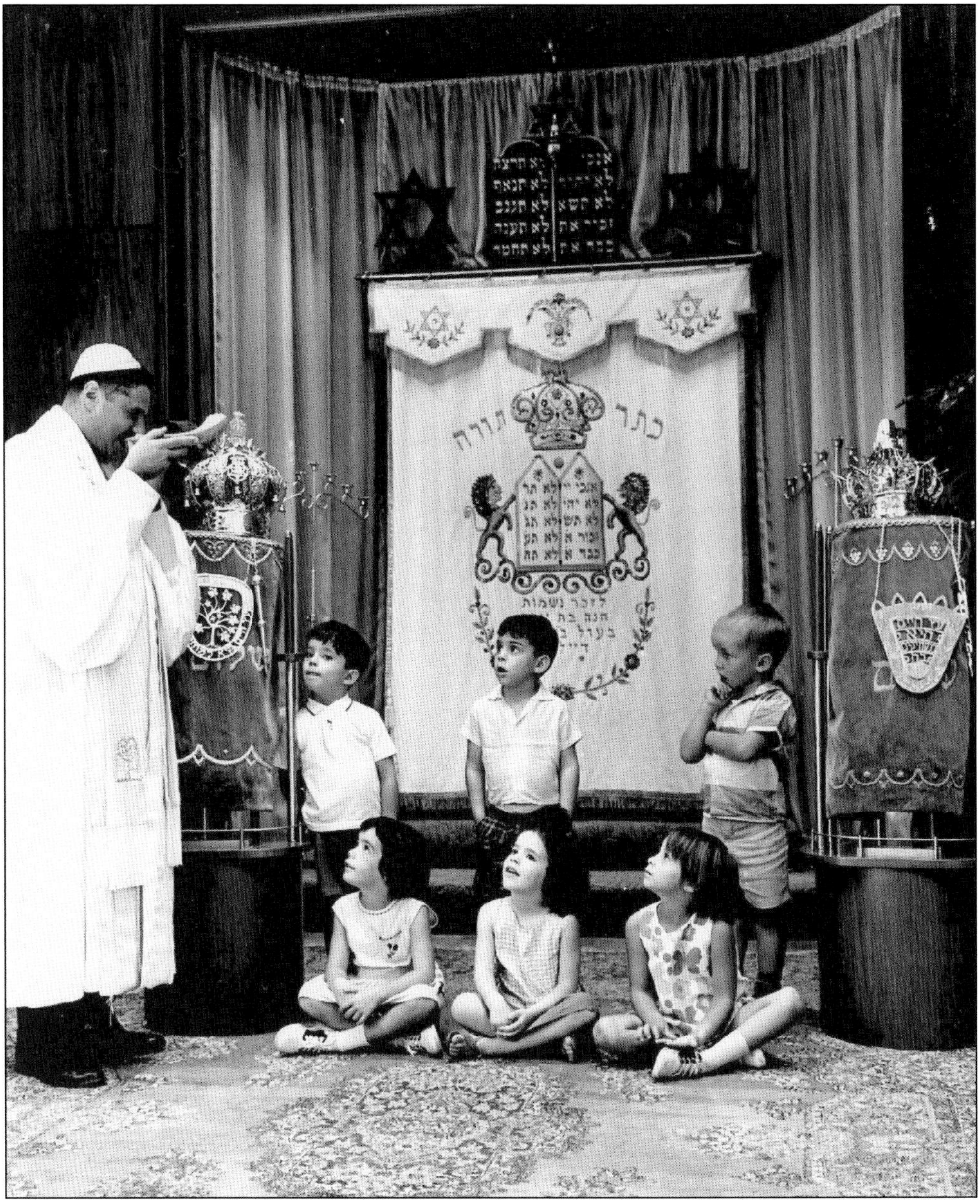


**RABBI HAROLD WHITE.** Among Rabbi White's initial concerns upon filling the position was the local perception in parts of the Christian community that Beth Israel was a "Jewish social club, only without golf." White immediately increased the visibility of the congregation, describing events in the local press, as well as stronger involvement in civic affairs. Along with other members of the congregation, Thomas Cook standing out in the rabbi's memory, White became prominent in issues of civil rights and racial equality, as well as the peace movement and antiwar activism. White also played a critical role in the evolution of Beth Israel's Social Action Committee as well as the Jewish Community Council, established during his tenure. Participation in interfaith and interracial organizations did not start with Rabbi White, but the Ann Arbor community at large became more aware of the role played by Beth Israel members in local events. (BIC.)

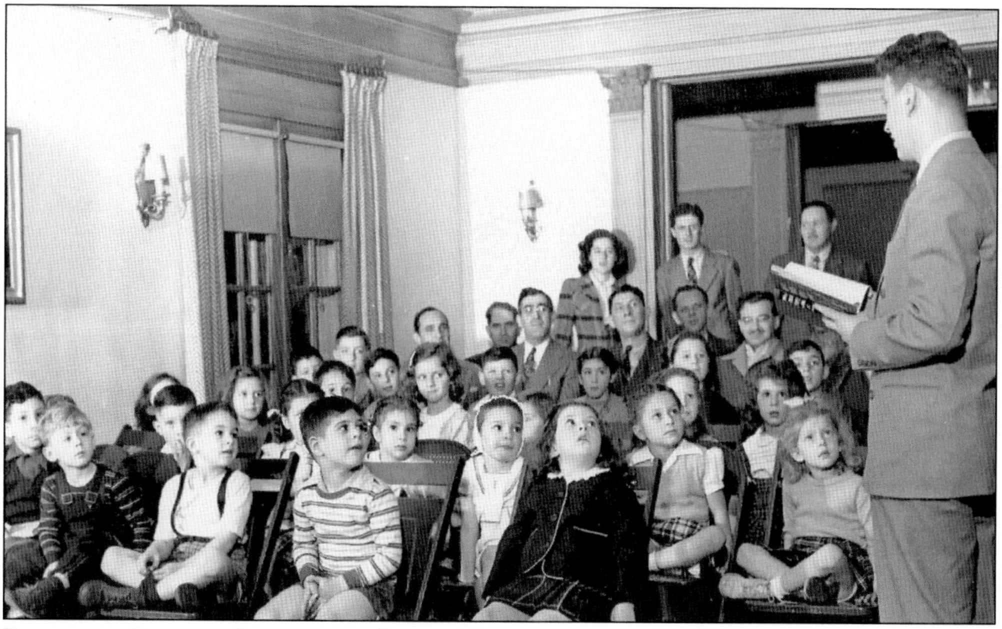

**RELIGIOUS SCHOOL CLASS WITH RABBI WHITE.** Among the changes instituted by Rabbi White was the joining of the congregation with the Conservative Jewish movement. Religious education supplemented that from the public schools, and White was always a ready participant to interact with the children. Ed Pear, son of Max and Ceil Pear, is among the children in the front. (BIC.)

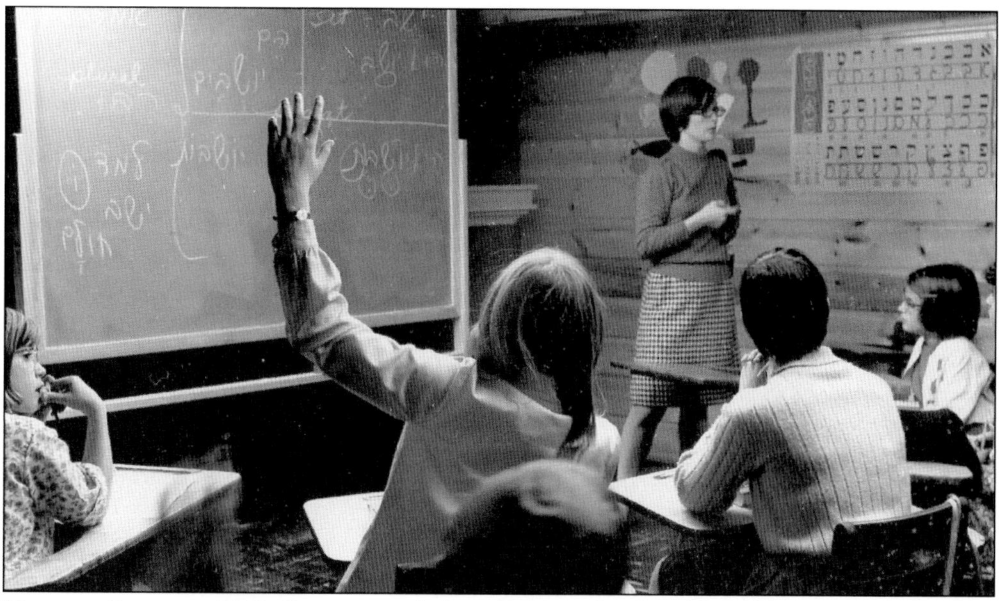

**HEBREW SCHOOL, 1967.** Expansion of the religious school and Jewish activities within the community was a primary goal during Rabbi White's tenure, establishing the congregation within the conservative movement. During these years, and indeed continuing until the larger synagogue was ready in 1978, the religious education program was challenged by a lack of space. Classes were often divided among several buildings. Nevertheless, dedicated teachers coped as best they could. (BIC.)

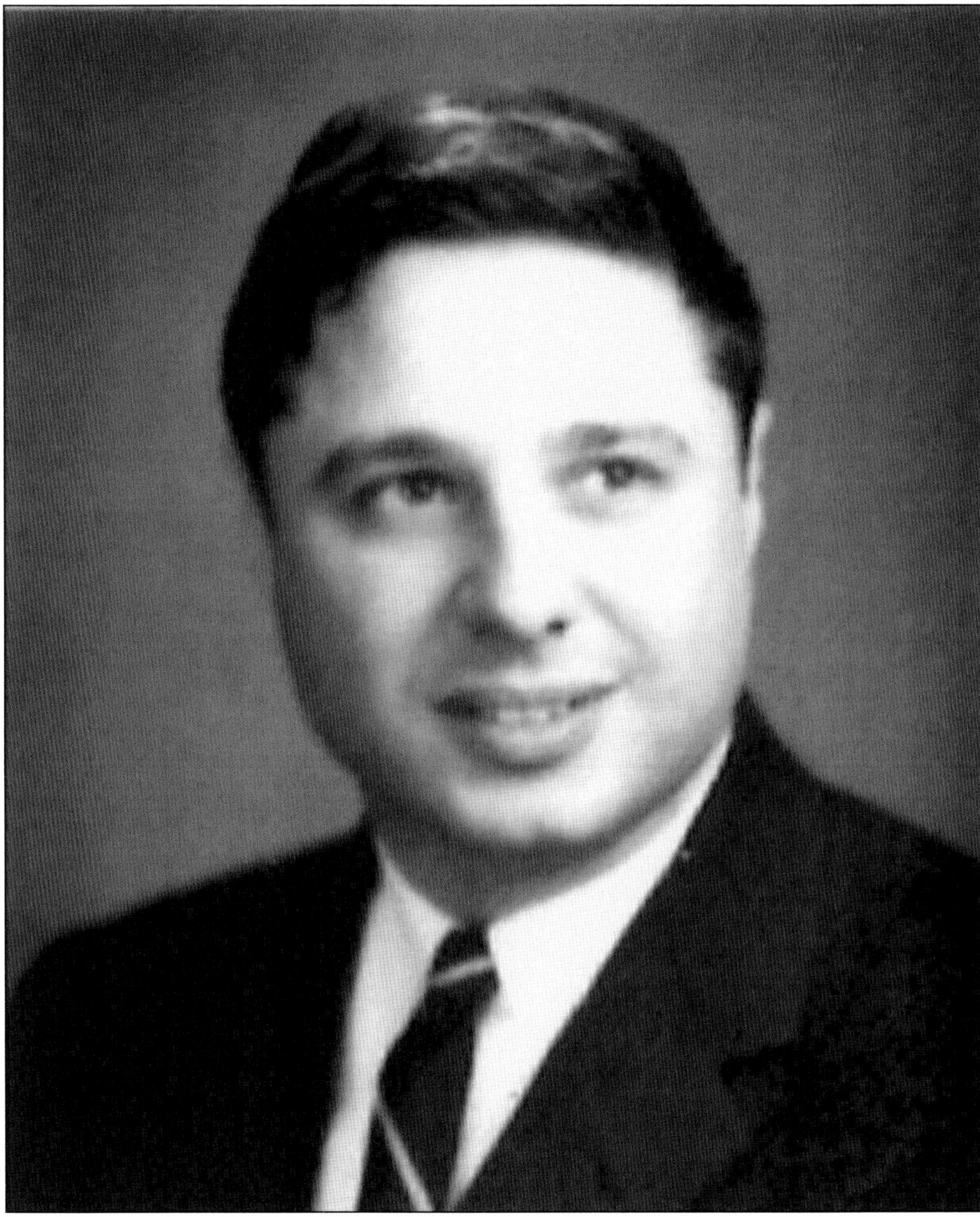

**RABBI HAROLD WHITE.** Rabbi White was born in 1932 in Hartford, Connecticut. Ordained at the Jewish Theological Seminary in 1959, he served several years as a navy chaplain with the Marines, first in South Carolina, then on the island of Okinawa. After serving a year as rabbi of Dublin (Ireland) Jewish Progressive Congregation, he came to Ann Arbor. Beth Israel represented his first American pulpit. The latter years of the 1960s were particularly stressful in Ann Arbor. White recalled a close working relationship with Fannie Haber, Professor William Haber's wife, on a variety of antiwar and civil rights committees. It was also during this period that plans were developed to seek a new site for a larger synagogue. In 1964, fund-raising activities began for that purpose. In May 1968, White resigned to direct the Hillel Foundation at American University in Washington and to teach at Georgetown University. In 1976, he became senior Jewish chaplain at Georgetown University. (BIC.)

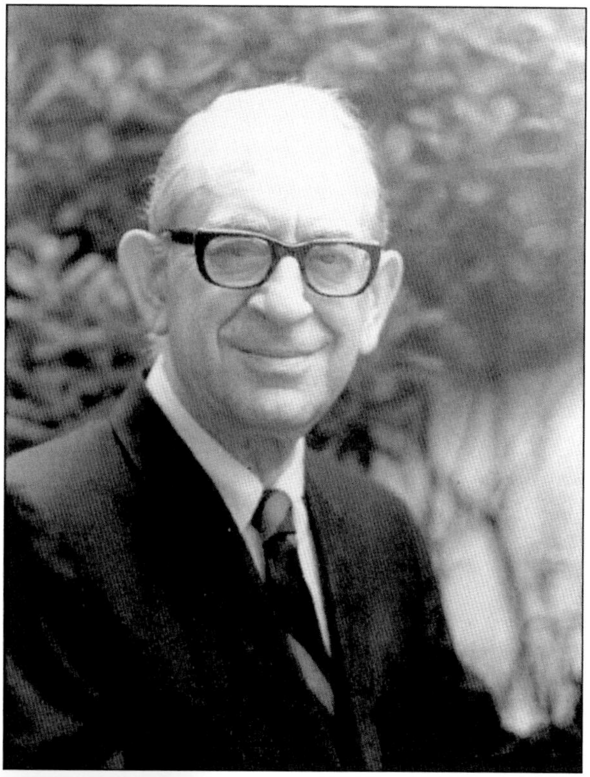

**RABBI JOSEPH KRICKSTEIN (1899–1971).** Rabbi White's relatively sudden departure left a vacuum in the position, one filled on an interim basis by Joseph Krickstein. Universally described as a "gentle, wonderful" man, Rabbi Krickstein had worked with White at Beth Israel since 1964. In recognition of his love for children, the congregation established a library, now called the Krickstein Youth Library, in his name. (Morgan Pressel.)

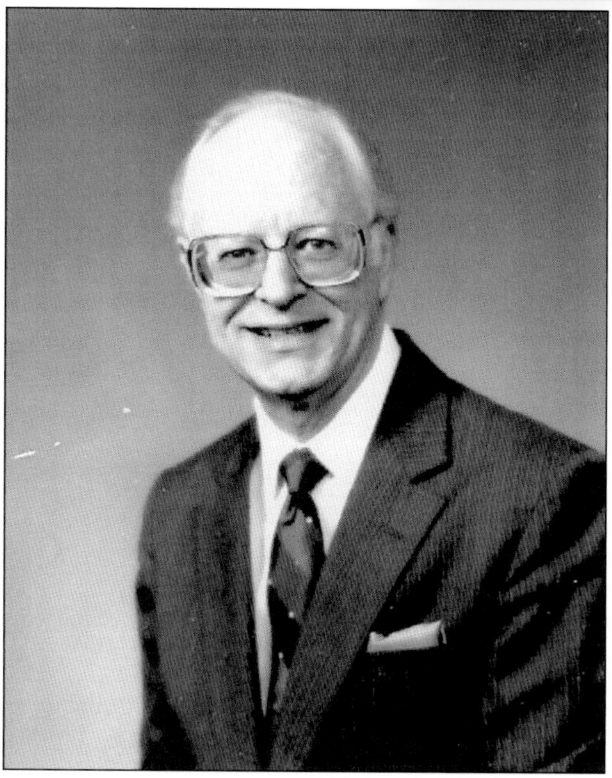

**RABBI MERVIN TOMSKY.** Born and raised in Minneapolis, Rabbi Tomsky, a World War II veteran, entered the rabbinate relatively late in life. Ordained at the Jewish Theological Seminary in 1956, Rabbi Tomsky, his wife Helen and their three children settled in the Ann Arbor community in March 1969, after serving in Oklahoma City. After 2½ years with Beth Israel, the Tomskys moved to Palos Verdes, California. (Mervin Tomsky.)

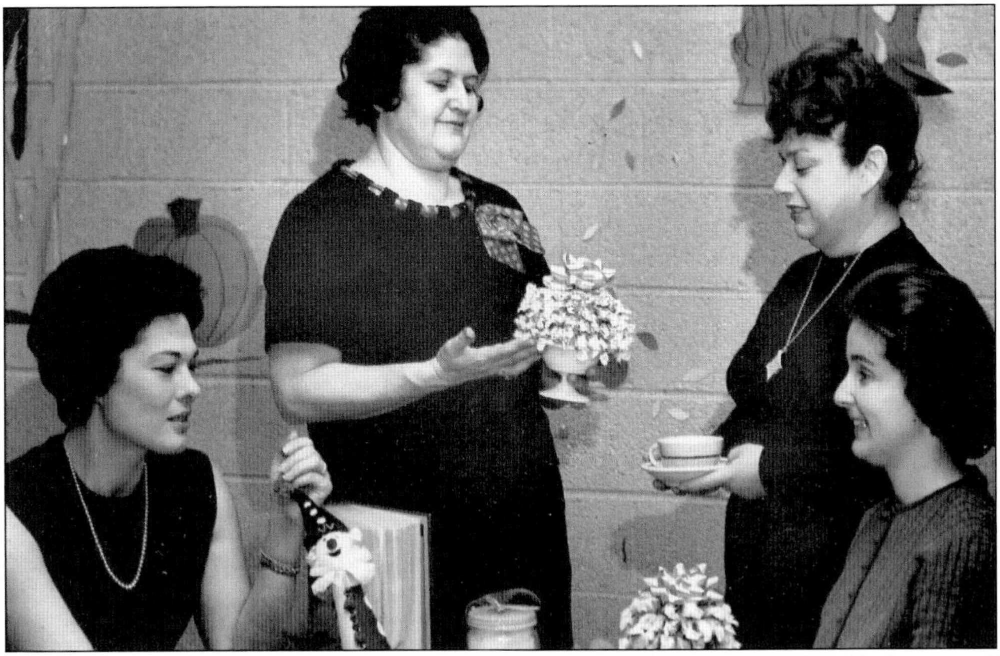

**SISTERHOOD TEA, 1970.** Shown here from left to right are (first row) Thelma Richman and Florence Gerber; (second row) Ada Margolis and Clara Seymour. The sisterhood was always ready to undertake many of the more "mundane" activities necessary for the function of Beth Israel. Purchase of kitchen material, interior requirements, and even a piano had been financed through the local organization. (BIC.)

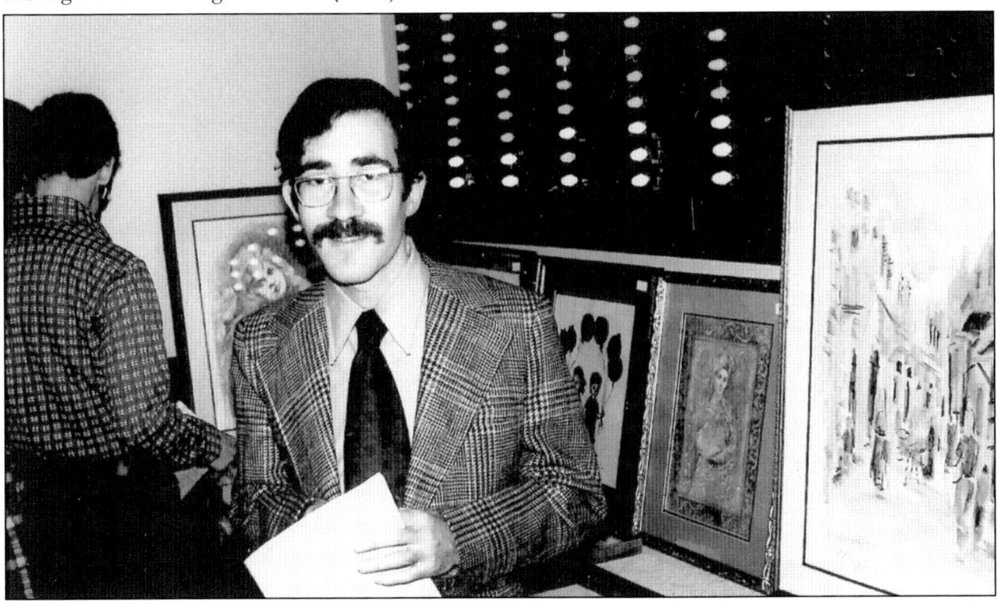

**RABBI ALLAN D. KENSKY.** Recently graduated from the Jewish Theological Seminary, youthful and "single," Rabbi Kensky was considered by members of the search committee as too young and consideration of his hiring was a source of contention among the members of the committee. Osias Zwerdling settled the issue: "Give him a year with this congregation. After that, he'll be old enough." (BIC.)

# *Six*

# A Permanent Home for Beth Israel

Beth Israel Congregation had grown to approximately 150 families by the mid-1970s. The question of a newer building had existed since the early 1960s. But outside of forming a building committee under Jack Sundelson along with the purchase of the property (Zeta Beta Tau fraternity) at 2006 Washtenaw Avenue, little in the way of actual movement on the issue had taken place. The original idea was to convert the house into a synagogue, but the age of the structure as well as a full understanding of the ultimate cost forced a postponement on the decision until an adequate building fund could be accumulated. A second Ann Arbor site was also being considered during the late 1960s. Near the present-day intersection of Eisenhower Boulevard and Packard Road, now the site of a bank but then open land, 19 acres were purchased with the idea of erecting a community center to serve both Beth Israel and Temple Beth Emeth. The idea never came to pass, and the land was ultimately sold, with the funds applied to the building fund at Beth Israel.

Difficulties delayed construction of a new synagogue, but once the decision had been made, it only remained for the congregation to develop an approach to overcome these problems. A building committee under the leadership of Henry Gershowitz visited other cities to determine the style to be incorporated. Questions revolved around funding, finding adequate space, and incorporating both offices and a religious school within the new building. On May 14, 1976, the Beth Israel board approved the funding for the building of a new synagogue, to be located at the site of the Zeta Beta Tau (ZBT) fraternity house at 2006 Washtenaw Avenue. Groundbreaking began on June 26, 1977. In a ceremonial parade on October 1, 1978, *Erev* Rosh Hashanah, the congregation carried the Torahs from the Hill Street location to the new synagogue on Washtenaw Avenue.

Rabbi Kensky continued to serve the congregation until 1988. The search committee for the new rabbi had one overwhelming criterion: in addition to knowledge, experience, and leadership, the new rabbi must be a *mensch*, a "human." In Rabbi Robert Dobrusin, the congregation found its mensch. One need only look at the length of his tenure—now in its 18th year.

Further change would be observed when, in 1994, a Reconstructionist *Havurah* was organized. Affiliated with the National Jewish Reconstructionist Foundation, the local organization consisted of approximately three dozen families by the end of the century.

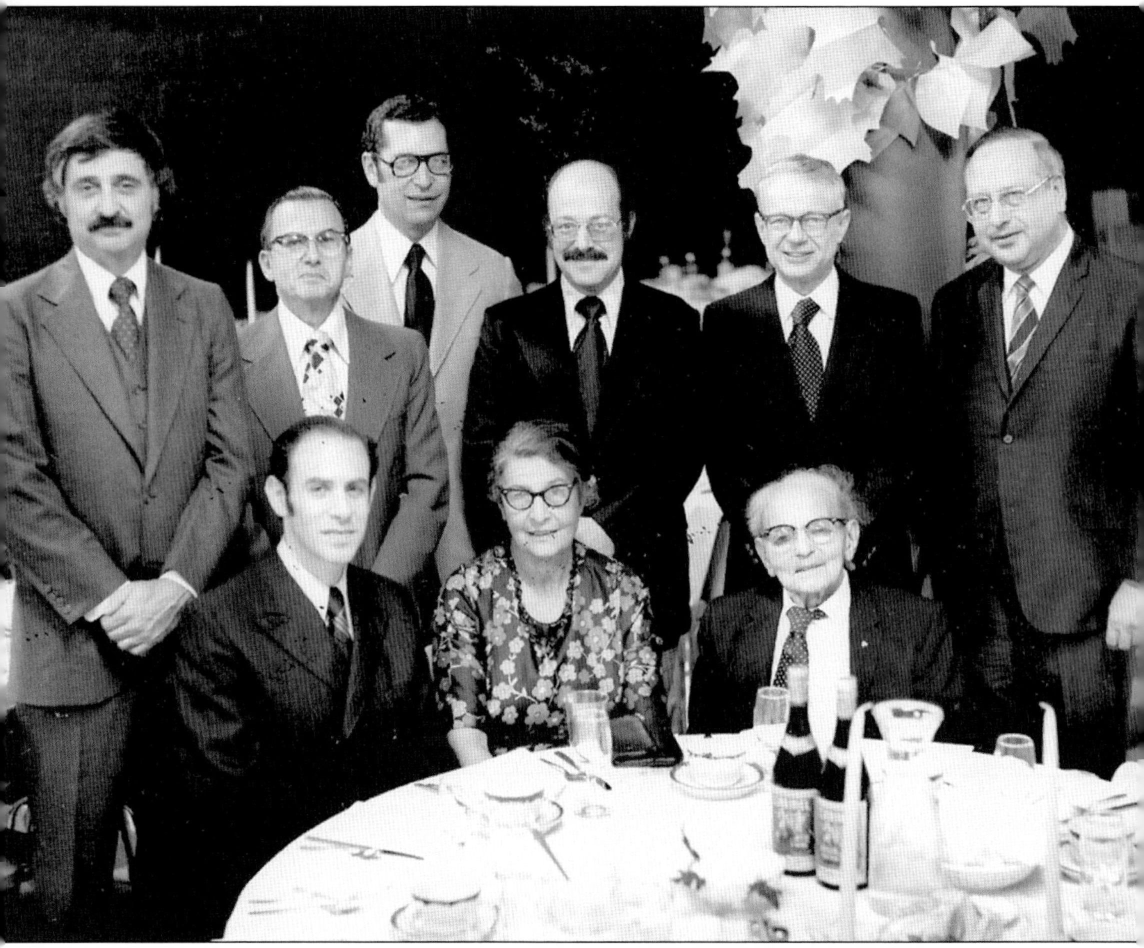

**BETH ISRAEL PRESIDENTS.** Pictured from left to right are (first row) Eduardo David Schteingart (1974–1978), Gerda Seligson (1971–1973), and Osias Zwerdling (1918–1958); (second row) Jarvis Franzblau (1960–1961), Henry Gershowitz (1970, 1994–1995), Morris Friedman (1959), Saul Hymans (1969), Marty Sichel (1966), and Paul Pressel (1967–1968). Osias Zwerdling was by far the longest "reigning" president of the congregation. Even after retirement, he maintained an honorary title to that position. The group represented most of the leaders of the congregation from its inception in 1916, until the new building was completed in 1978. The years were marked by significant change. From humble beginnings, it remained until the early 1950s until a permanent site could be found to house a growing congregation. The presidency required an individual who wore many hats, both serving as a leader as well as a fund-raiser, and often a referee able to mediate disagreements as to synagogue politics and philosophies. Slowed only by advancing age, Zwerdling for decades was the man for this position. Arguably, future presidents succeeded Zwerdling; they did not replace him. (BIC.)

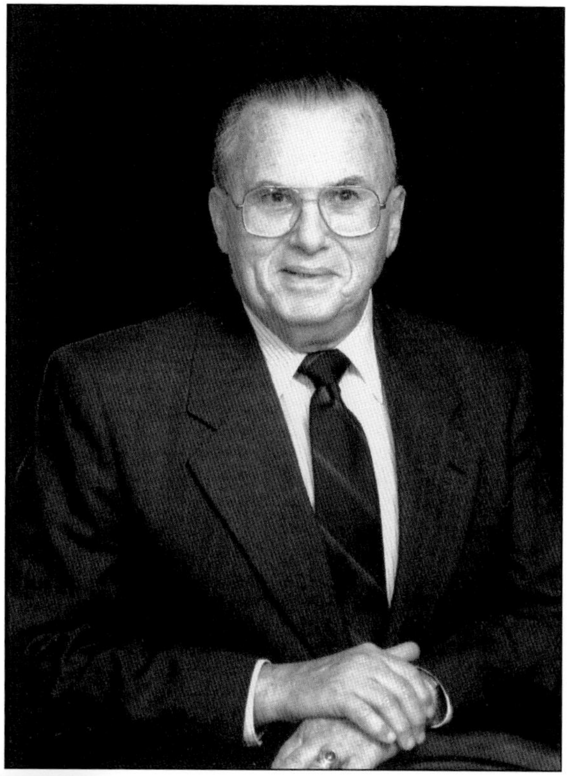

**Henry Gershowitz (1925–1998).** Twice elected president of the congregation, Henry Gershowitz represented as dominant a figure at Beth Israel as had Osias Zwerdling. Gershowitz entered college at 16, dropping out following the death of his father. Following service in the war, he returned to college, earning a Ph.D. in genetics. Gershowitz and his wife Beverly came to Ann Arbor in 1956, where he was one of the few Jewish members of the medical school. (Beverly Gershowitz.)

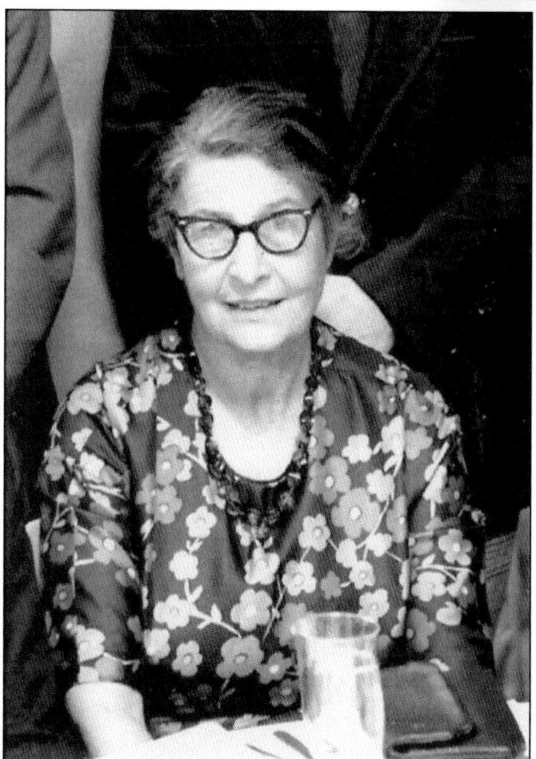

**Gerda Seligson (1909–2002).** Gerda Seligson was president of Beth Israel from 1971 to 1973. With her election in 1971, Seligson became one of the first women to serve as president of a conservative congregation. As Professor Emerita in the Department of Classical Studies at the University of Michigan, Seligson was well known and respected in the study of classical languages such as Latin and Greek, each of which she could speak and read fluently. (BIC.)

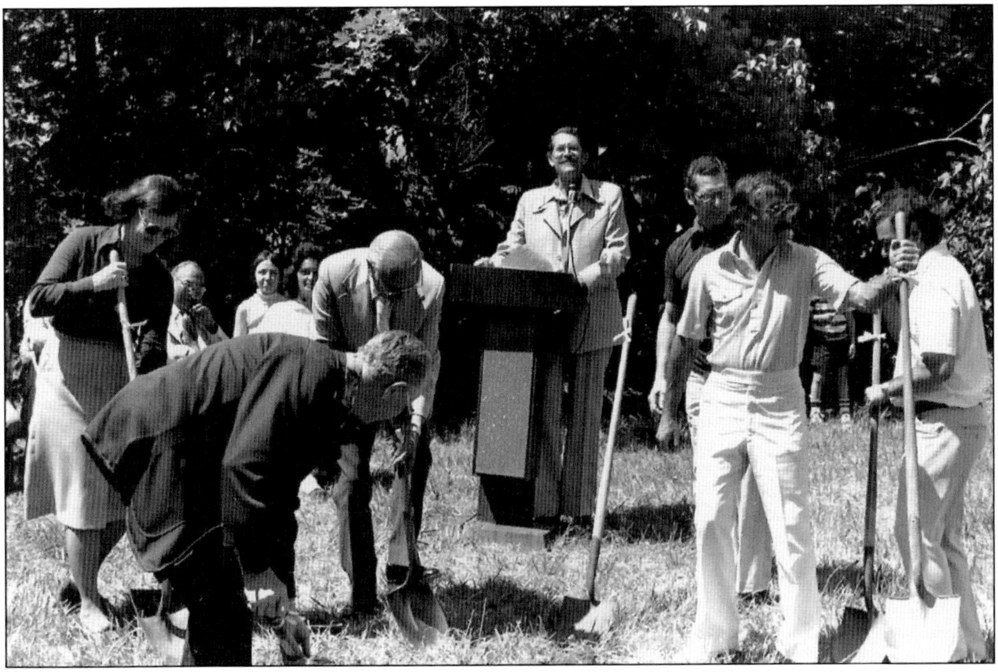

**BREAKING GROUND FOR THE NEW SYNAGOGUE.** On June 26, 1977, Morris Friedman (from right, holding shovel), a former president of the congregation and son of Israel Friedman, one of the founders, is shown preparing to break ground for construction. The site for the new building was long a source of contention, with some favoring a place within walking distance to campus and others arguing for a more distant site with more parking. (BIC.)

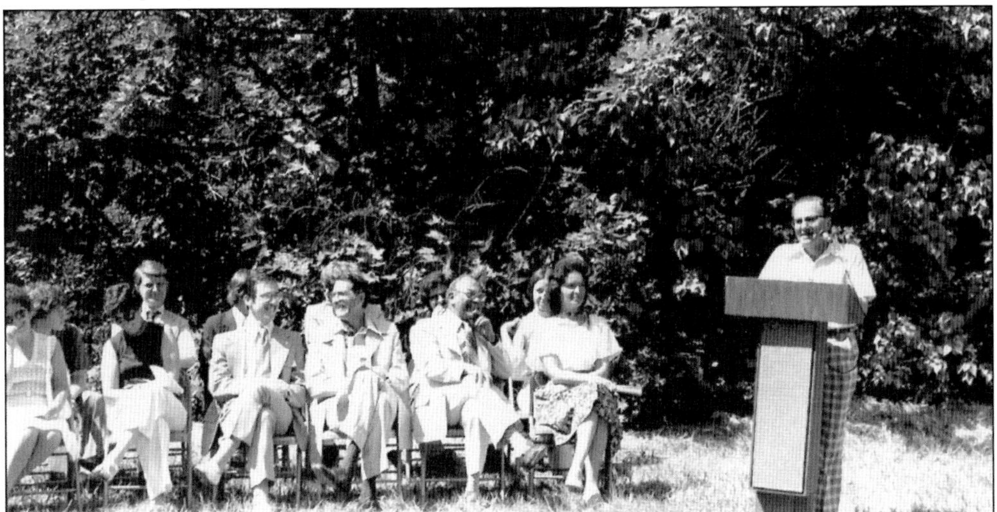

**SYNAGOGUE GROUNDBREAKING.** Henry Gershowitz is shown speaking at the groundbreaking. Gershowitz, then a former (and future) president of the congregation, was a key member of the building and search committee, which finally settled on the Washtenaw Avenue site. Building plans were four years in the making. The contractor for construction was Jeffries-Dyer. (BIC.)

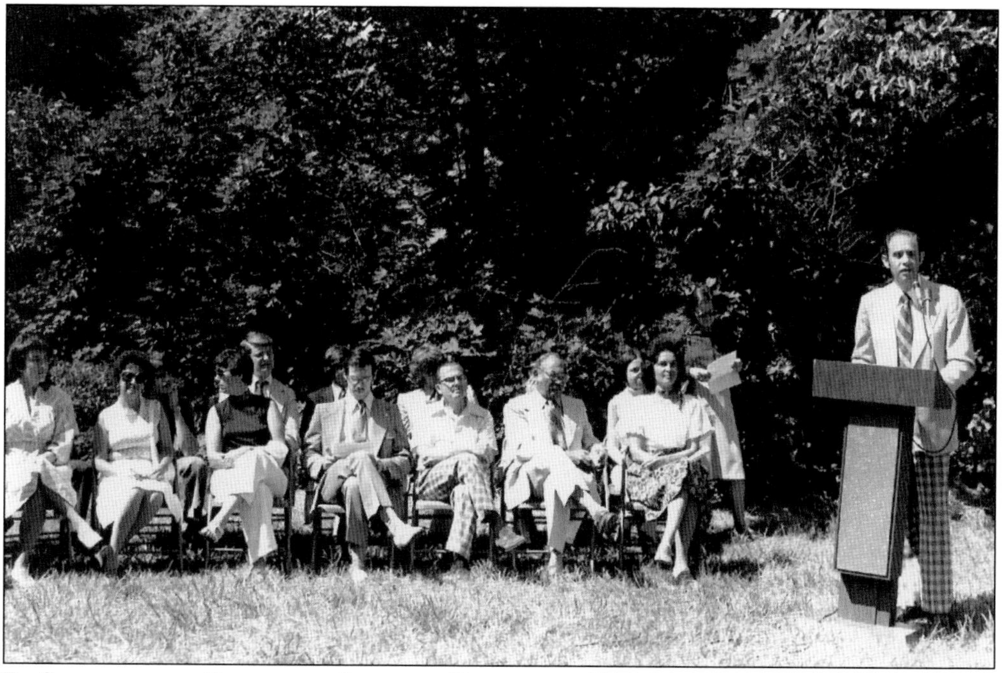

**Ed Schteingart, President, Board of Directors.** Ed Schteingart provided a few words at the groundbreaking. His tenure as president (1974–1978) corresponded with the final decision as to the site and plans for the new building. He was still congregation president at the time of the groundbreaking and would serve through its completion the following year. (BIC.)

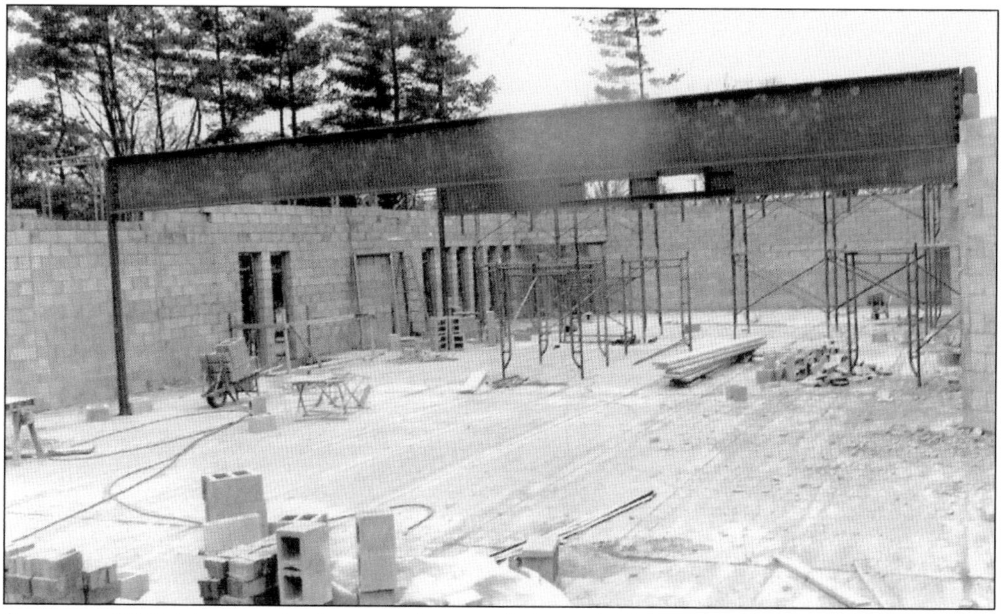

**Summer, 1977.** Construction began and proceeded on schedule. Even after the groundbreaking, followed by the work itself, significant problems still existed. Changes or additions were still being considered. Strikes were possible. Given the often long and harsh Michigan winters, delays were always possible. Not least of the concerns was the significant costs that the new building would incur. The architects were Hobbs and Black and Associates. (BIC.)

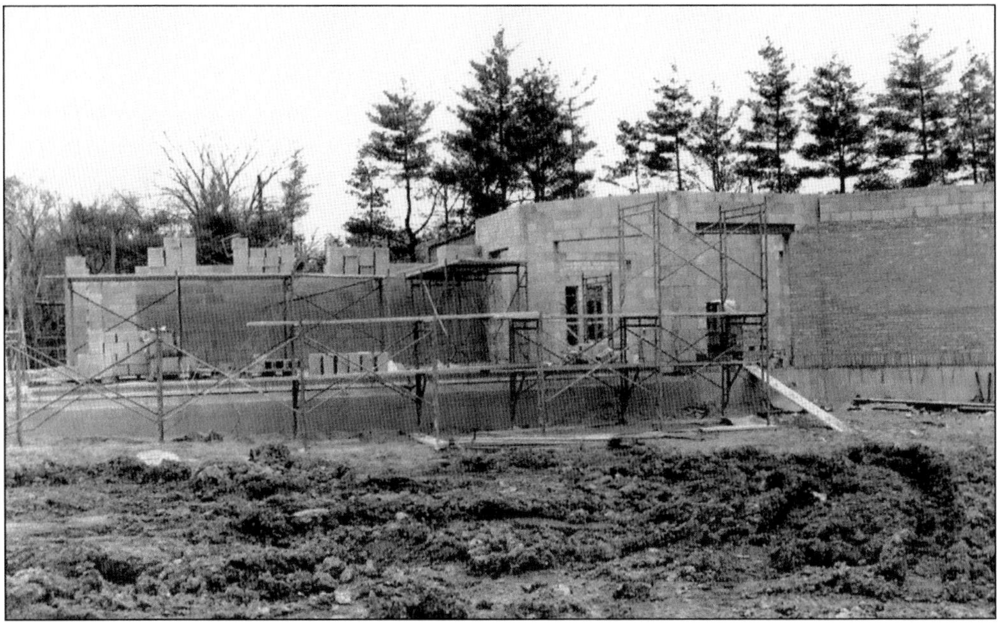

**Construction of the Sanctuary.** The new sanctuary would serve as the new site of worship for a growing congregation. The size of the sanctuary was one of the major decisions for the new synagogue. At the Hill Street site, particularly during High Holy Day ceremonies, congregants were often crowded together, sight lines were effectively nonexistent. Problems such as these limited the ability of the congregation to grow in numbers. (BIC.)

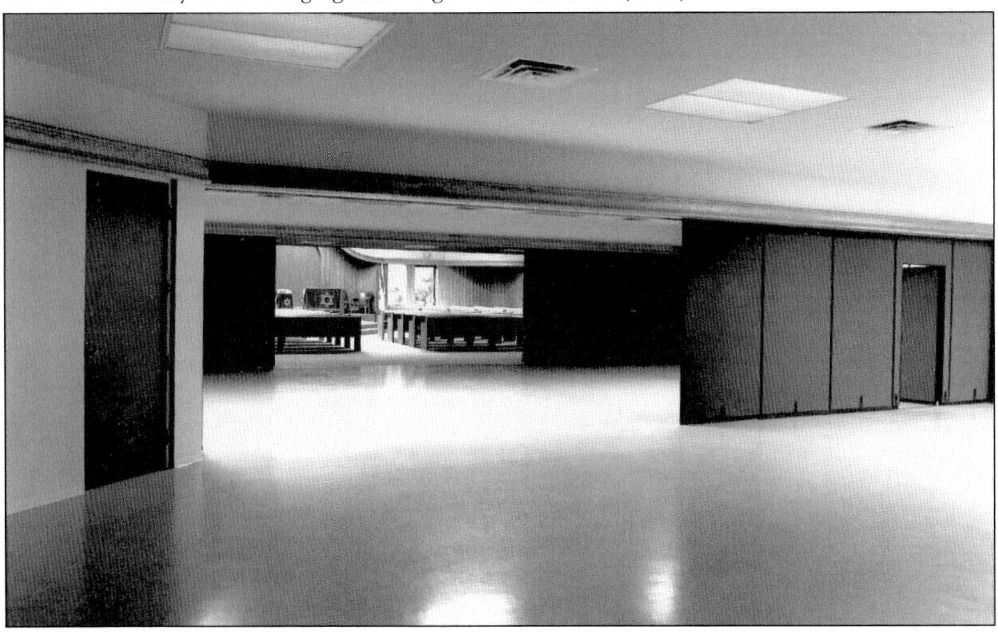

**Completed Sanctuary.** By the fall of 1978, the building was finished. The larger sanctuary, formed as a semicircle, faced the *bima*, "stage," and ark in the front. To accommodate larger crowds for special events or High Holy Day services, a second adjacent room was available. A partition, which opened, would also allow the room to serve as a social hall with a kitchen in back. (BIC.)

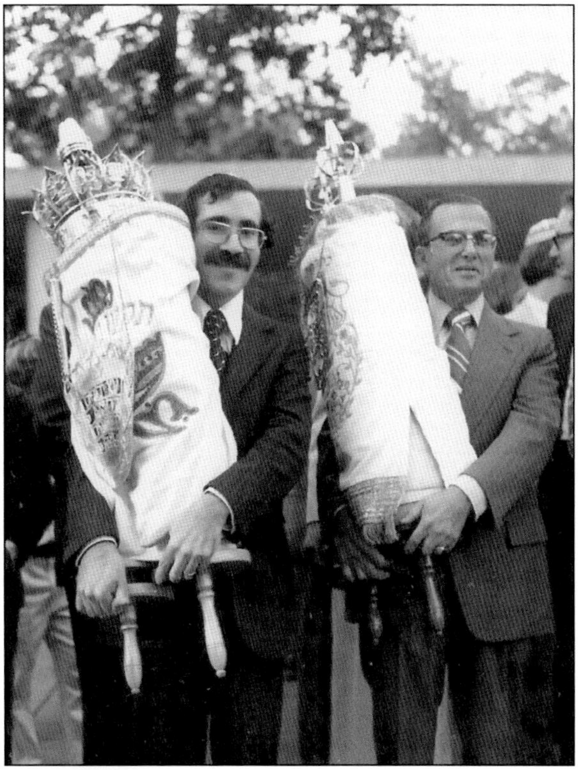

EREV ROSH HASHANAH, **OCTOBER 1, 1978.** Rabbi Allan D. Kensky (left) and Henry Gershowitz prepare to lead the march from the Hillel Building to the new synagogue at 2000 Washtenaw Avenue. The Torah scrolls were removed from the ark housed in the Hill Street site of the synagogue and, at the time the photographs were taken, were carried to the new site approximately one mile away. Kensky, as spiritual leader of the congregation, was given the honor of helping lead the procession. Gershowitz, former congregation president and key member of the building committee, was given the honor of accompanying Kensky at the head of the procession. (BIC.)

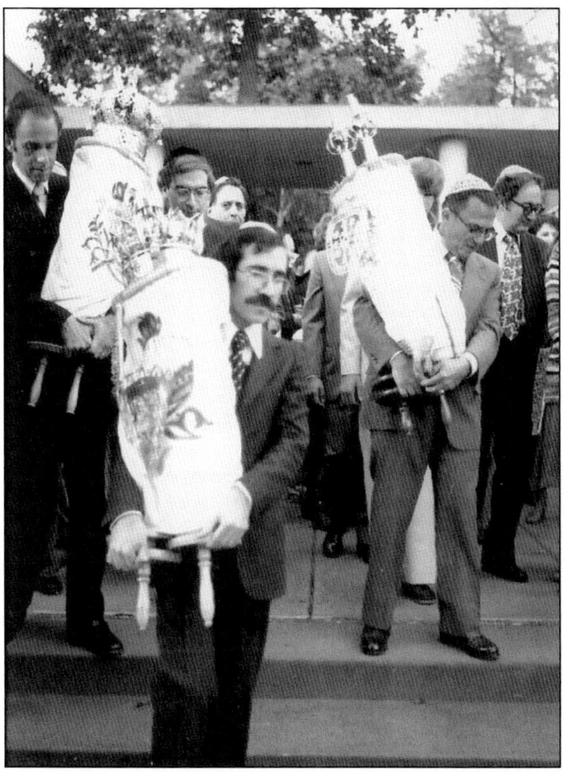

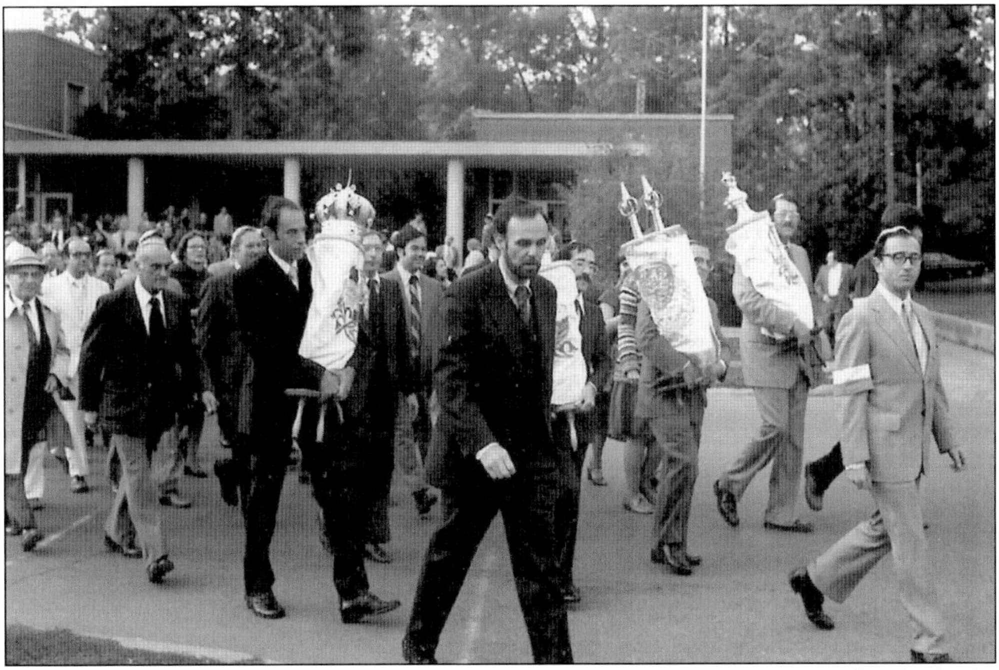

**CARRYING THE TORAH TO THE NEW SYNAGOGUE.** Congregant Monroe Hafter leads the procession (right). The privilege of carrying a Torah scroll to a new home, while available to any congregant of the synagogue, is considered a significant honor and is carried out by those members who represent leadership or who are standouts among the congregation. (BIC.)

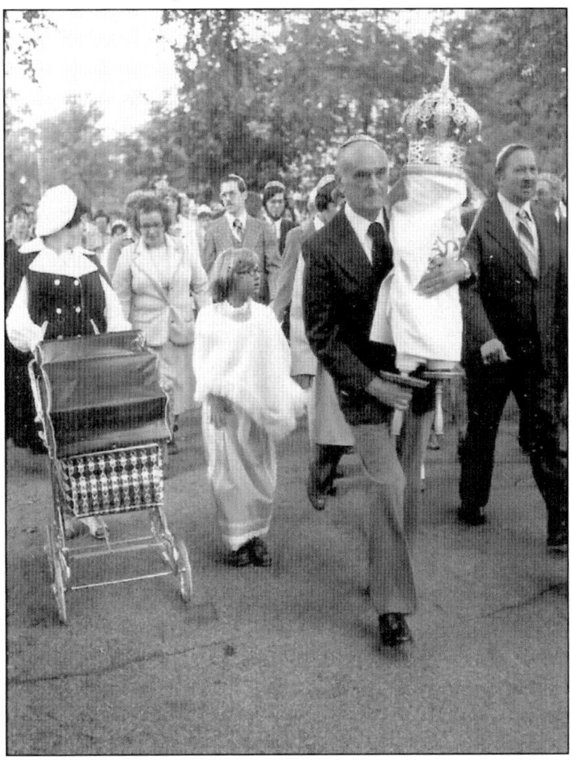

**SAM BENJAMIN.** Sam Benjamin, with his wife Eva, were prominent members of the congregation, and in recognition, he carried one of several Torahs to its new site. Eva Benjamin had significantly contributed to both Hadassah and sisterhood during a period covering several decades. Their many years of membership in the Beth Israel family also allowed the Benjamins to serve as historians when it came time to first record a Beth Israel history. (BIC.)

**GERDA SELIGSON.** Gerda Seligson was one of the first women presidents of a conservative congregation. Arguably, the fact that Rabbi Kensky was hired could even be contributed to Seligson, as the first function she carried out was to travel to the Jewish Seminary in New York in 1971 to recruit a new rabbi for the congregation. (BIC.)

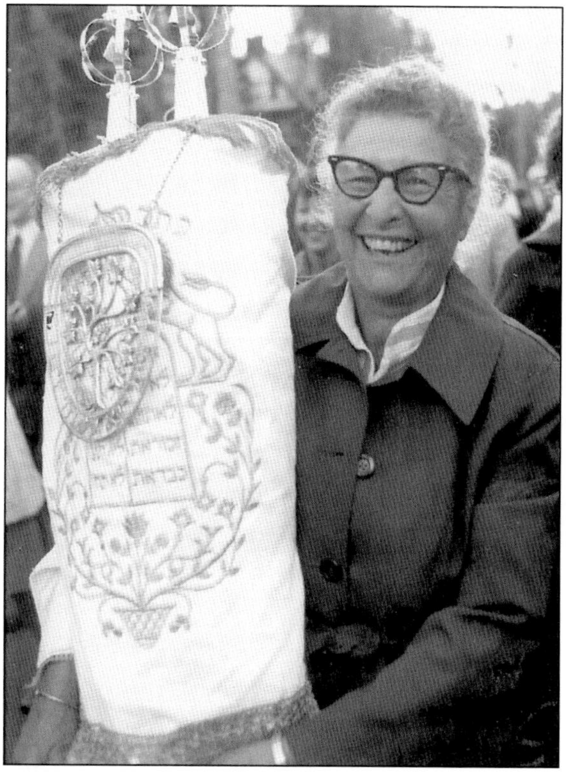

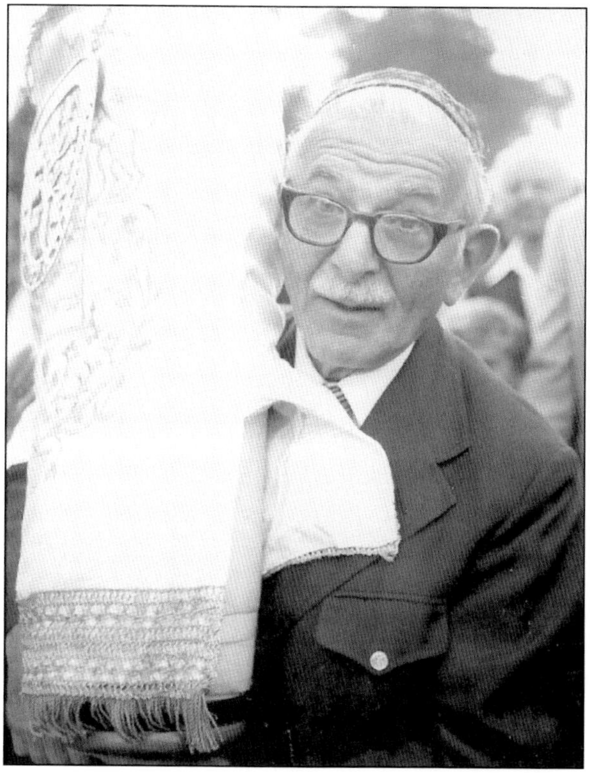

**HERMAN JACOBS (1902–1987).** In 1953, following Rabbi Lymon's departure for California, Herman Jacobs, then executive director of the Detroit Jewish Community Council, succeeded Rabbi Lymon as Hillel director. Jacobs served in that capacity for 15 years and remained involved in Hillel activities on an informal basis even after retirement. (BIC.)

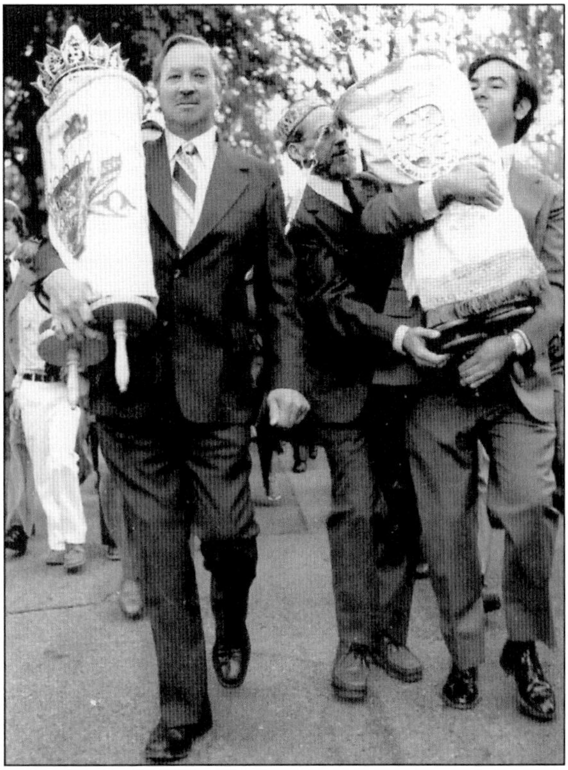

**GILBERT LANSKY (1919–1997).** Gilbert Lansky's parents were Eva and Phil Lansky, one of the founders of Beth Israel in 1916. Gilbert was married to Ida Lansky, who, as of this writing, survives. The Lansky family was one of the larger ones in Ann Arbor, consisting of six children—four sons, George, Aubrey, and Sam, in addition to Gil; and two daughters, Ellyn and Gertrude. Sam Lansky married Naomi Kamenetzky, daughter of the 1920s spiritual leader. (BIC.)

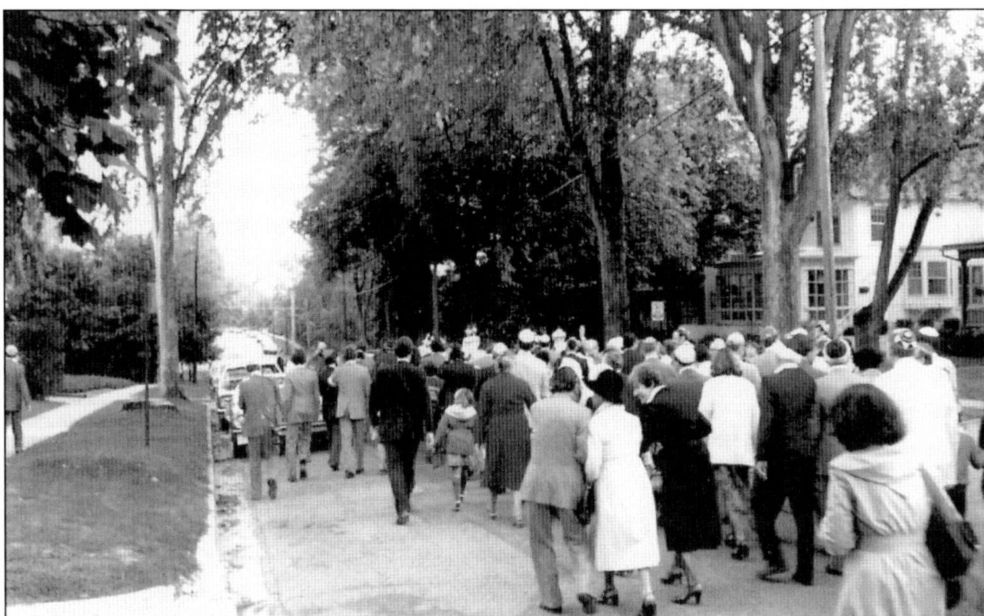

**TORAH PROCESSION.** The procession continued to 2000 Washtenaw Avenue, approximately one mile, as the congregation prepared to enter its new home. Moving into a new home was a significant event for the congregation, which now had grown to well over 200 families. Led by Rabbi Kensky, dozens of congregants participated in the procession to the new synagogue. (BIC.)

**PLACING THE MEZUZAH.** Jewish law requires a mezuzah, a small scroll containing words from the Torah, on the doorposts of structures. Rabbi Allan D. Kensky is placing the mezuzah on the doorpost of the new synagogue. The angle of the mezuzah is not an accident, but represents an early compromise resulting from the Jewish schools of thought as to whether it should be horizontal or vertical. (BIC.)

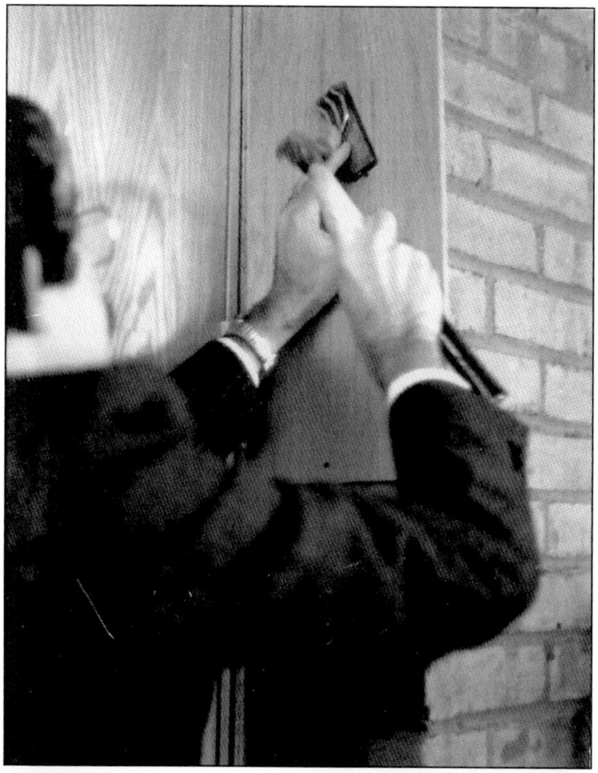

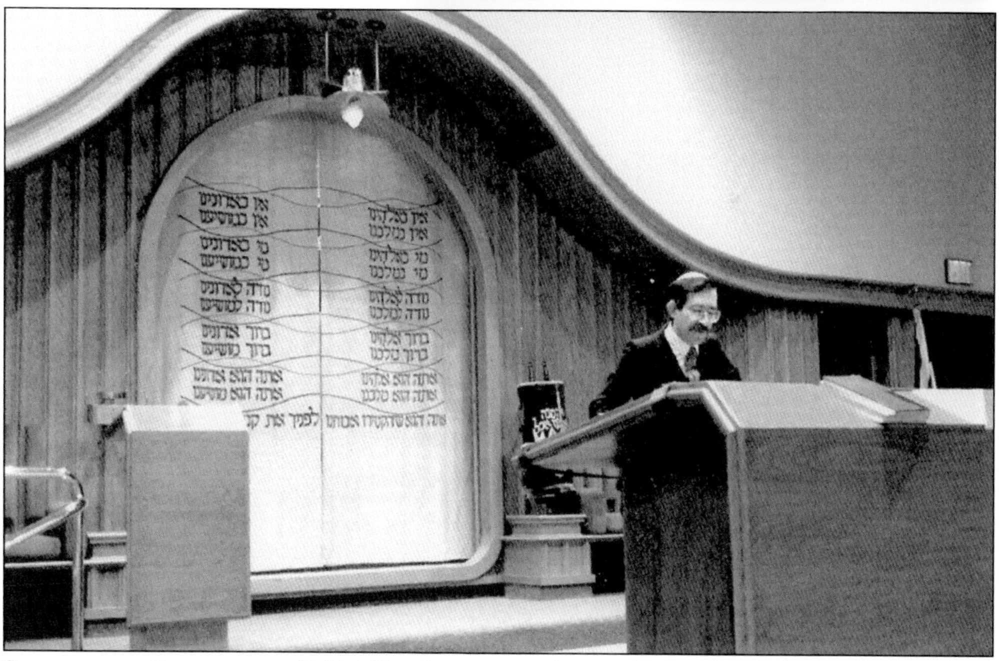

**SYNAGOGUE SANCTUARY.** Rabbi Kensky presented remarks at the dedication of the new synagogue. The Torahs have been placed in the ark standing behind Kensky. Although the sanctuary has undergone some reconstruction in ensuing years, it remains largely unchanged from its original form. (BIC.)

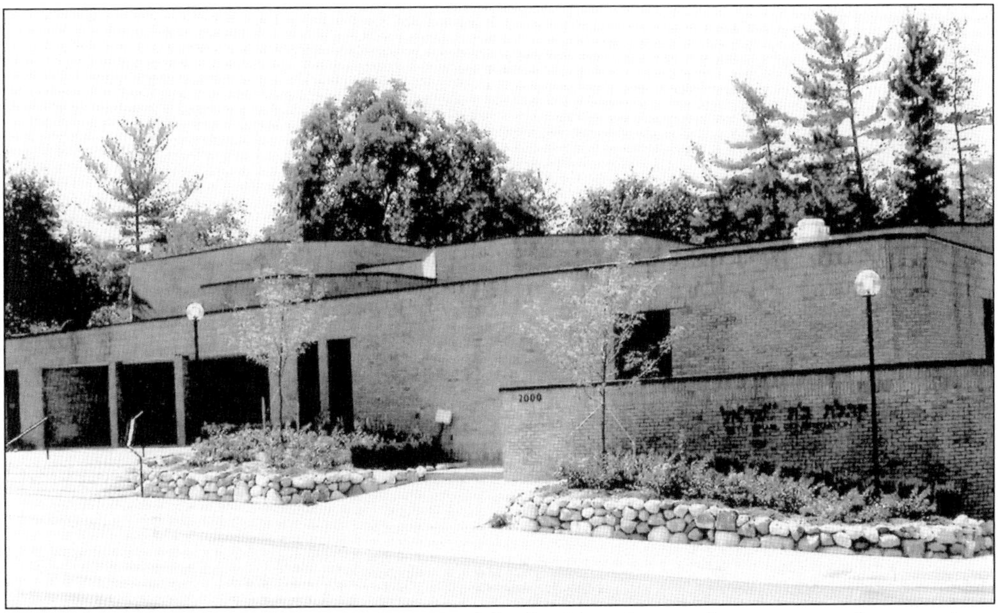

**SYNAGOGUE, 2000 WASHTENAW AVENUE.** The building has undergone several renovations since the 1970s, most notably increasing the size and utility of the social hall and increasing the number of classrooms for the religious school. The building sits on the site originally owned by the Jewish ZBT fraternity. In a sense coming full circle, among the members of that fraternity were descendants of the original Weil family who attended school in Ann Arbor. (Authors.)

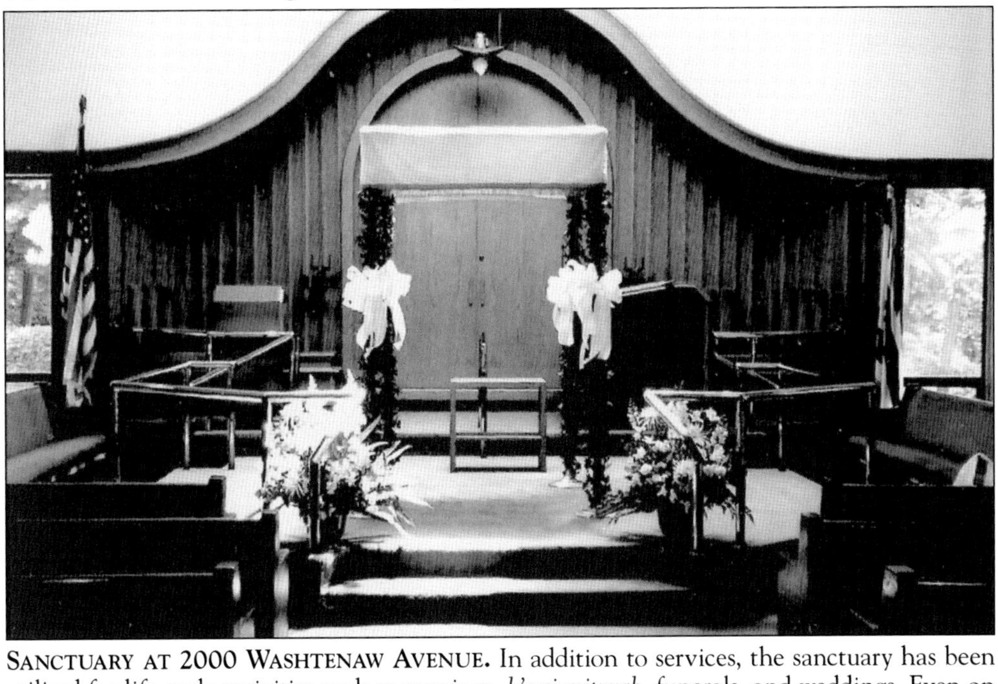

**SANCTUARY AT 2000 WASHTENAW AVENUE.** In addition to services, the sanctuary has been utilized for life cycle activities such as namings, *b'nai mitzvah*, funerals, and weddings. Even an Eagle Scout ceremony has been carried out here. The wedding of Richard Adler's daughter Rebekah Adler to Justin Gamble would take place beneath the chuppah, or canopy, seen in the photograph. (Authors.)

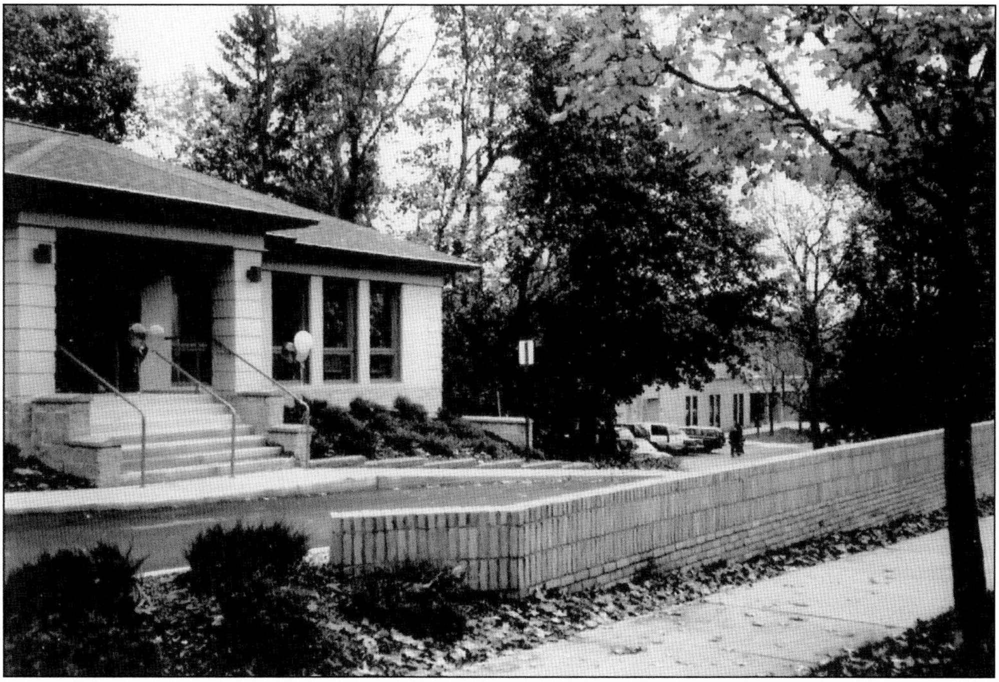

**2010 WASHTENAW AVENUE.** The property next door was owned by the congregation for several decades, serving as one of the sites for the Hebrew School and as the original site for the Krickstein Youth Library. With construction of the new synagogue, 2010 Washtenaw Avenue also was used for some social functions. By the end of the 20th century, however, the building had badly deteriorated from age and was replaced with a new, more modern structure. Housing the Garfunkle-Schteingart lounge, the building contains classrooms and a social area for synagogue youth. An urban legend associated with the original house suggested it to be the site at which a ransom letter associated with the Leopold-Loeb kidnapping and murder case in the 1930s had been mailed. (BIC.)

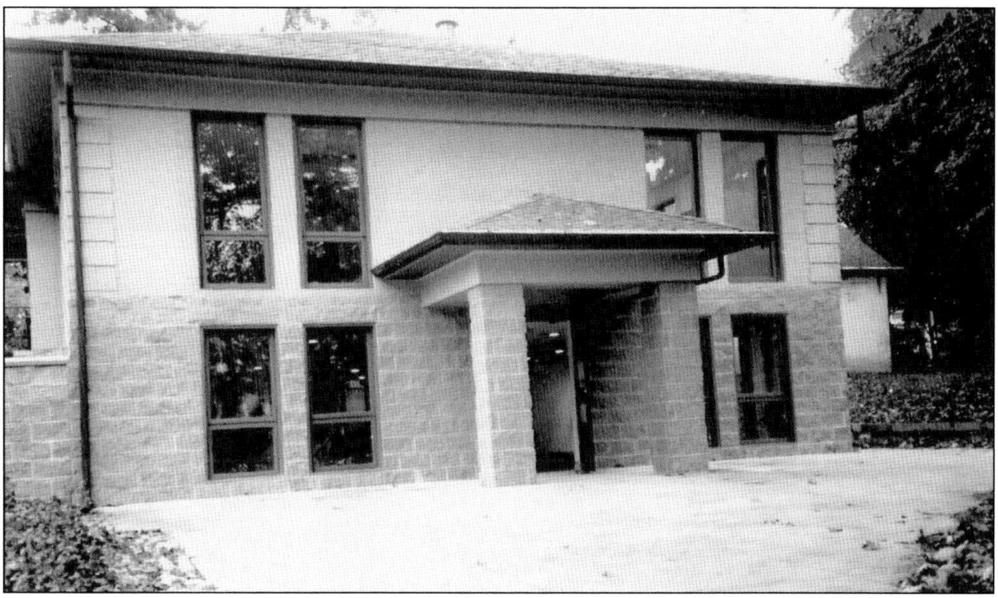

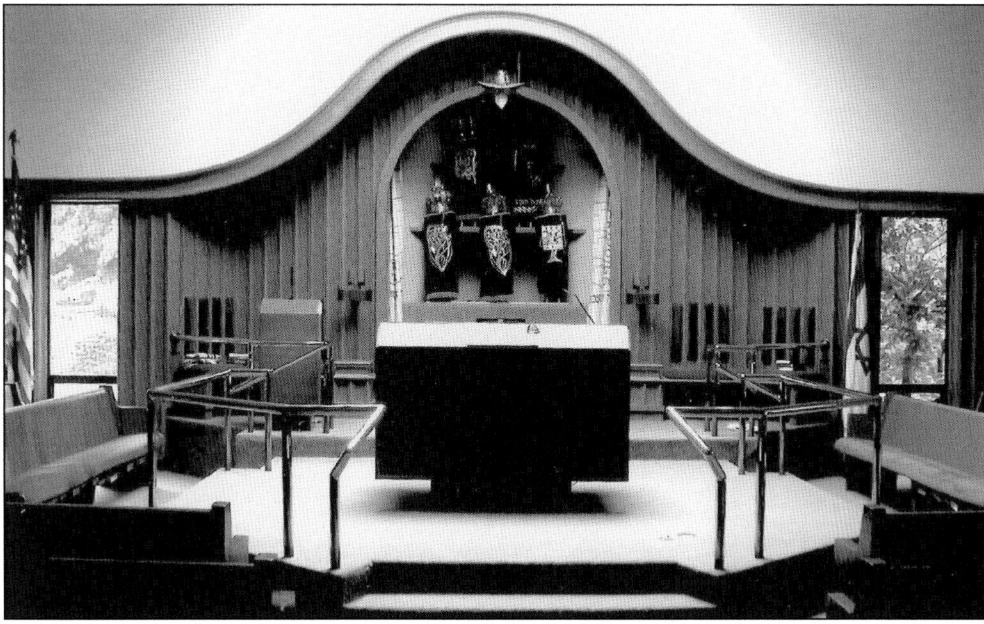

**TORAH SCROLLS.** A section of the Torah is read each Saturday, followed by a section from the Books of the Prophets. The first Torah acquired by the congregation was donated by the Hoffman family of Flint, whose son graduated from the University of Michigan Law School in 1929. The Israel Friedman family donated a second scroll in 1939, honoring their son Morris, who had graduated from the University of Michigan Dental School. (Authors.)

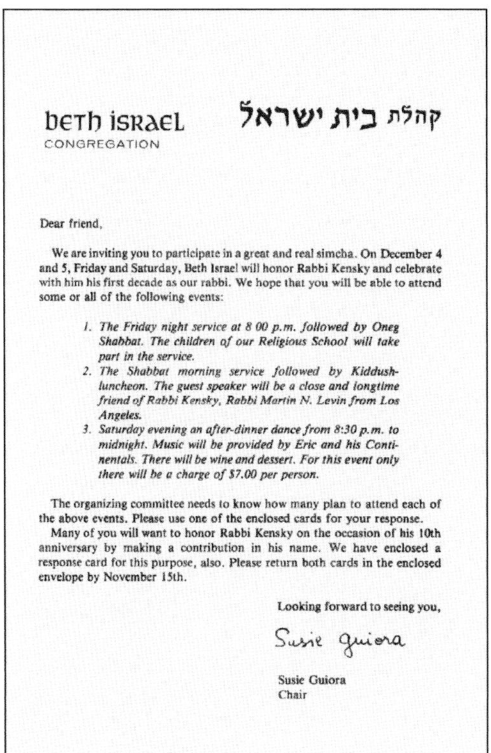

beth israel קהלת בית ישראל
CONGREGATION

Dear friend,

We are inviting you to participate in a great and real simcha. On December 4 and 5, Friday and Saturday, Beth Israel will honor Rabbi Kensky and celebrate with him his first decade as our rabbi. We hope that you will be able to attend some or all of the following events:

1. *The Friday night service at 8 00 p.m. followed by Oneg Shabbat. The children of our Religious School will take part in the service.*
2. *The Shabbat morning service followed by Kiddush-luncheon. The guest speaker will be a close and longtime friend of Rabbi Kensky, Rabbi Martin N. Levin from Los Angeles.*
3. *Saturday evening an after-dinner dance from 8:30 p.m. to midnight. Music will be provided by Eric and his Continentals. There will be wine and dessert. For this event only there will be a charge of $7.00 per person.*

The organizing committee needs to know how many plan to attend each of the above events. Please use one of the enclosed cards for your response.

Many of you will want to honor Rabbi Kensky on the occasion of his 10th anniversary by making a contribution in his name. We have enclosed a response card for this purpose, also. Please return both cards in the enclosed envelope by November 15th.

Looking forward to seeing you,

Susie Guiora

Susie Guiora
Chair

**TENTH ANNIVERSARY INVITATION.** In December 1981, the synagogue celebrated the 10th Anniversary of the rabbi once considered too young to lead the congregation. Ultimately, Rabbi Kensky served 17 years, the longest tenure of a rabbi at Beth Israel through 1988. During this period, he introduced a number of changes once considered controversial. (BIC.)

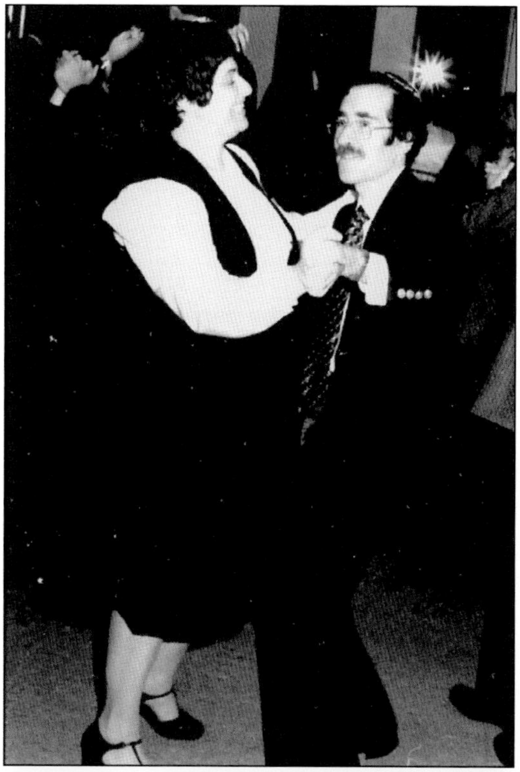

**RABBI KENSKY AND TIKVAH FRYMER.** Rabbi Kensky danced on the occasion of his anniversary party. Dr. Tikvah Frymer, a well-known and respected scholar of the Hebrew Bible, and Rabbi Kensky met in Ann Arbor and would ultimately marry. Tikvah Frymer-Kensky has contributed significantly to interpretation and knowledge on the subject of women and the Bible. (BIC.)

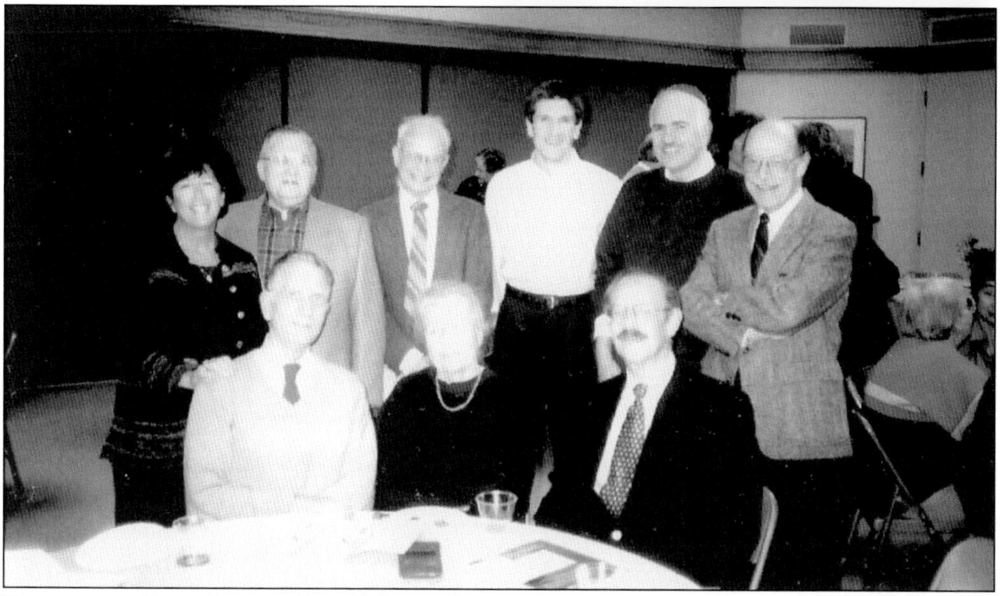

**PRESIDENTS, BETH ISRAEL.** From left to right are (first row) Carl Cohen (1979), Gerda Seligson (1971–1973), and Ed Schteingart (1974–1978); (second row) Suzi Coran (1981–1985), Henry Gershowitz (1970, 1994–1995), Marty Sichel (1966), Errol Soskolne (1996–1997), Richard Seid (1998–1999), and Saul Hymans (1969). The period covered by these individuals, primarily 1974–1998, represented one of significant growth in the local Jewish community in general, and membership in the Conservative congregation in particular, an increase in size of 50 percent. (BIC)

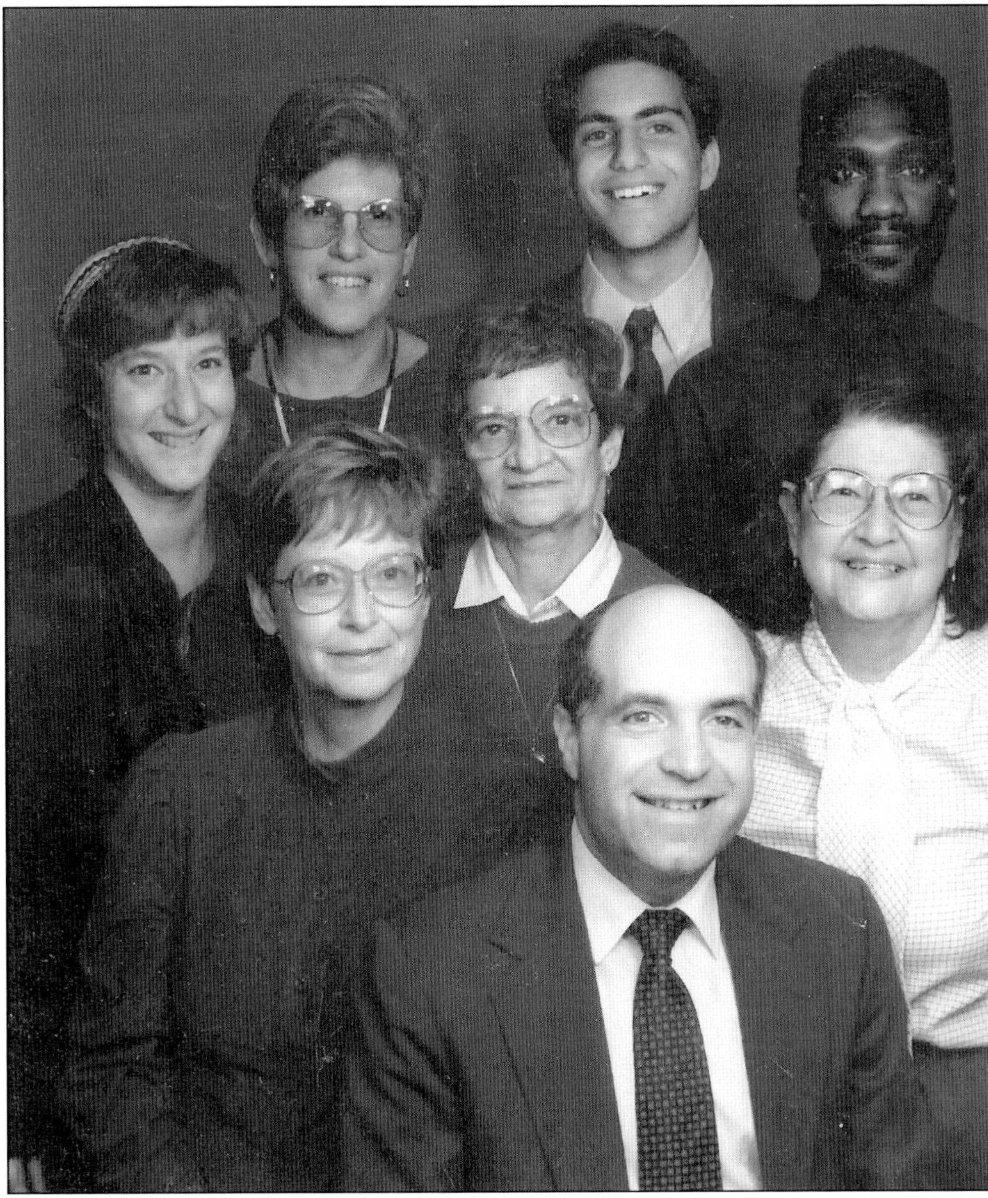

**BETH ISRAEL "FAMILY," AROUND 1992.** From left to right are (first row) Rabbi Robert Dobrusin; (second row) Martha Oleinick, office; Shirley Norton, librarian; and Hilma Geffen, bookkeeper; (third row) Aviva Panush, director of Beth Israel Religious School; Stacey Tessler, school secretary; Michael Pont, youth director; and Jonathan Warren, custodian. Aviva and her husband Mitch Silverman along with daughter Shoshana, were among the more active members during the 1980s and 1990s. Aviva was a teacher in the religious school during the late 1970s. In 1982 she became the director of the school. She served in this position until 1997, a period during which the school outgrew its facilities. The increase in student population required a number of classes to be split. Finding an increasing number of qualified teachers was among the challenges faced. Michael Pont was one of several youth directors during this era. Synagogue youth have a number of national organizations with which they can be affiliated—United Synagogue Youth as well as B'nai Brith Youth Organization. (BIC.)

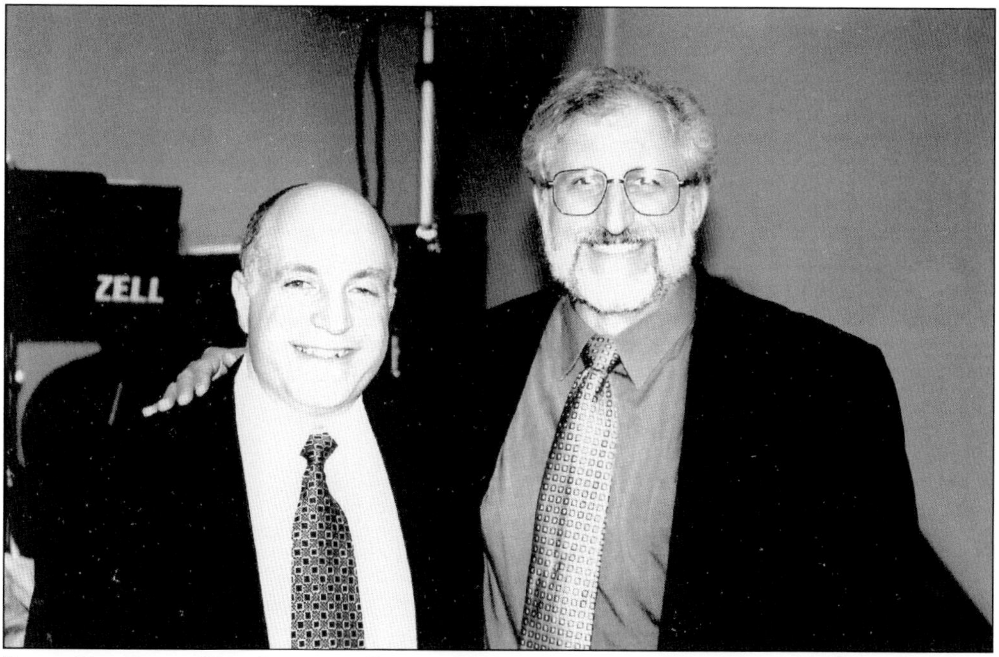


**RABBI DOBRUSIN, RON SUSSMAN, RITUAL ASSISTANT AND TUTOR.** This is the occasion of the 10th anniversary of Rabbi Dobrusin as spiritual leader, in 1998. Ron and his wife Elana "Lonnie" Sussman can generally be observed reading or assisting in the reading of the Torah during Sabbath services. In addition, each is among the more popular tutors for b'nai mitzvah. (BIC.)

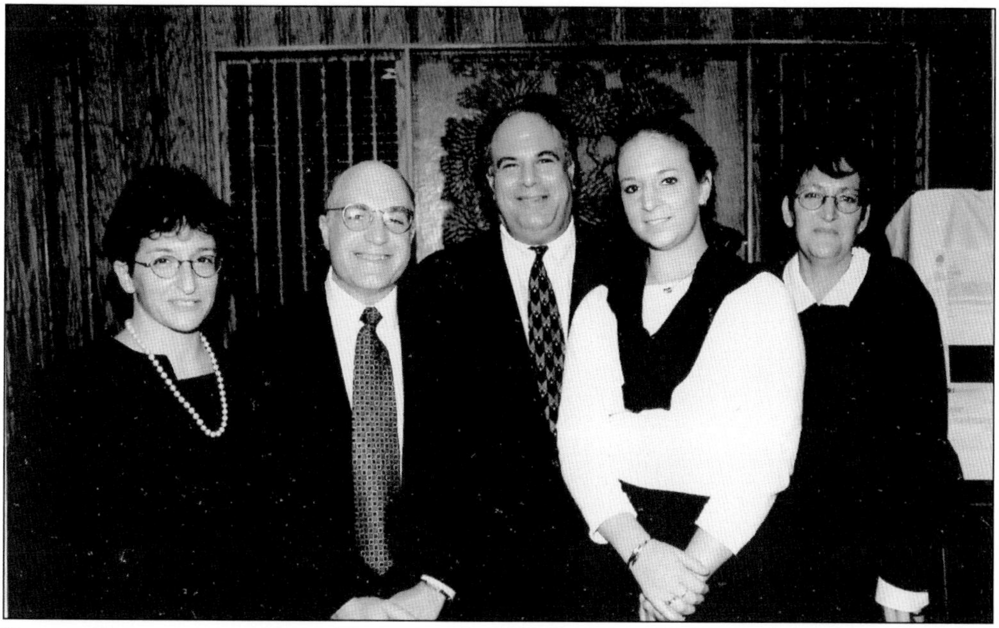

**ROBERT DOBRUSIN AND ELLEN DOBRUSIN.** In 1988, Beth Israel celebrated the 10th anniversary of Rabbi Dobrusin. From left to right are Ellen Dobrusin, Rabbi Robert Dobrusin, Rabbi Charles Dobrusin, Nami Dobrusin, and Deborah Dobrusin. Rob and Ellen Dobrusin met at Beth Israel and were subsequently married by his brother, Rabbi Charles Dobrusin. There was precedent. Rabbi Kensky also met his future wife, Tikvah Frymer, at Beth Israel. (BIC.)

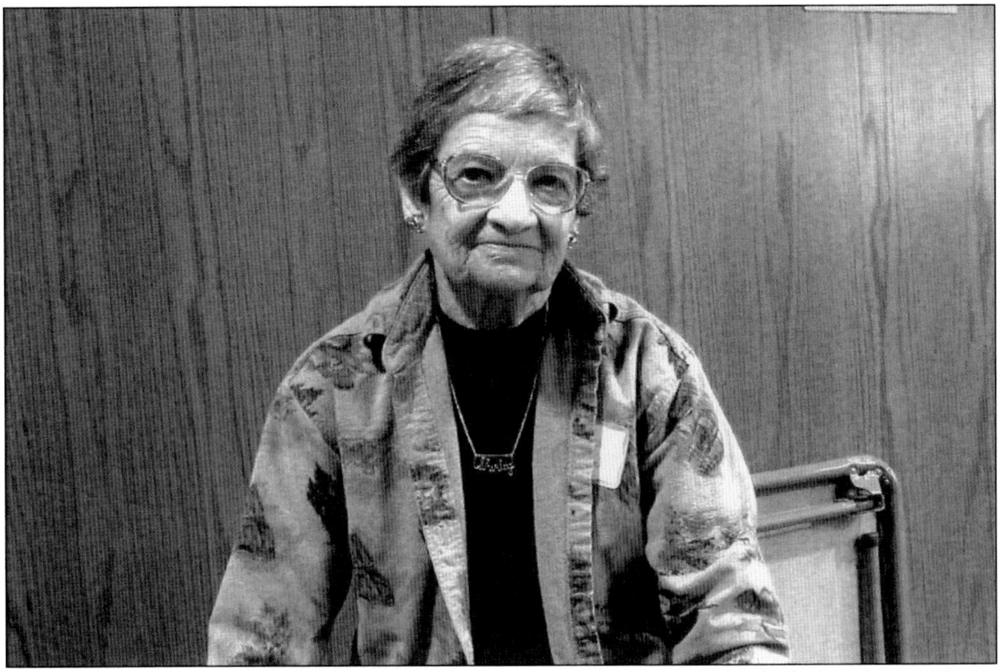

**SHIRLEY NORTON.** Shirley Norton has been the longtime librarian for both the Krickstein Youth Library as well as the adult library at Beth Israel. The youth library is a staple of the religious school and has been housed in several buildings over the years. (Authors.)

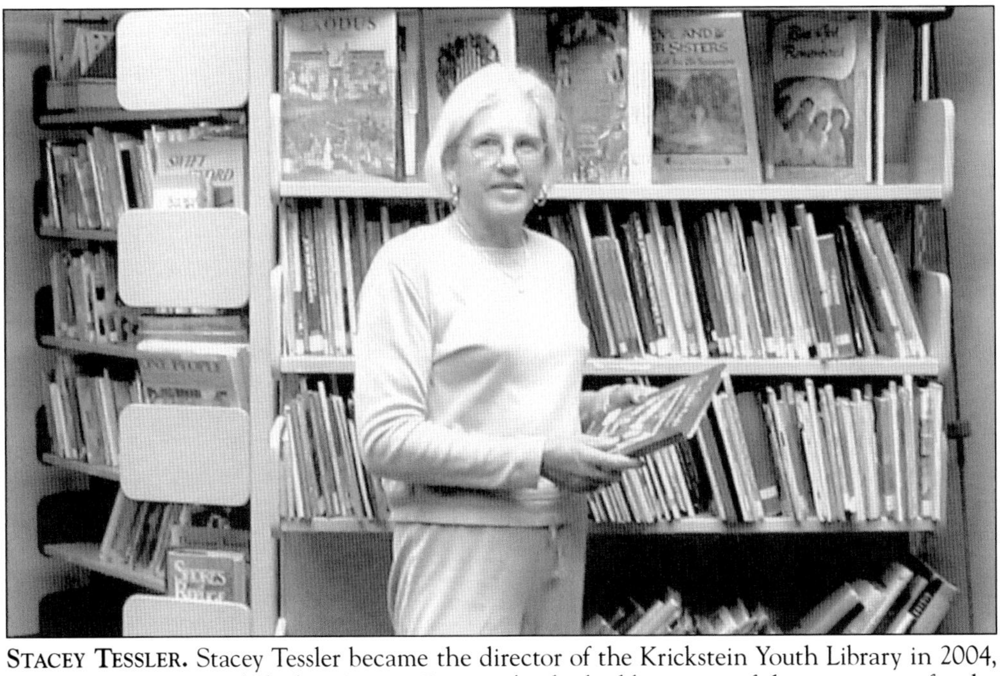

**STACEY TESSLER.** Stacey Tessler became the director of the Krickstein Youth Library in 2004, upon the retirement of Shirley Norton. Previously, she had been one of the instructors for the kindergarten class and secretary at the Beth Israel Religious School. In addition to maintaining the library collection, Tessler interacts with the children working on research or projects associated with classroom activities. (Authors.)

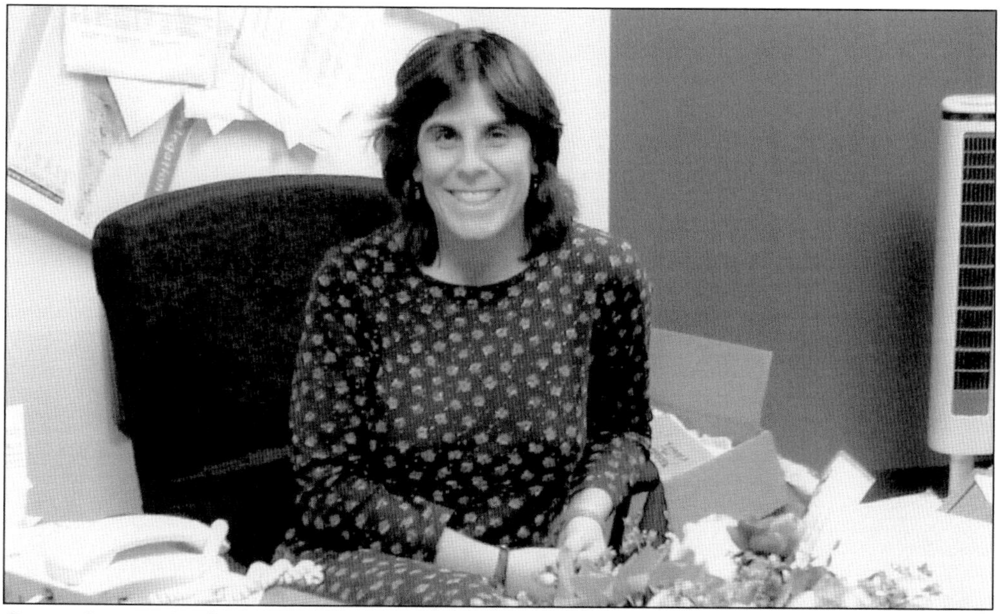

**CINDY SAPER.** Cindy Saper is currently the director of the Beth Israel Religious School. With over 20 years experience in fields of education, Saper became assistant director of the religious school in 1996 and director in 2004. Prior to coming to Ann Arbor, her experience included roles as curriculum coordinator at Harvard Hillel Children's School and similar positions at Beth Israel Religious School and Irvin M. Shlenker Day School in Houston, Texas. (Authors.)

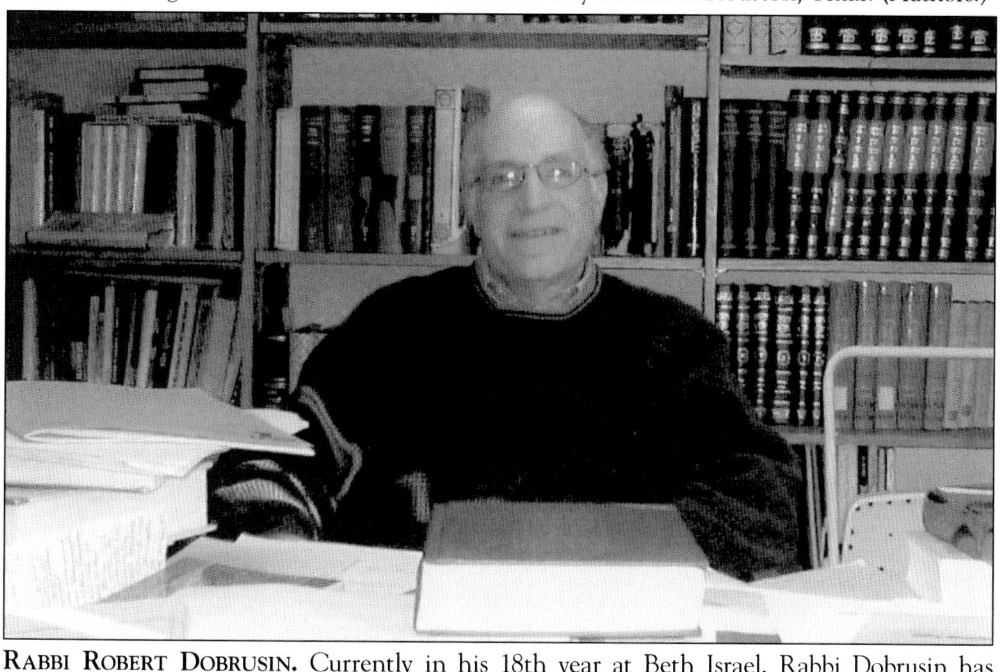

**RABBI ROBERT DOBRUSIN.** Currently in his 18th year at Beth Israel, Rabbi Dobrusin has become the longest serving rabbi for the community, a testament to his popularity within the congregation. Patience may be a virtue, and if so, he is among the most virtuous—a mensch in every sense of the meaning. Dobrusin is also a rabid Boston Red Sox fan, reflecting his heritage from that city. (Authors.)

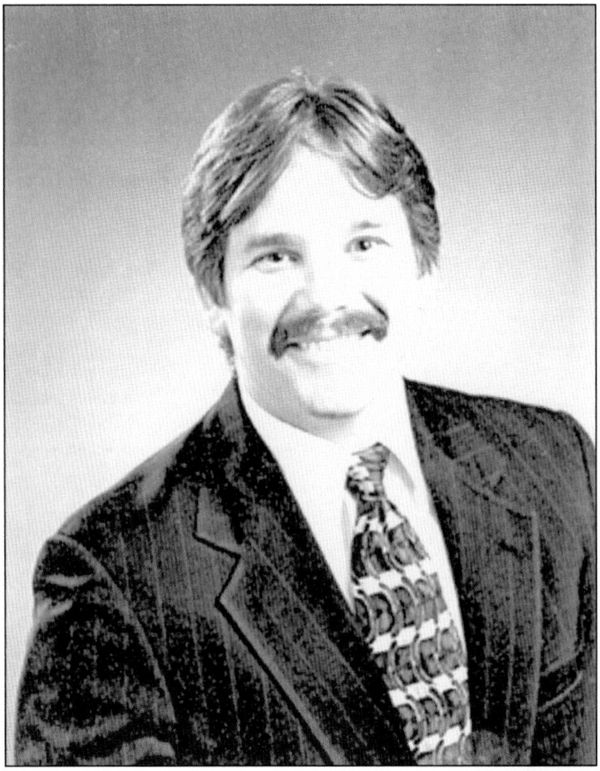

EDWARD D'ANGELO. PRESIDENT OF BETH ISRAEL, 2000–2005. The longest serving president since Osias Zwerdling, Ed D'Angelo's tenure culminated in the most significant building renovation since its inception. Reflecting the greater needs of the congregation, the social hall and sanctuary were integrated into a more useful service area. Housekeeping functions such as kitchen renovations and a new roof likewise required imagination in fund-raising. (BIC.)

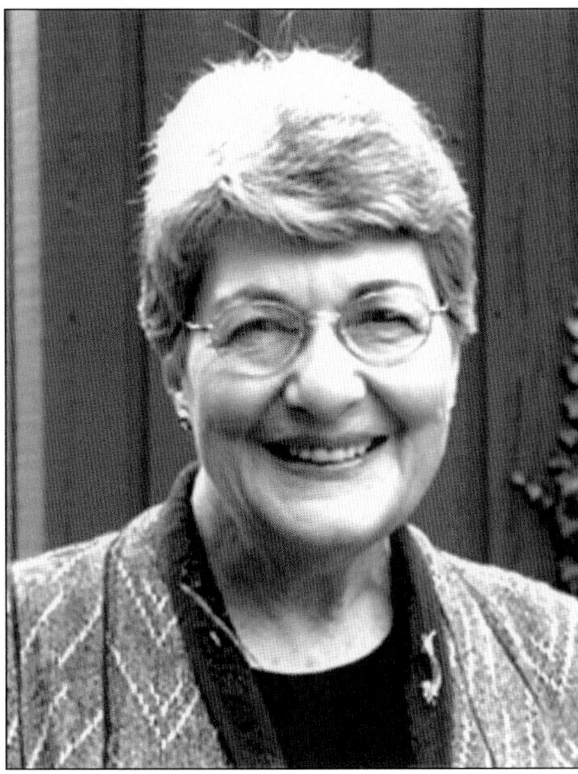

CAROL FINERMAN. Elected in 2005 as the new president of Beth Israel, Carol Finerman inherited many of the problems faced by her predecessors: raising funds for additional needs, refereeing different interpretations of functions or activities, and maintaining the interest of young people after undergoing b'nai mitzvah, among other challenges. (BIC)

# *Seven*

# TEMPLE BETH EMETH

Beth Israel Congregation had outgrown its home. In addition to sharing quarters with Hillel, the religious school and youth library were housed in an old home farther south on Washtenaw Avenue, now the newly constructed building at 2010 Washtenaw Avenue. Consequently, the Beth Israel Board of Directors was seriously considering the purchase of land elsewhere in the city for construction of a new synagogue, a proposition that would inevitably require significant expense. In addition, while the conservative approach to Judaism was fine with much of the Beth Israel membership, others were more interested in the more liberal reform movement.

In February 1966, at the home of Ron and Rita Tikofsky, a meeting was held to discuss the possibility and mechanics of a new Reform Judaism congregation. Each had been an active member at Beth Israel but was more comfortable with a reform service. Other families or individuals present at the meeting included Paul and Linda Vanek, Ken and Marilyn Bronson, George and Lenore Mencher, and Ellen Landau. The primary result of that first meeting was to establish the logistics for holding services and setting up a religious school. At a later meeting, a name for the congregation was decided upon: *Beth Emeth*, the "House of Truth."

The initial site at which services would be held for the new congregation was the First Congregational Church on East William Street. Although only two services and several organizational meetings were held at the church, one of the deacons, Glen McDowell, a local dentist, would play an unusual part in Rosh Hashanah services later that year.

High Holy Day services for 1966 were held that month at the newer location. Dr. Robert Katz, a professor and rabbi from Hebrew Union College (HUC) in Cincinnati presided. McDowell, a deacon from the Congregational Church and a dentist, produced a mouthpiece for the shofar and was given the honor of blowing the instrument at services. The Vanek family would later donate a *yad*, "pointer" in McDowell's honor. As noted in Linda Vanek's history of Temple Beth Emeth (TBE), this was probably "the first yad ever dedicated in honor of a deacon of a Congregational Church." The first life cycle event took place on October 27, as David Lazarus became a bar mitzvah.

By 1970, the Temple Beth Emeth family had grown to include nearly 100 families. That year, a search committee, established to address the problem of space, recommended a move to St. Clare of Assisi Episcopal Church at 2309 Packard Road.

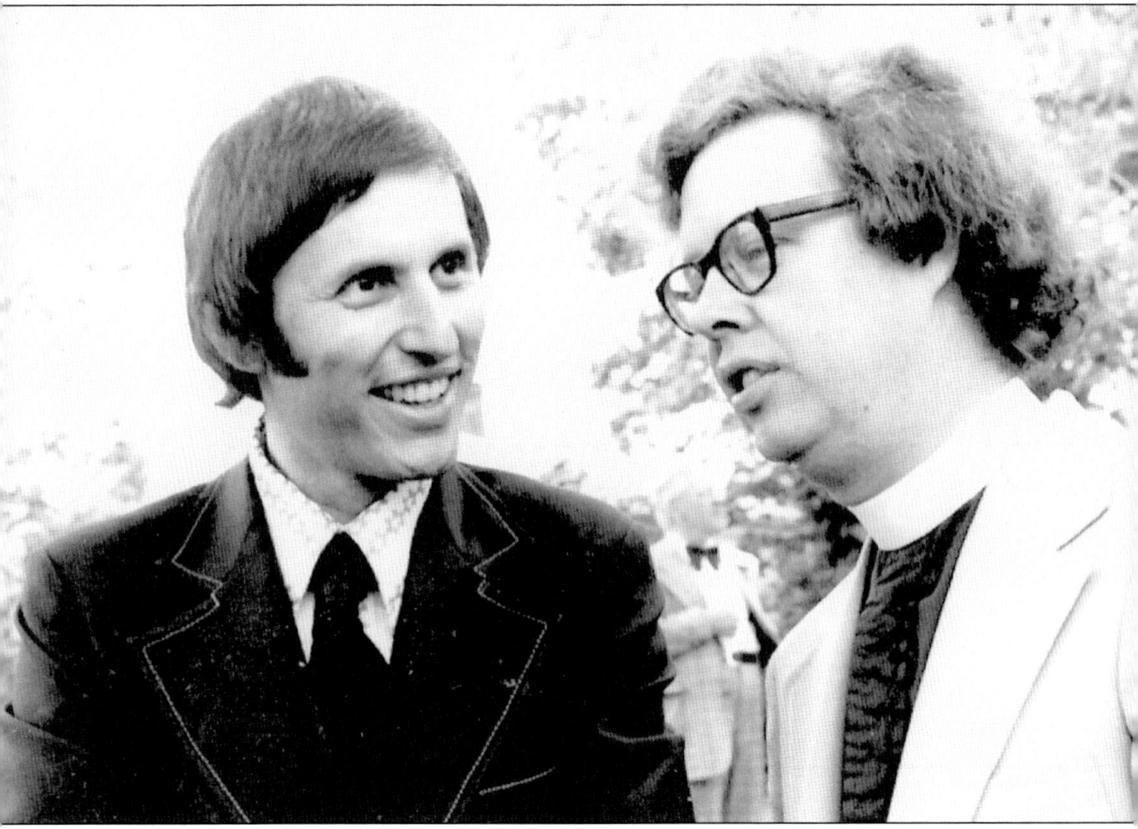

**RABBI BRUCE WARSHAL AND FR. DAVID EVETT.** While Beth Emeth required more suitable facilities, St. Clare's was encountering financial challenges. Temple Beth Emeth becoming a tenant addressed each problem. Nevertheless, challenges still existed. Foremost was the issue of space. As a later search committee would note, "the Rabbi had his office in his home, and the religious school is in a public school building. . . . Our relationship with St. Clare Episcopal Church has been the ray of sunshine in an otherwise difficult situation." The arrangement between Temple Beth Emeth and St. Clare's could in a sense be described as made in heaven. A primary factor in the success of the move was the professional and friendly relationship that developed between Rabbi Warshal and the Reverend Evett. The successful union between St. Clare's and Beth Emeth occurred "not because Bruce Warshal and I [Father Evett] had a dream, but because the people of Beth Emeth and St. Clare's decided to pull it off," according to *Temple Beth Emeth: The First Fifteen Years, 1966–1981* by Linda Vanek and Rose Vainstein. (BHL.)

Temple Beth Emeth
Ann Arbor, Michigan

379 Brookside Drive

April 4, 1966

Dear

It has long been felt that a need exists for a Reform Jewish congregation in Ann Arbor. As a result of a recent resurgence of interest, I am pleased to extend a warm invitation to you, and to other interested friends, to join in the planning of our new congregation.

During the last few weeks a number of us have met to discuss preliminary plans for our congregation. We have adopted the name, Beth Emeth, and have decided to affiliate with the Union of American Hebrew Congregations. Further, we plan to have a religious school in operation in the Fall of 1966. The First Congregational Church has graciously offered the use of its facilities for our religious school and worship services.

Our first general meeting will be held at the church (corner State and William streets) on Sunday, April 24, 1966, at 8:00 p.m. I'm sure you will be interested to hear of our plans and to join with us in evolving this exciting program.

It is not our intention to draw anyone away from established affiliations, but rather, to provide an opportunity for those who wish to worship and to give their children religious education in the Reform tradition.

We look forward to meeting with you on April 24th.

Sincerely,

Ronald Tikofsky
Chairman, pro-tem
662-9319

Steering Committee

**COMMUNITY LETTER ANNOUNCING REFORM CONGREGATION.** In April 1966, a mailing went out announcing the formation of the new reform congregation. In May, the board of Temple Beth Emeth was formally established, with Ron Tikofsky as the first president. The first official service was held on August 19 at the Congregational church. Rabbi Richard Hertz from Temple Beth El in Detroit conducted the service. To perhaps underscore the significance of the event, a daughter was born to Linda Vanek, the congregation's religious education chair, that same day; Temple Beth Emeth's first Torah fund was established in her honor. Prayer books were obtained from Temple Beth El in Detroit. A congregant, Mark Solent, built a portable ark for housing the Torah, a 200-year-old scroll donated by B. L. Maas. The date marked the last service held at the Congregational church, as the congregation moved to the First Unitarian Church at 1917 Washtenaw Avenue. On September 10, Beth Emeth Saturday morning religious school opened in the house adjacent to the main building. (TBE.)

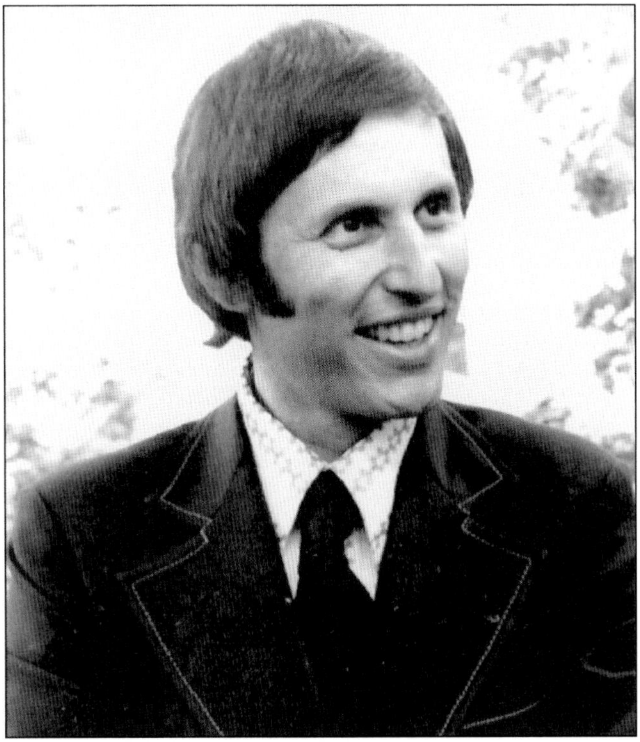

**Rabbi Bruce Warshal.** As a student at HUC in Cincinnati, Rabbi Warshal traveled to Ann Arbor during the period from July 1968 to the following June to conduct services. On July 12, Warshal presided over the bar mitzvah of Mark Richter. Already licensed to practice law, Warshal was ordained in 1969, and was hired as full-time rabbi by Beth Emeth in June 1969. (BHL.)

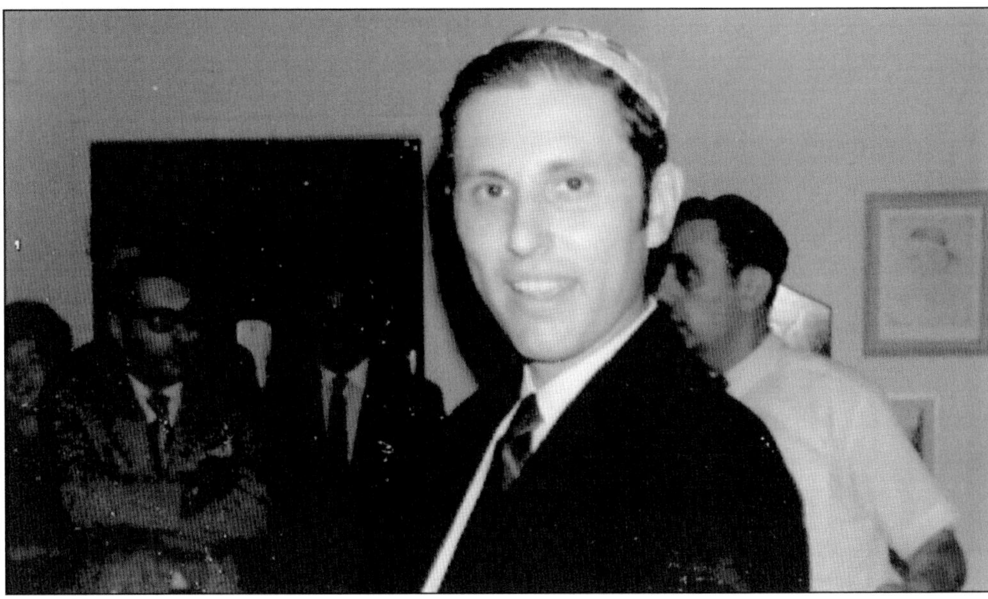

**Warshal Bris.** Rabbi Warshal brought an enthusiasm to his work that energized his audience. The Beth Emeth congregation was more than simply present—they listened. As Warshal reminisced, in *Temple Beth Emeth: The First Fifteen Years, 1966–1981* by Linda Vanek and Rose Vainstein, if the response was, "Good sermon, Rabbi," it was not perfunctory. Whether it was Warshal "bounding off a plane at seven in the morning" or complaining about a speeding ticket, when Warshal joined the Temple, the congregation knew "things were not going to be dull. . . ." (Bruce Warshal.)

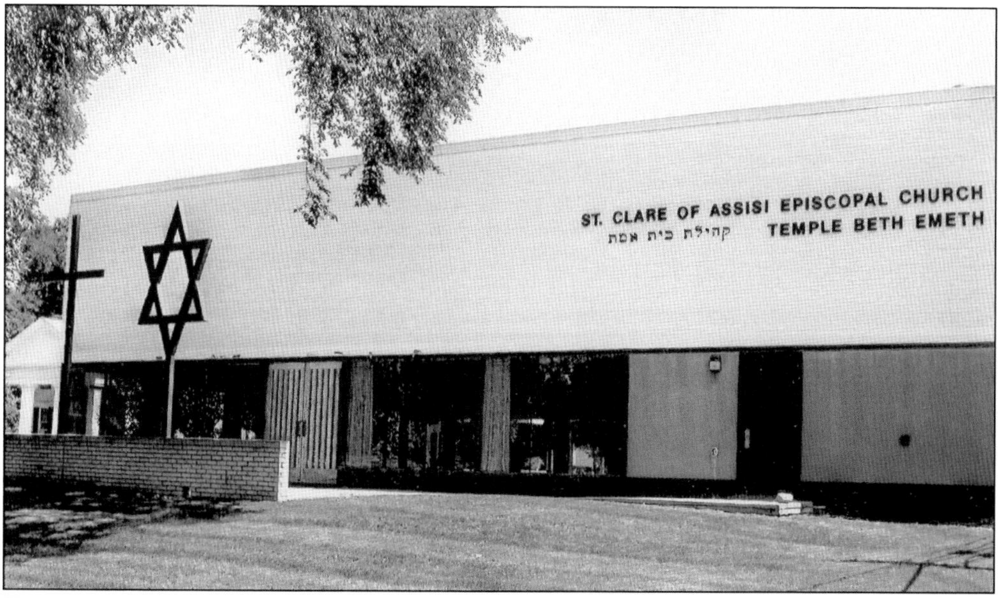


**TEMPLE BETH EMETH/ST. CLARE EPISCOPAL CHURCH.** In a board meeting held on April 3, 1974, a resolution was passed to establish joint ownership between St. Clare's and Temple Beth Emeth; the resolution was approved by the congregation on June 10th. Temple Beth Emeth purchased a half interest in the facility, with new additions to serve as a site for the religious school and social hall. While the joint ownership is no longer unique, it has continued to flourish for over 35 years. (Authors.)

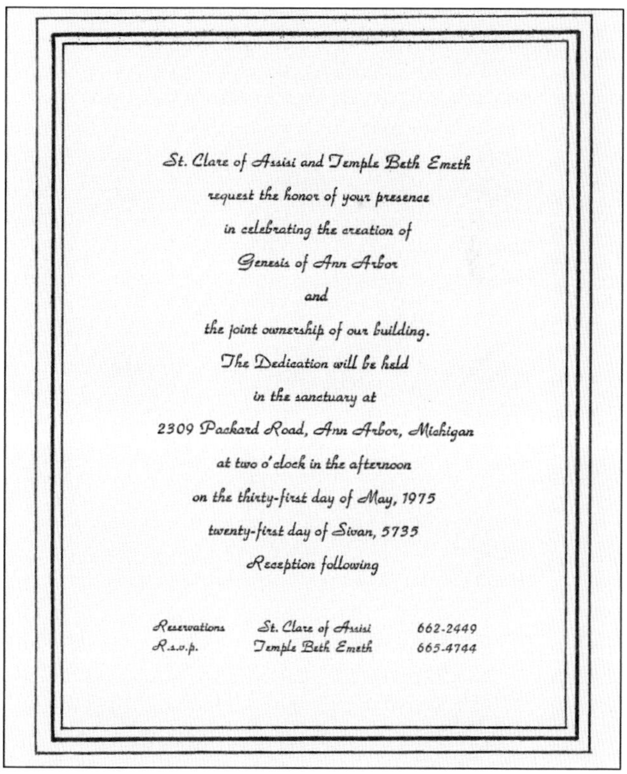

St. Clare of Assisi and Temple Beth Emeth
request the honor of your presence
in celebrating the creation of
Genesis of Ann Arbor
and
the joint ownership of our building.
The Dedication will be held
in the sanctuary at
2309 Packard Road, Ann Arbor, Michigan
at two o'clock in the afternoon
on the thirty-first day of May, 1975
twenty-first day of Sivan, 5735
Reception following

Reservations St. Clare of Assisi 662-2449
R.s.v.p. Temple Beth Emeth 665-4744

**INVITATION FOR CELEBRATION OF GENESIS OF ANN ARBOR.** To oversee financial issues, a nonprofit corporation, Genesis of Ann Arbor, was formed, and an agreement was signed in December. The corporation "will own, maintain, and improve the buildings." On Wednesday, May 28, 1975, the Mogen David star was placed in the front of the building, where it remains until this day. The mezuzah was placed on Friday, May 30, and a formal dedication was held that Sunday. (BHL.)

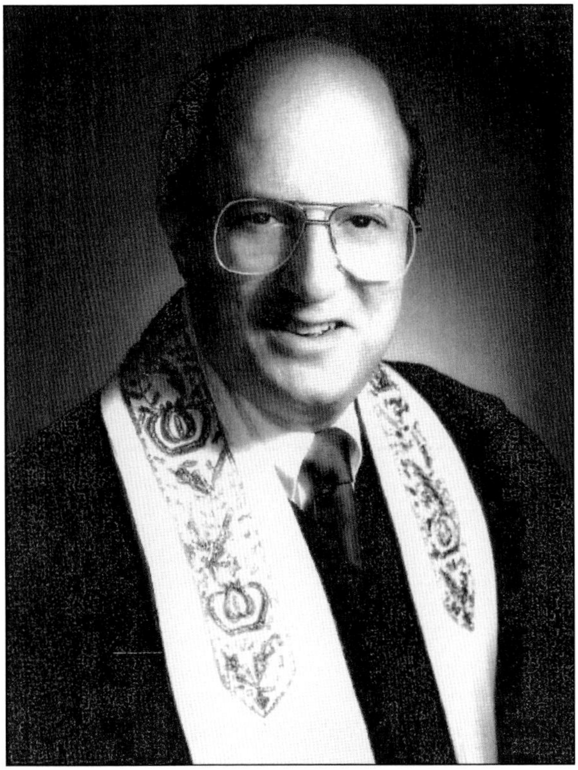

**RABBI RALPH MECKLENBURGER.** Originally from the Chicago area, Rabbi Mecklenburger was ordained in 1972 at Hebrew Union College, Institute of Religion, in Cincinnati. After a three year tenure at Temple Emmanuel in California, Mecklenburger succeeded Bruce Warshal as spiritual leader at Temple Beth Emeth, serving from 1975 to 1984. In 1984, he joined Beth-El Congregation in Fort Worth, Texas. His tenure in Ann Arbor marked the strengthening of the ties between the temple and St. Clare's. (Ralph Mecklenburger.)

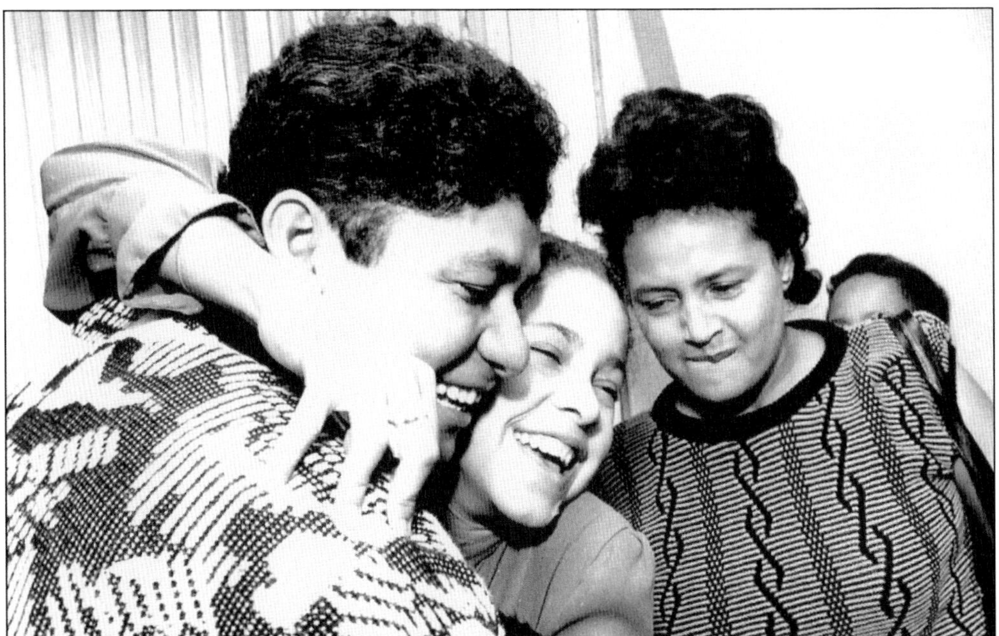

**MARIO VASQUEZ FAMILY, AROUND 1987.** Temple Beth Emeth, as well as the Jewish community at large, has always provided support for human rights. In the late 1980s, Temple Beth Emeth was prominent in their support for the Vasquez family. Mario, Mirian, and their seven children fled Honduras because of his opposition to the Honduras government. (BHL.)

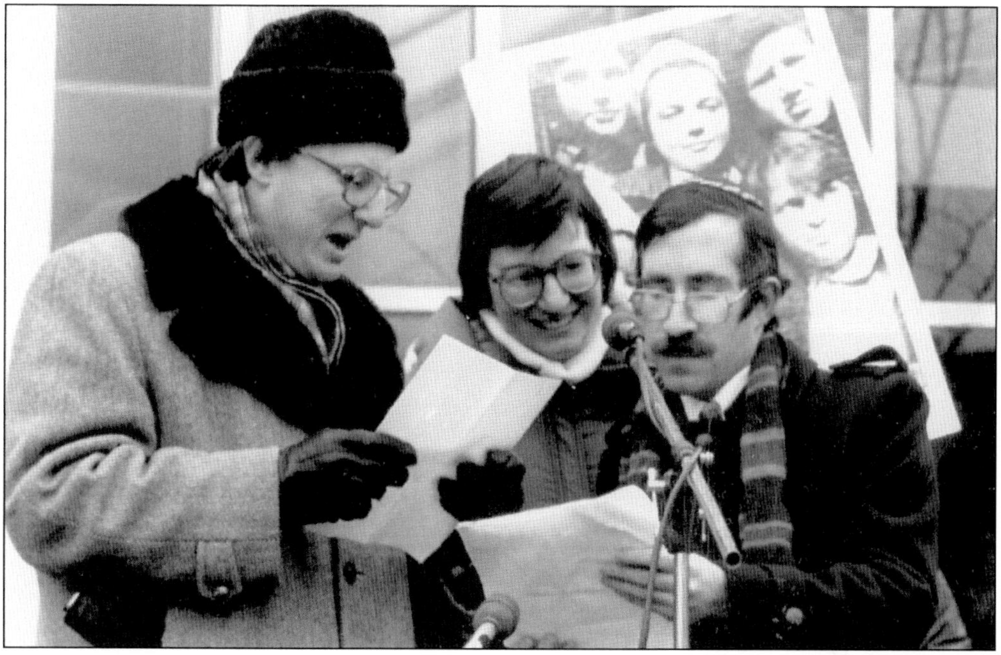

**RALLY AGAINST NUCLEAR PROLIFERATION.** Rabbi Ralph Mecklenburger (TBE), Rabbi Allan D. Kensky (BI), and Rabbi Ellen Dreyfus attended a March 20, 1982, community rally in front of the Federal Building. The three were guest speakers at a rally for civil rights as well as participants in arguments against nuclear proliferation. (BHL.)

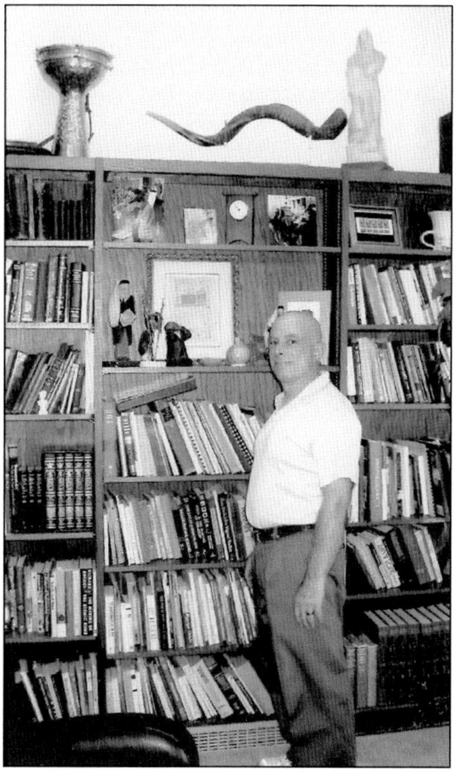

**RABBI ROBERT D. LEVY.** Born in New York City, Rabbi Levy graduated from Boston University in 1974, with a degree in Biblical studies. After earning a master's degree in Hebrew Letters from Hebrew Union College, he was ordained at Hebrew Union College-Jewish Institute of Religion in 1979. Levy joined Temple Beth Emeth in April 1984. (Authors.)

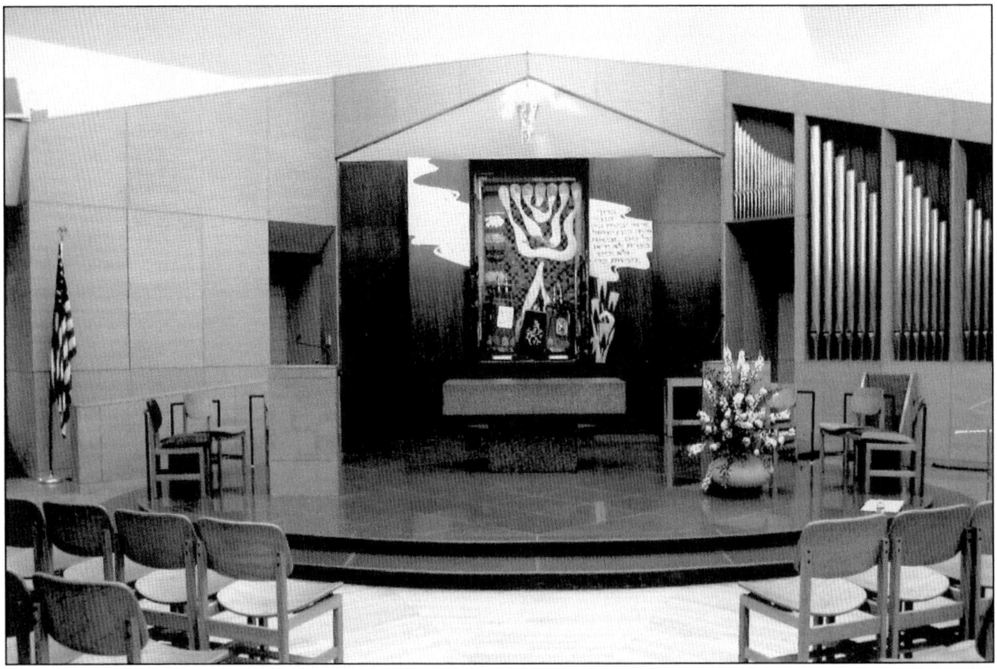

**MAIN CHAPEL AT TEMPLE BETH EMETH.** Services for both the St. Clare Church as well as the temple are held in this room, religious artifacts are mobile and can be moved or hidden as necessary. As well, special events, such as choir concerts, are also held in the main sanctuary. (Authors.)

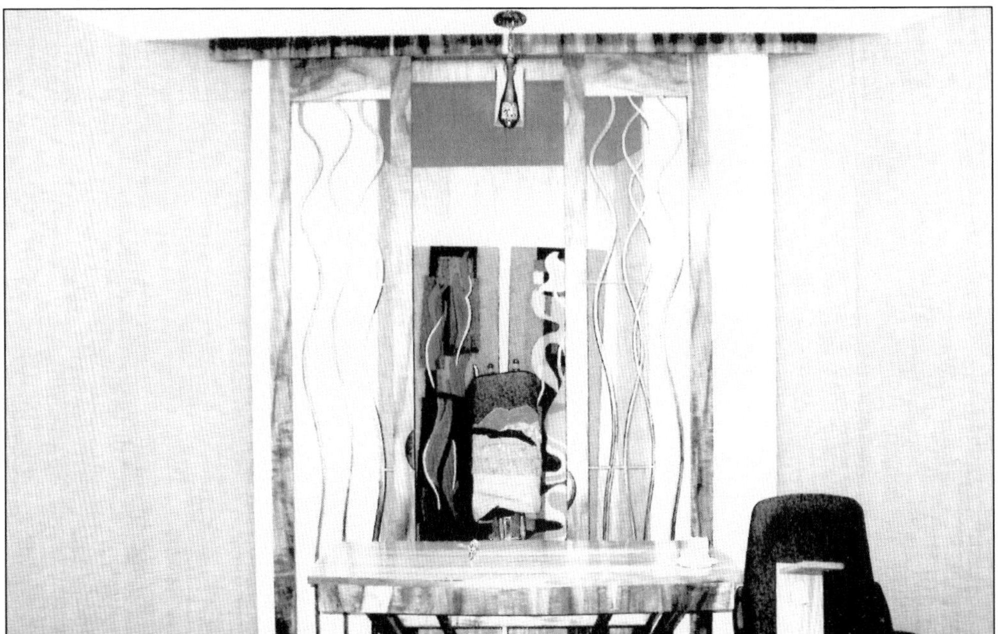

**SECONDARY CHAPEL, TBE.** This chapel is used for smaller services or events. The decorative cover behind the Torah was at one time part of the original sanctuary. The cover was a gift from the Vanek family. At that time, the cover helped frame the ark when it was in the front of the building. (Authors.)

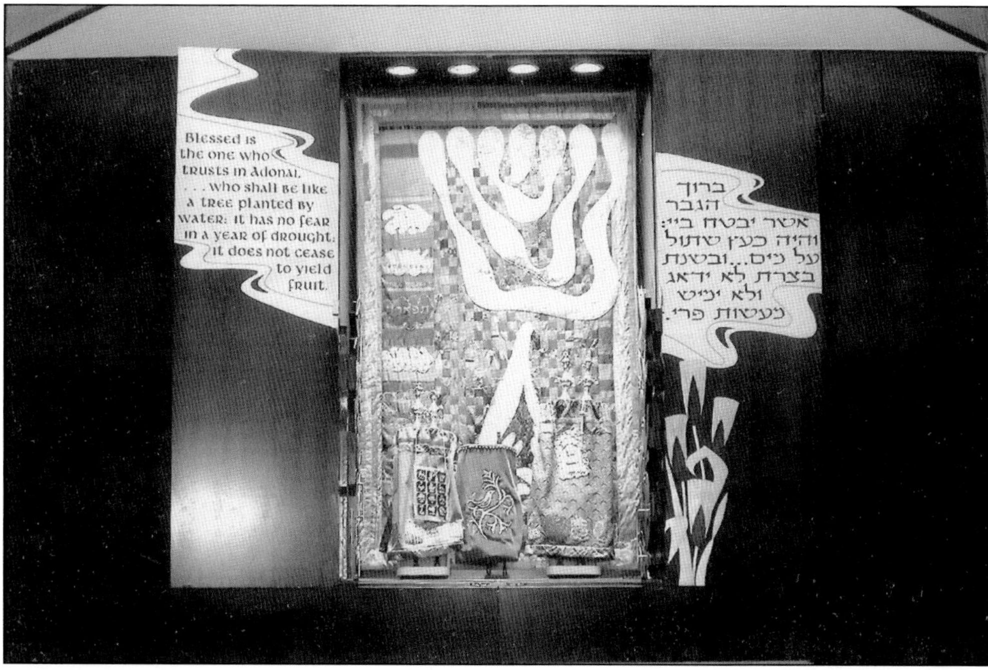


**TBE Torah Scrolls.** Scrolls include both the Torah as well as other readings. The scroll in the center is a haftorah scroll, containing the Books of the Prophets. Temple Beth Emeth also owns several scrolls not in general use; a 200-year-old gift too worn for use and a Torah rescued from the Holocaust. (Authors.)

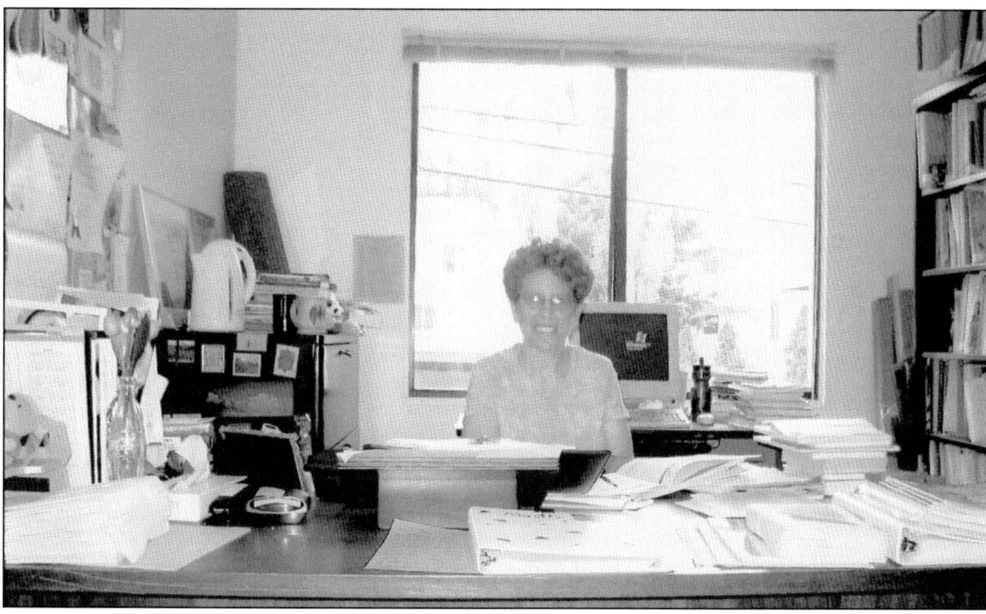

**Terri Ginsburg.** The 10th Anniversary of Terri Ginsburg as the director of the Temple Beth Emeth Religious School was in 2005. The Temple Beth Emeth Hebrew and Religious School has some 450 students enrolled, with classes from preschool through 12th grade. In addition, Ginsburg supervises 40 teacher helpers, teenagers in the *madrichim* program. Ginsburg herself has taught both Jewish and special education classes. (Authors.)

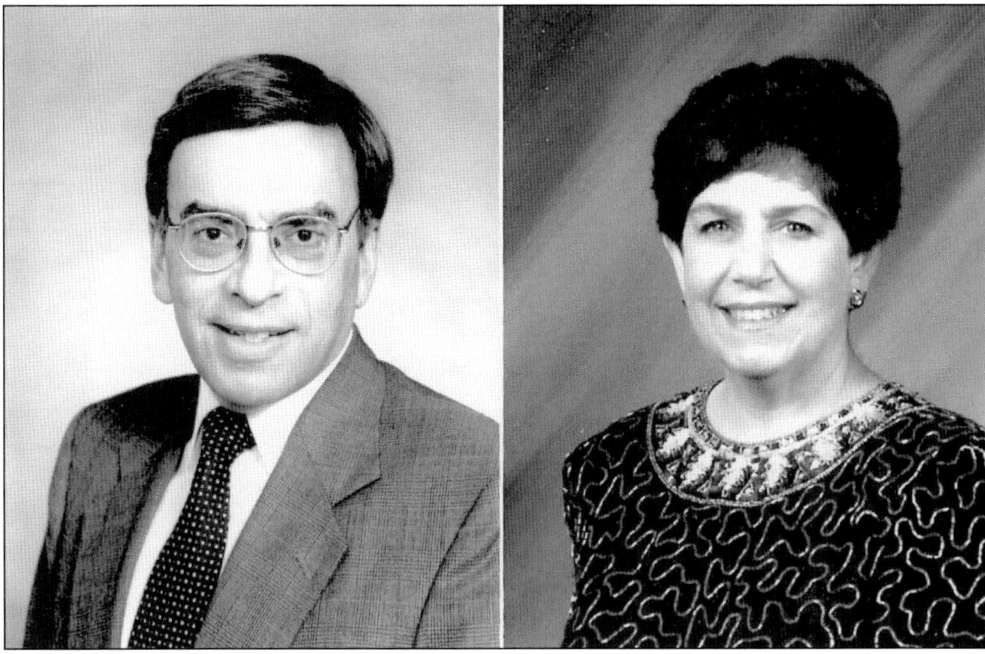

**Stu Simon and Barbara Heilveil.** Stu Simon served as president of Temple Beth Emeth from 1991 to 1993. Barbara Heilveil served as president of Temple Beth Emeth from 1993 to 1997. (TBE.)

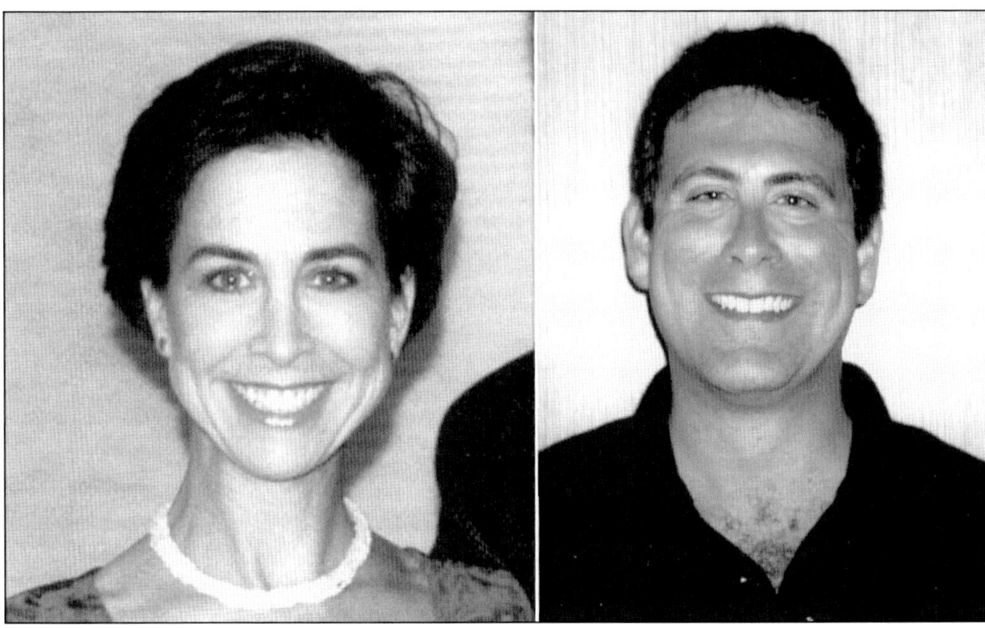

**Pat McCune and Bill Parkus.** Pat McCune served as president of Temple Beth Emeth from 1999 to 2001. Bill Parkus followed as president of Temple Beth Emeth from 2001 to 2003. (TBE.)

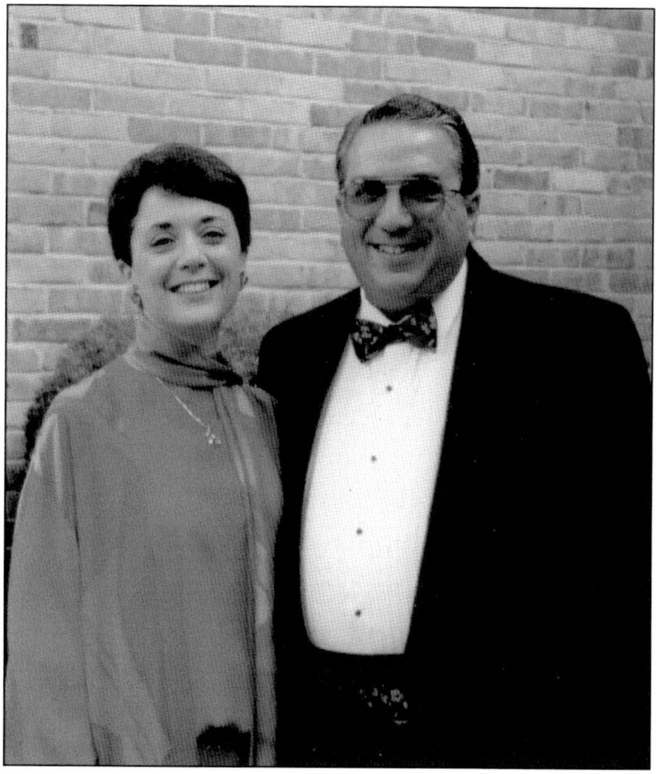

**ALAN AND BETTE COTZIN.** Alan Cotzin served as Temple Beth Emeth president from 1985 to 1989. During his tenure, Rabbi Robert Levy was hired to replace Rabbi Mecklenburger. The congregation grew during this period from 175 to 225 member units. Following an interim of eight years, Bette Cotzin was elected president in 1997. During her tenure, Mitzvah Day, a one-day volunteer service event, was initiated. The inaugural event was highlighted by a concert featuring Peter and Bethany Yarrow. (Bette Cotzin.)

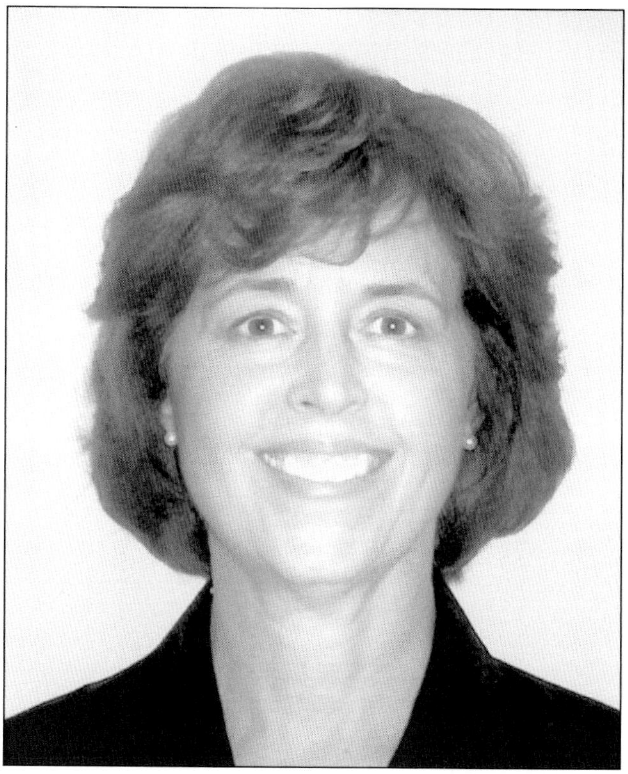

**GRETTA SPIER.** Spier served as president of Temple Beth Emeth from 2003 to 2005. Highlights of her tenure included a *Shabbaton* with rabbi and author Lawrence Kushner to honor Rabbi Levy on the occasion of his 25th year at the Temple Beth Emeth pulpit. The adult choir, under the direction of Annie Rose, toured and sang in Eastern Europe. The temple also carried out a series of Middle East "teach-ins," culminating in an exchange of visits with the local Islamic mosque. (TBE.)

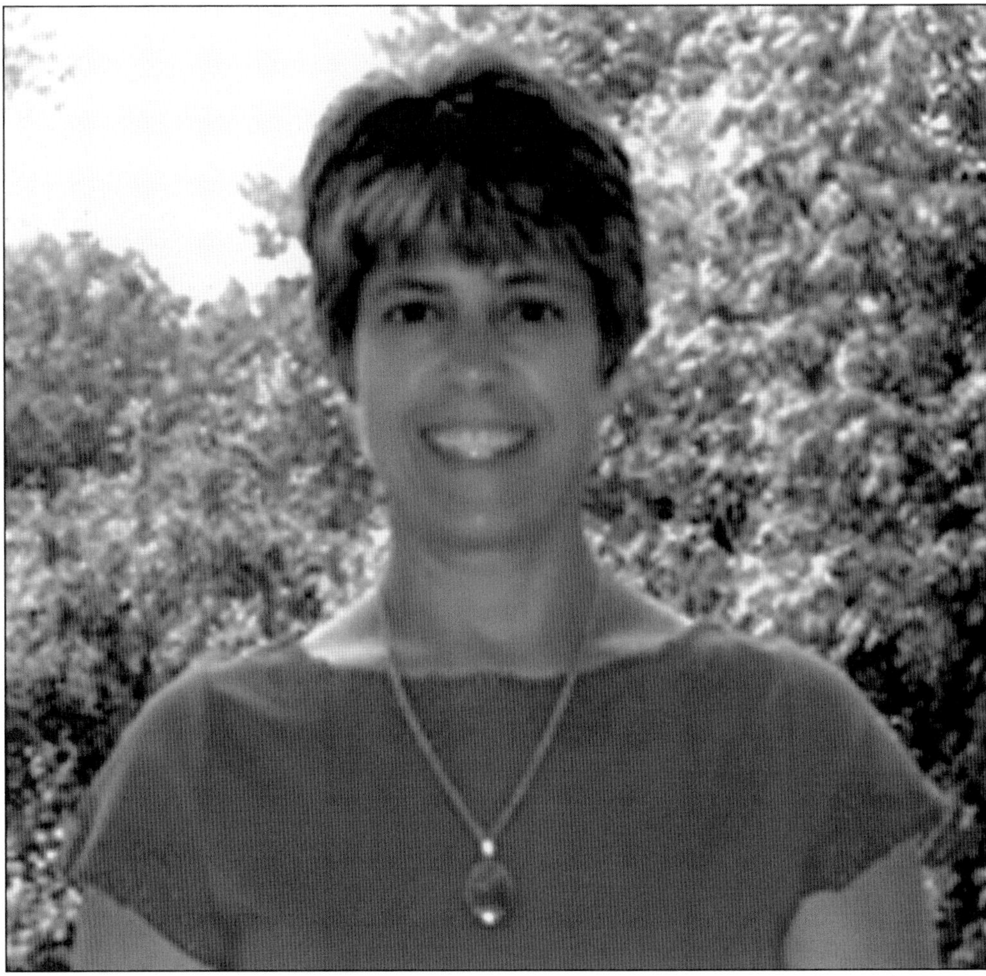

**WENDY LAWRENCE.** Wendy Lawrence is the current president of Temple Beth Emeth. Despite the size of the congregation, Lawrence is faced with issues such as limited space, the need for an assistant rabbi, and the near universal difficulties of financial planning. Such needs are balanced with the challenge of maintaining a warm home for temple members. As is the situation with each congregation in Ann Arbor, Temple Beth Emeth "strives to create a sense of family" within the context of a reform congregation. Shabbat services are held on Friday nights, reflecting the needs of its diverse membership; if life cycle events such as b'nai mitzvah take place, services may also be held on the more traditional Saturday. The temple president also oversees the Social Action Committee, which addresses issues such as human rights and interfaith relationships. (TBE.)

# *Eight*

# Ann Arbor Chabad

The Chabad organization represents a movement based upon a traditional interpretation of the Torah. Its origins date from an 18th century movement in the Russian town of Lubavitch, with the philosophy of Chabad based in part upon the teachings of the first of seven leaders, Rebbes, of the movement. Since then, the Chabad is often referred to as the Chabad-Lubavitcher movement. Each subsequent Rebbe was a descendant from Rabbi Schneur Zalman (1745–1812), the most recent being Rabbi Menachem Mendel Schneerson (1902–1994).

The term "Chabad" is an acronym originating from the Hebrew terms denoting intellectual activities: *chachmah* "wisdom," *binah* "understanding," and *da'at* "knowledge." Each member of the movement is taught to carry out his or her life based upon the teachings and interpretations of the Torah. Ideally, aspects of intellectual pursuit are incorporated into the Jewish lifestyle of the individual.

January 1975 marked the 25-year celebration of the leadership of Lubavitcher Rebbe Menachem Mendel Schneerson in the movement, as well as the 25th *yahrzeit* of the passing of the previous Rebbe. As a gift for the Rebbe, the Detroit Chabad community was inspired to establish a more formal center for Chabad activity in Ann Arbor. The original idea was to build a house, but the Rebbe's response was that his preference was for a building to be purchased in time for his upcoming birthday. Several choices were presented to Rabbi Schneerson, who chose the house at 715 Hill Street based upon its location, as well as its appearance and history. The purchase was carried out, and the keys for the building were presented to the Rebbe in time for his birthday on the 11th of Nisan (March 23, 1975).

The home was purchased by Chabad in March 1975, and in June, it opened as Chabad House for Jewish students. Rabbi Aharon Goldstein, recently completing his graduate work in Brooklyn, became the first spiritual leader for the Ann Arbor Chabad, a position he holds to this day with his son and assistant, Rabbi Alter Goldstein. Approximately 250 students participate in a variety of Chabad functions. The building contains the only *mikveh*, "ritual bath," in Ann Arbor, and from 1975 to 1980, it contained the only kosher restaurant in the city.

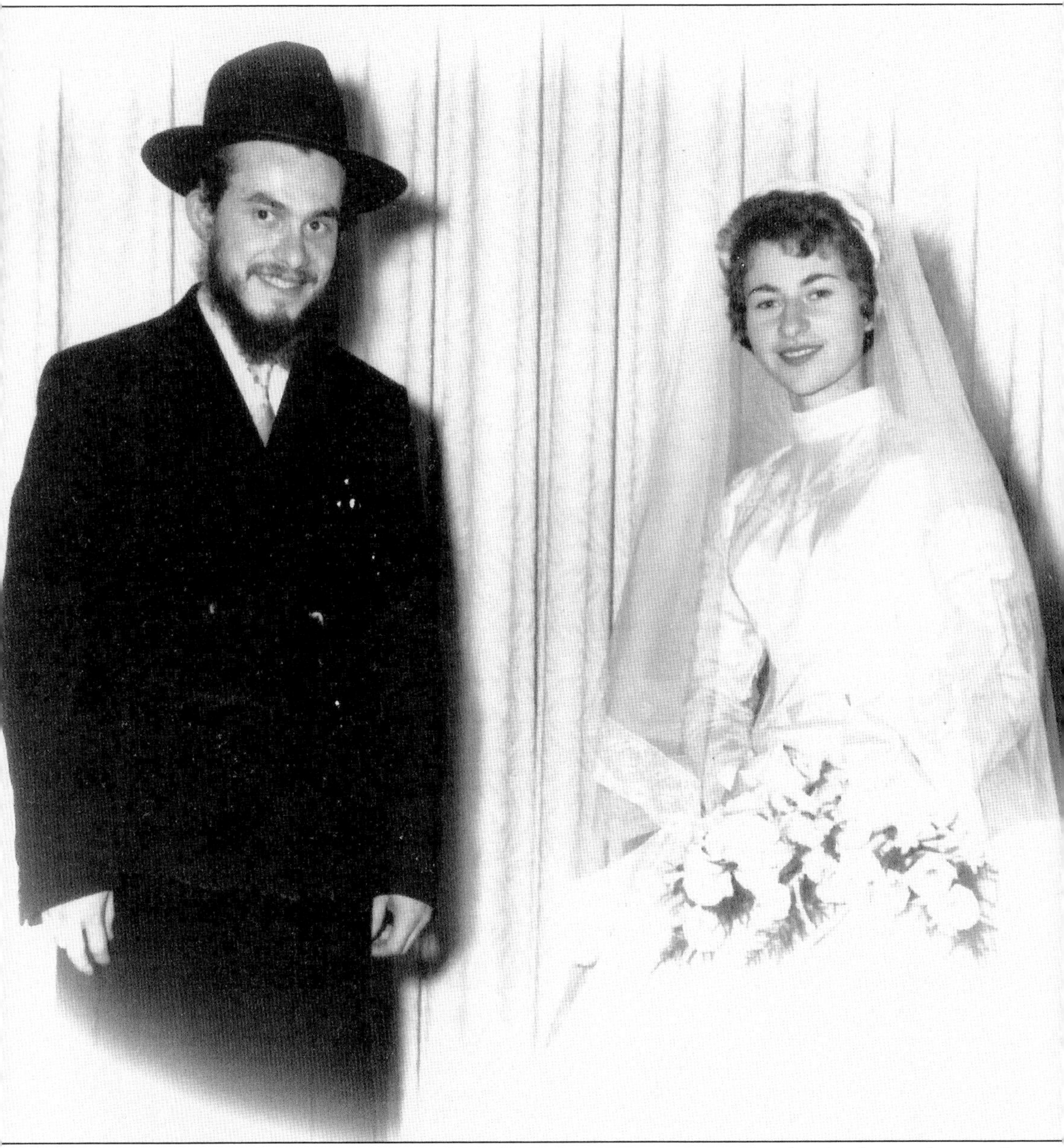

**Rabbi Sholom Ber Shemtov.** The Chabad movement came to the Midwest during the mid-1950s, with the arrival of the Lubavitcher-Chabad Rabbi Sholom Ber Shemtov. Prior to that period, Chabad was limited primarily to the eastern cities of the United States. Rabbi Shemtov was instrumental in the establishment of the first student branch of Chabad in Ann Arbor in the early 1960s, although no formal gathering place had yet been established. At the time, Chabad rabbis from the Detroit area held classes at various sites in Ann Arbor, commonly working from the Hillel Foundation. In time, classes were also held in private homes, most notably that of Arthur and Sarah Mendel. Among the initial goals was to either build or purchase a more formal, and permanent, location. Rabbi Shemtov is currently regional director of Michigan Chabad. (Rabbi Sholom Ber Shemtov.)

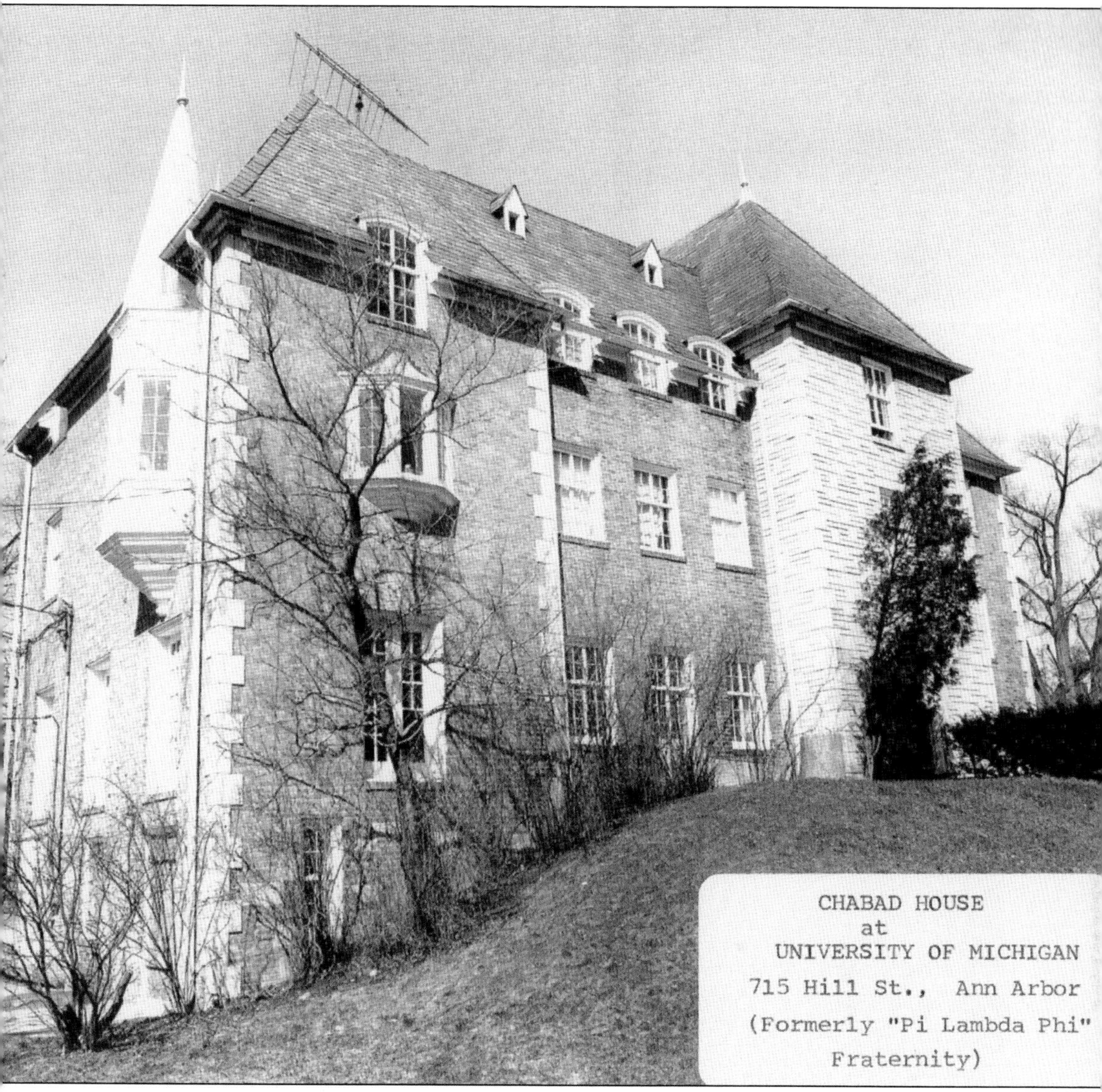


**CHABAD HOUSE AT TIME OF PURCHASE.** Located at 715 Hill Street, the building was built in 1927 as a Jewish fraternity, Pi Lambda Phi, at approximately the same time as the Theta Chi house located at Washtenaw Avenue and South University Avenue. It may be noted that both the exterior trim and floor plans for the two buildings were similar. In subsequent years, the building had undergone several alterations and renovations. During the war years, patriotic students removed the radiators and pipes from the dormitory sleeping area for use as steel in the war effort. For a time, the building was also leased to the university as league housing, functioning as a dormitory used by women while many of the men were in the service. The sorority Alpha Xi Delta was among the tenants during the early war years. In 1964, the building underwent a significant face-lift, and early in the in 1970s, it was sold to a private investor. (Rabbi Sholom Ber Shemtov.)

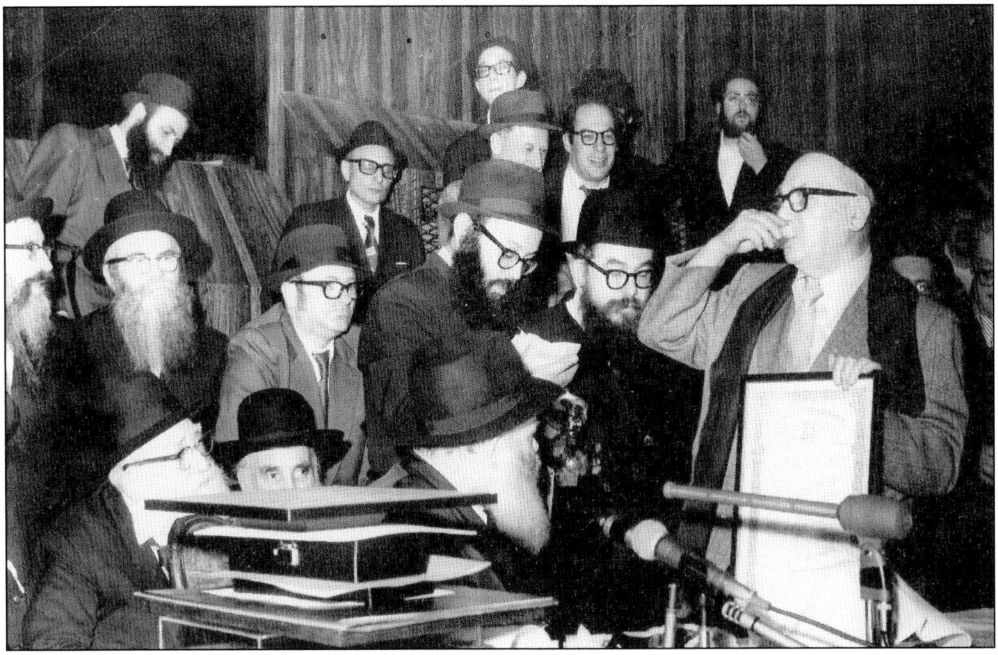

**PRESENTATION OF THE KEYS.** In 1975, the keys to the Ann Arbor Chabad House were given to the Rebbe (Rabbi Schneerson) in New York. Timing of the purchase was intentional and was meant as a gift to the Rebbe. Rabbi Shemtov from Michigan stands just to the right, behind the microphone. (Rabbi Sholom Ber Shemtov.)

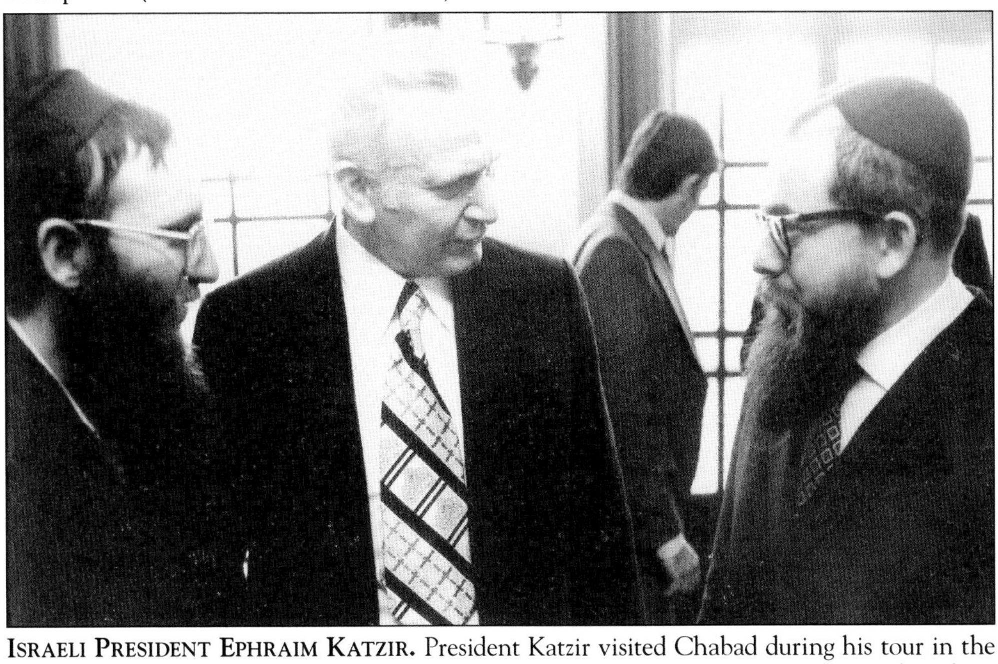

**ISRAELI PRESIDENT EPHRAIM KATZIR.** President Katzir visited Chabad during his tour in the United States in 1975. Rabbi Shemtov is on the right. Katzir served as Israeli president from 1972 to 1978. In addition to his political roles, Katzir earned a Ph.D. in chemistry from Hebrew University in 1941 and was a founding member of the Weizmann Institute of Science in 1949. (Rabbi Sholom Ber Shemtov.)

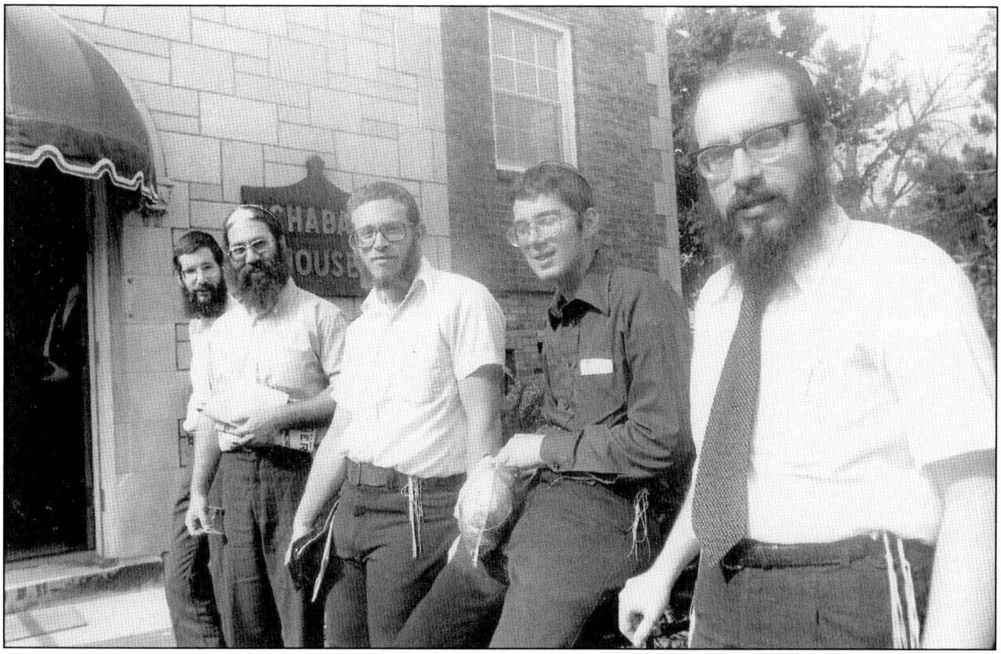


**Rabbi Aharon Goldstein.** The rabbi is standing with several student rabbis outside Ann Arbor Chabad in 1975. Rabbi Goldstein (right) was ordained at Chabad-Lubavitch Yeshivah in Brooklyn in 1972 and is the only rabbi to have served Chabad in Ann Arbor. (Rabbi Sholom Ber Shemtov.)

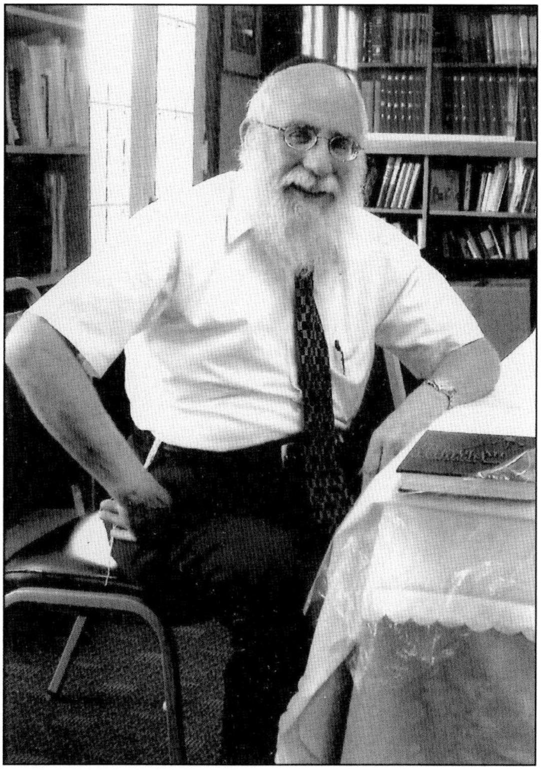

**Rabbi Aharon Goldstein.** The more traditional interpretation of Jewish law and traditions had given rise in Michigan to the Chabad movement. The result in 1975 was the establishment of a Chabad House, located near Hill and State Streets in what was once a fraternity house. Under the leadership of Rabbi Aharon Goldstein, Chabad has proven successful with both students as well as other local Jewish families interested in such a traditional approach. (Authors.)

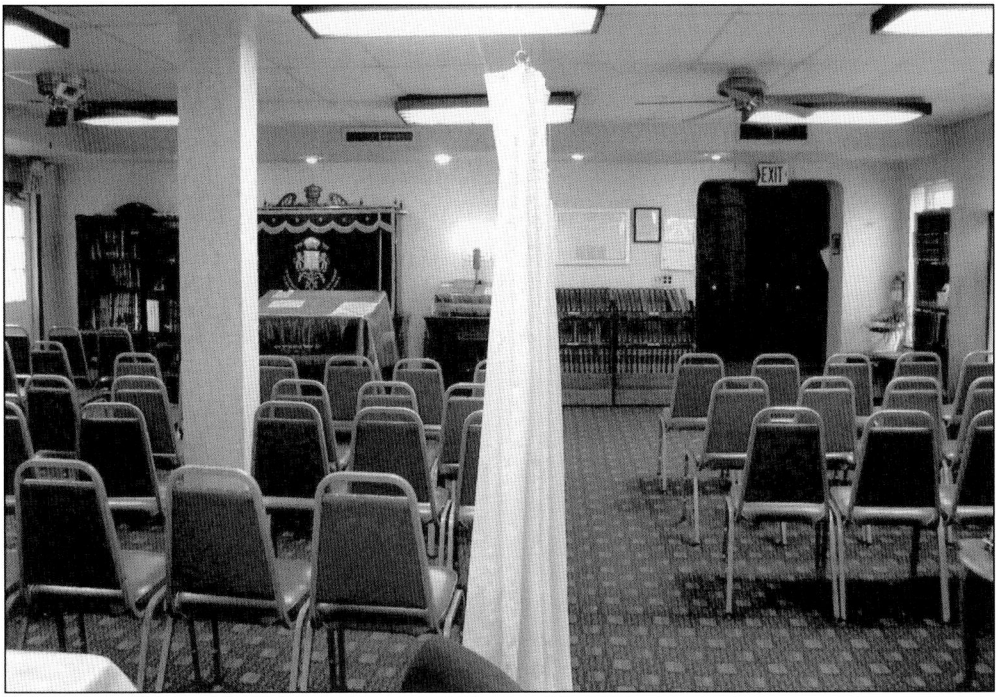

**SANCTUARY AT CHABAD HOUSE, ANN ARBOR.** The *mechitzah*, "curtain," is used to separate men and women during prayer services. The separation of men and women by a wall or curtain, or in some cases by placing the women in a separate gallery, can be traced to early Judaism. Most conservative and reform congregations no longer utilize the mechitzah. (Authors.)

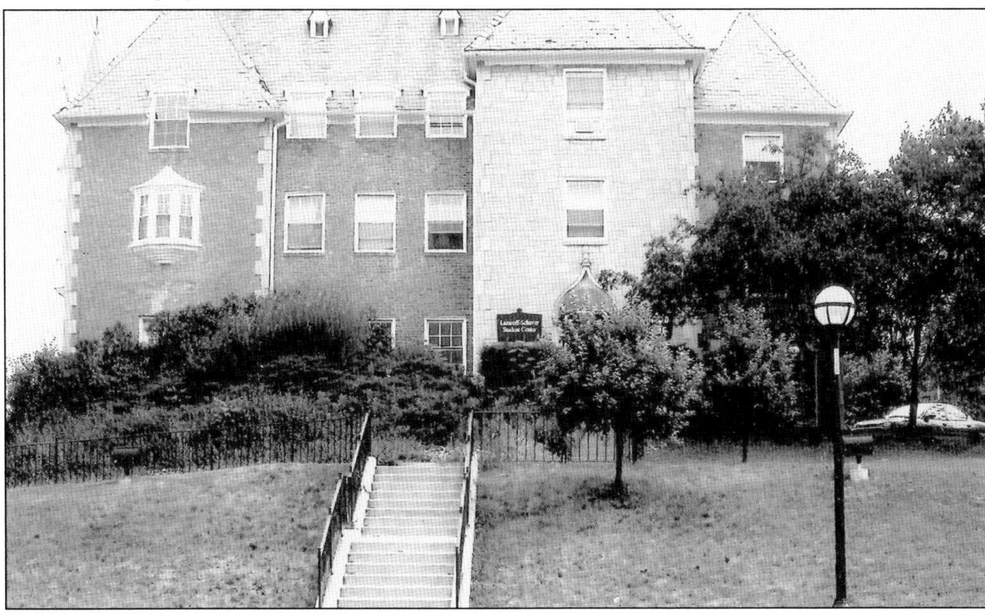

**CHABAD HOUSE, 2005.** Despite attempts by the university to purchase the property, the site retains much of its earlier character. The university continues to build on adjacent property, leaving the land on which Chabad House sits as one of the few locations of open land on the edge of campus. During Hanukkah, a large menorah is erected on the property. (Authors.)

# *Nine*

# DEDICATION OF THE ORIGINAL JEWISH CEMETERY

Knowledge of the Jewish cemetery itself and the role played by the Weil family, both in establishing the cemetery as well as in providing a significant Jewish presence in the community, was the result of a series of fortuitous events. As described by Helen Aminoff, a local fraternity during the fall of 1980 discovered that what they were using as a stepping-stone for the house was actually a face-down tombstone. The stone, with preserved Hebrew script, was first presented to Rabbi William Rudolph, then director of the Hillel Foundation near campus, and then passed on to the rabbi of Beth Israel Congregation, Allan D. Kensky. Rabbi Kensky determined the name on the stone was that of Reila Weil, the wife of Moses Weil, with the date of death listed as 1858. In a ceremony held June 12, 1983, the stone became part of a dedication to the Weil family, some of whom were buried at Forest Hill Cemetery in Ann Arbor.

The June ceremony over which Rabbi Kensky presided represented the culmination of a project which required the cooperation of several organizations in addition to the local community: the University of Michigan, which owned the property; the state of Michigan; and the city of Ann Arbor. Those dedicating the plaque included university president Harold Shapiro, Michigan Secretary of State Richard Austin, local historian Wystan Stevens, and Helen Aminoff, the driving force behind the project. In addition, several descendants of the Weil family participated in the ceremony. Following the dedication, participants traveled to the Forest Hill Cemetery, where a service was held at the Weil grave sites.

*The Jewish Historical Society of Michigan*
*Washtenaw County Jewish Community Council*
*Beth Israel Congregation*

*cordially invite you and your family*
*to the*

*DEDICATION CEREMONY*

*of a*

*STATE HISTORICAL MARKER*

*on the site of*

*THE FIRST JEWISH CEMETERY IN MICHIGAN*

*Sunday*
*June 12, 1983*
*11:30 a.m.*

*East Courtyard, U-M Rackham Building*
*Fletcher between Huron & Washington Streets*
*Ann Arbor, Michigan*

*Luncheon following at Beth Israel Congregation*
*RSVP by $7.50/Person Check No Later Than May 31 To*
*Beth Israel, 2000 Washtenaw, Ann Arbor, MI 48104*

INVITATION TO DEDICATION CEREMONY. On June 12, 1983, a ceremony was held dedicating the first Jewish cemetery in Michigan, with invitations sent to members of the local Jewish communities and other Ann Arbor communities. As part of the occasion, a plaque was unveiled, which rests at the corner of Huron and Fletcher Streets. (BIC.)

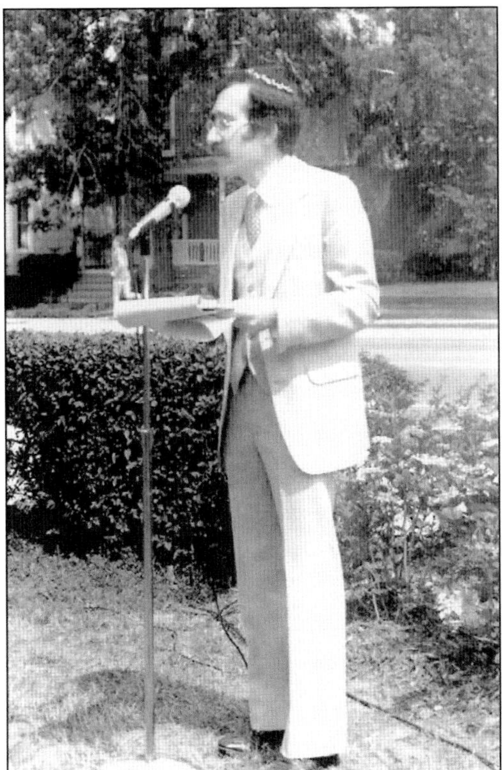

RABBI ALLAN D. KENSKY. Rabbi Kensky opened the ceremony with remarks appropriate for the occasion. "Today we celebrate completion, the completion of a project which began some four years ago, when . . . the monument of Reila Weil, dated 1858, was returned to the Jewish community. That monument . . . was to become the cornerstone for our entire project of restoration and research." (BIC.)

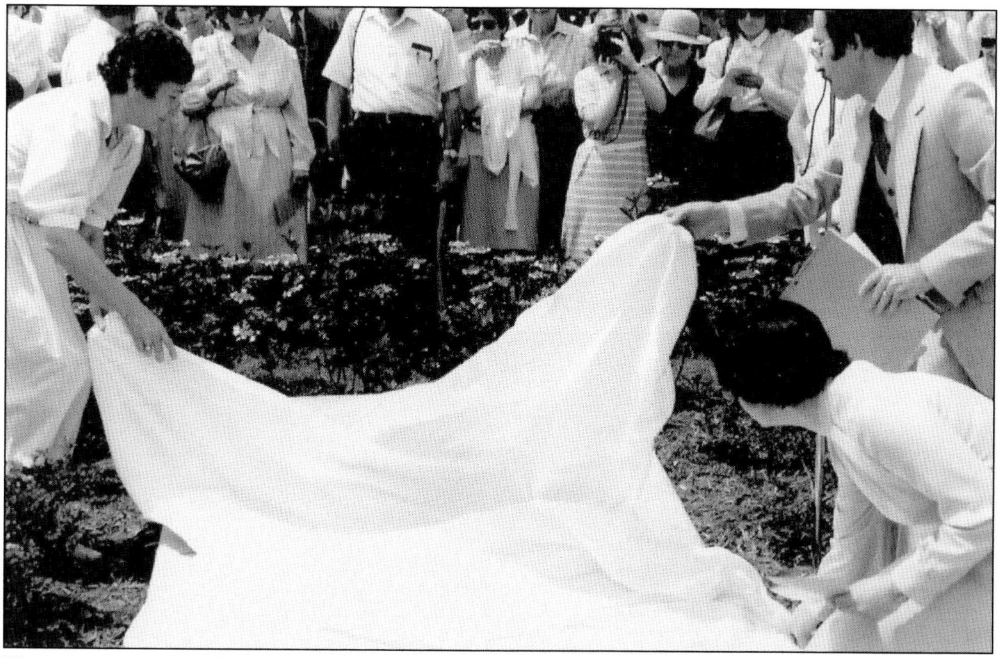

**UNVEILING OF THE PLAQUE.** Following brief remarks from Rabbi Kensky, as well as those from invited members of the local community and the Weil family descendants, the rabbi prepared to unveil the plaque. Much of the community was present during the historic ceremony. (BIC.)

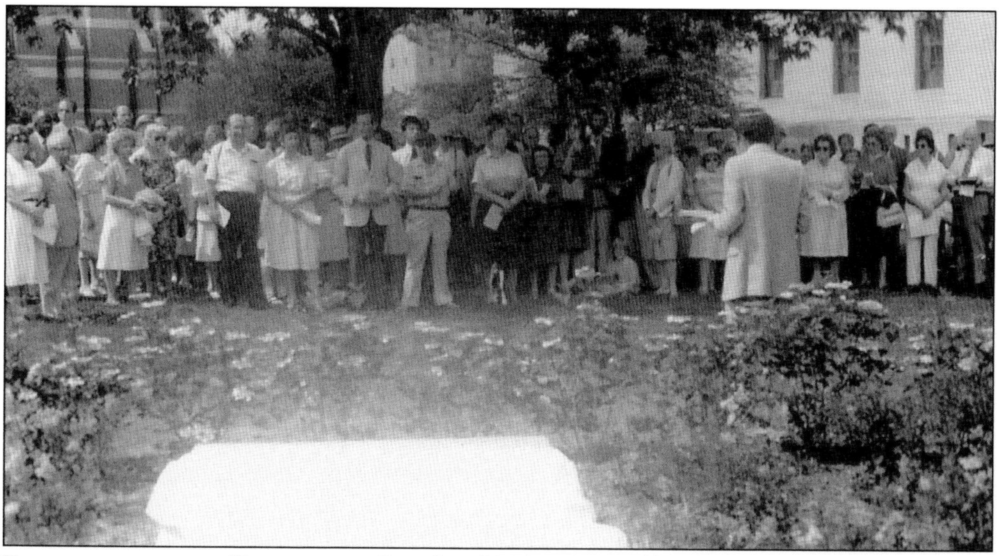

**PREPARING FOR THE DEDICATION.** David and Helen Aminoff and Pres. Harold Shapiro of the university acknowledged the occasion with a few words. Following Helen Aminoff's publication of her work on the early Jewish community, she was contacted by Jane Berliss, a Weil descendant who had just come to the university. (BIC.)

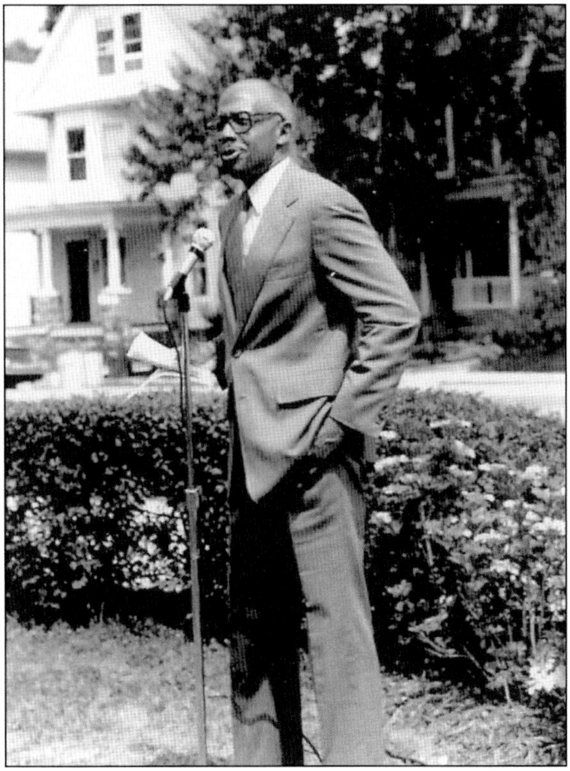

**Richard Austin, Michigan Secretary of State.** "In this rapidly changing society of ours, as we plan for the future and try to make the most of the present, we often take glances to the past . . . and look for guidance from a time when existence was rugged, less complicated, and the future was more predictable." (BIC.)

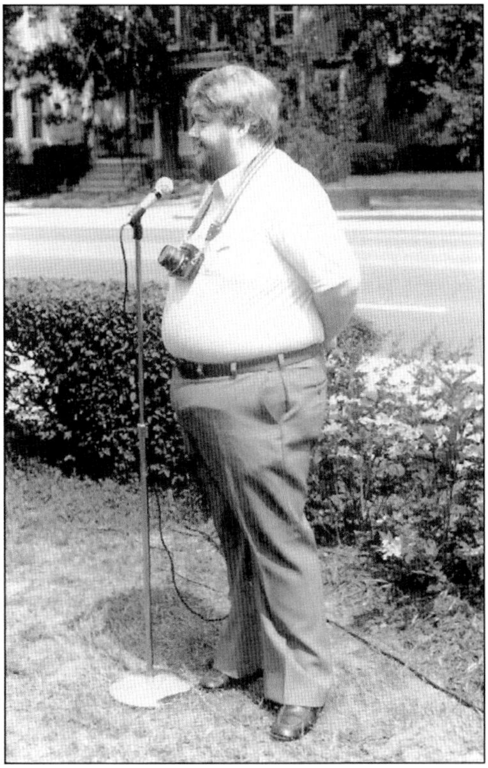

**Wystan Stevens.** Wystan Stevens for many years had served as the official Ann Arbor city historian. His presentation was highly appropriate for the occasion. "This is a kind of history people are dying to know more about. We are on a site now which almost was forgotten." (BIC.)

UNIVERSITY PRESIDENT HAROLD SHAPIRO. "Bearing witness to our history is one of the most human things of all. It is very human to care about history, and it is very human to need our history. It really helps place all of ourselves in that long stream of human history, helps us tell us where we are going, why we are going there, and if we should be heading somewhere else." (BIC.)

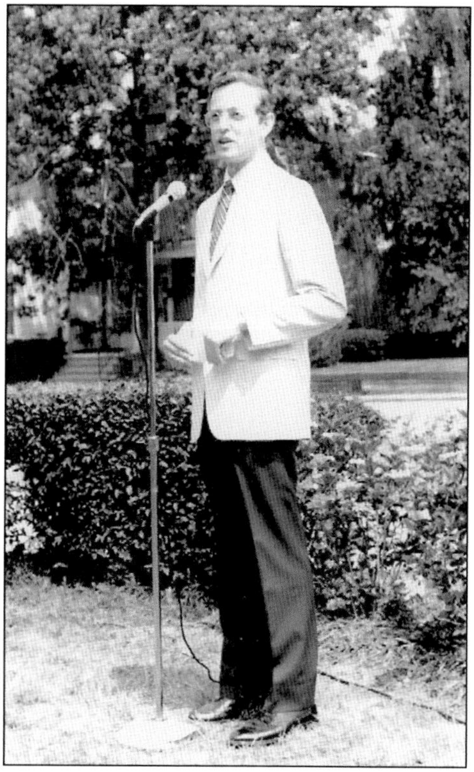

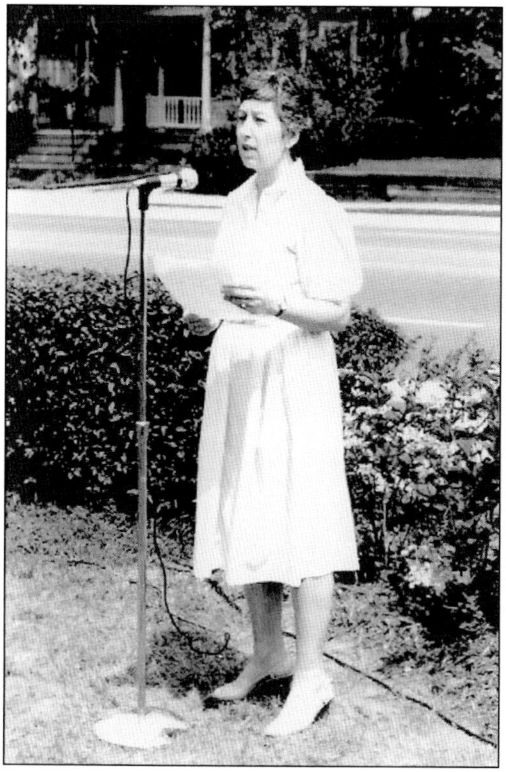

HELEN AMINOFF. "Little did I realize when I began my search to discover the origins of the beautifully inscribed Hebrew tombstone that was turned over to Rabbi Kensky that I would be standing here with you today. . . . It seems fitting that the site of the first Jewish cemetery in Michigan now should be the site of one of the university's most prestigious buildings, here where the past looks to the future. (BIC.)

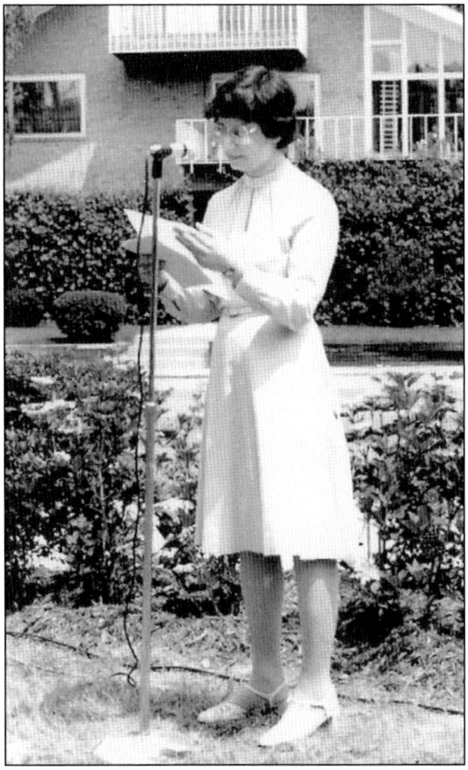

**Jane Berliss, great-great-granddaughter of Solomon Weil.** "When Helen [Aminoff] told me . . . that the marker had been placed in the Rackham courtyard, I ran over there and stood for a while in the dead quiet of the rainy dusk, and thought about my great-great-grandfather and his brothers and their wives . . . . Thank you all for being here to share a part of history." (BIC.)

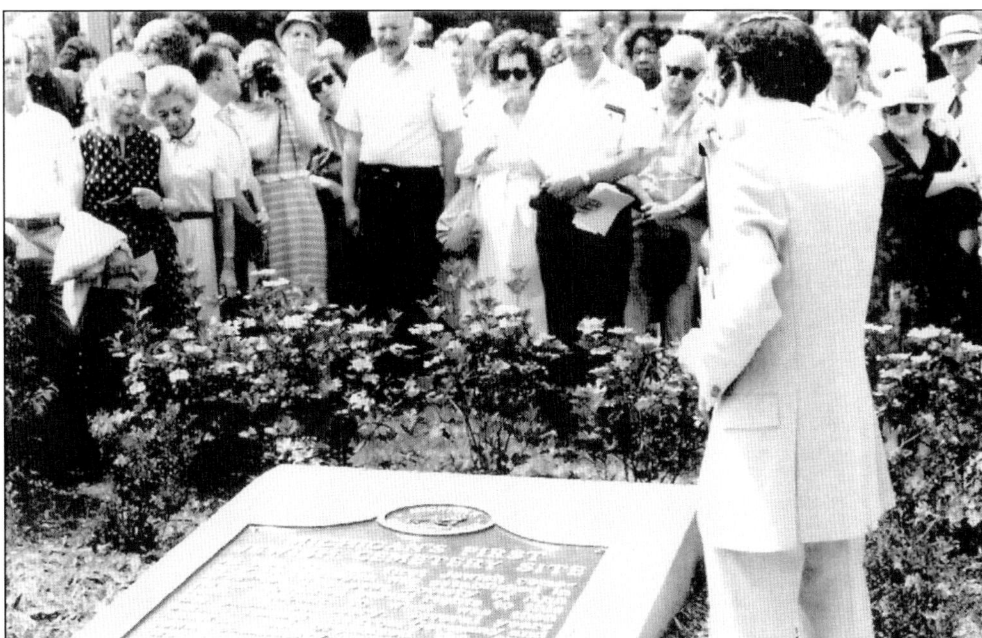

**Closing Remarks by Rabbi Kensky.** At the completion of the ceremony dedicating the original cemetery grounds, Rabbi Kensky read aloud the words on the plaque: "The Jews Society in Ann Arbor acquired burial rights to this land adjacent to what was then the public cemetery." (Now the site of the Power Center.) (BIC.)

**Historic Plaque.** The plaque, located in the ground at the corner of Huron and Fletcher Streets, commemorates Michigan's first Jewish cemetery site. A similar plaque is located in Elmwood Cemetery in Detroit. The mistake was due to a misinterpretation of the designation of the Ann Arbor site as being a private family burial site in plat maps. (BIC.)

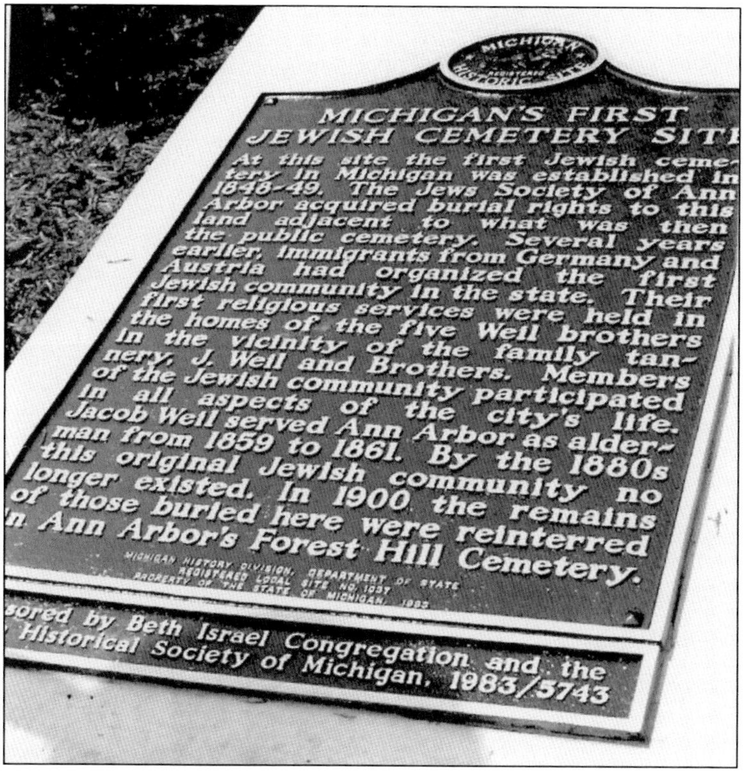


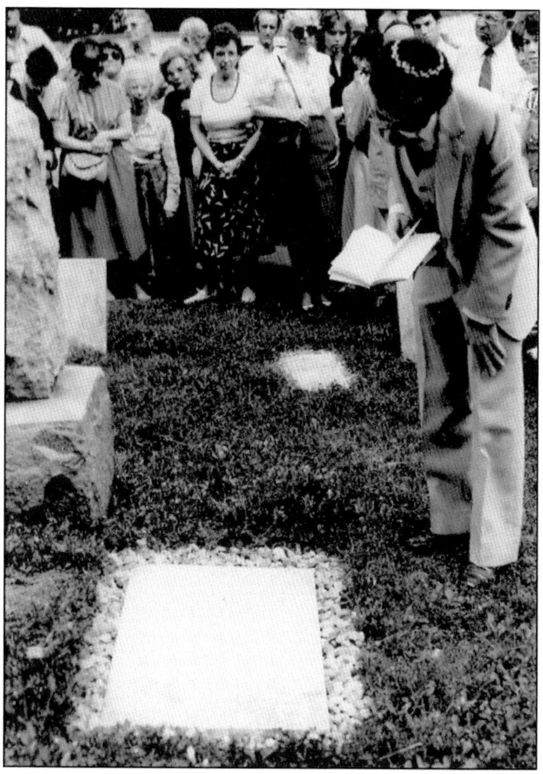

**Weil Plot, Forest Hill Cemetery.** At the completion of the ceremony commemorating the establishment of the first Jewish cemetery in Michigan, members of the congregation traveled the mile to visit the permanent resting place for the Weil family. Rabbi Kensky conducted services at the Weil plot in Forest Hill Cemetery. (BIC.)

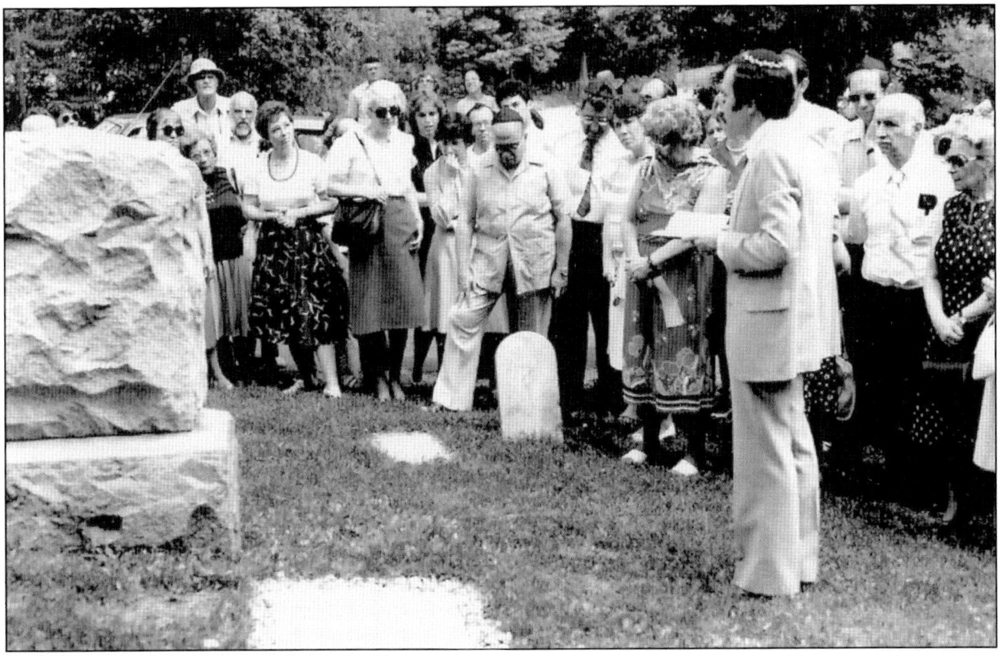

**WEIL GRAVE MARKERS.** The several grave markers in the Weil plot, located now in Forest Hill Cemetery, are original. The 1980 discovery of the Reila Weil tombstone, at the time serving as a stepping-stone in front of a local fraternity house, became the key to opening the story of the Jewish community in Ann Arbor. (BIC.)

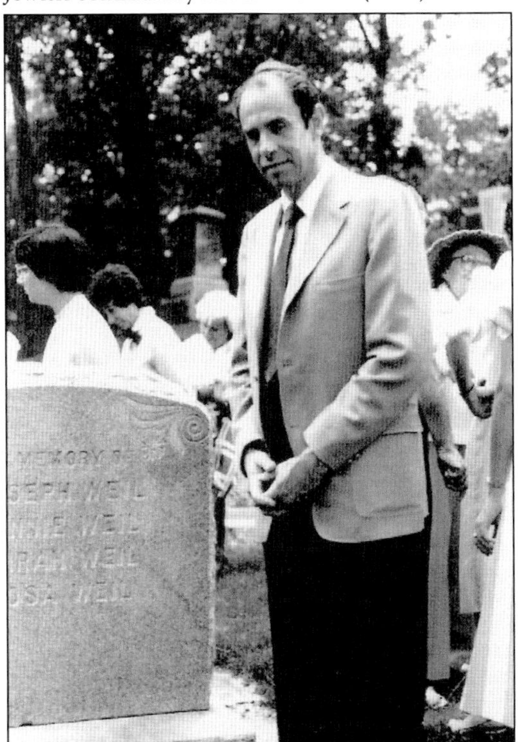

**DAVID SCHTEINGART.** The former president of the Beth Israel Congregation (1974–1978) stood in silence near the Weil grave marker as a service was carried out. Following the ceremony in the cemetery, the members dispersed, having honored the earliest known members of the Jewish community. Despite an earlier attempt at restoration, the markers have been weathered by nature; the graves lie peacefully in their own section of the cemetery. (BIC.)

# *Ten*

# Legacies of the Past, Confidence in the Future

The new century found the Jewish community of Washtenaw County in general, and Ann Arbor in particular, vibrant and diverse. Membership in the two major congregations had increased to over 3,000 members (approximately 1,200 family units). The numbers do not reflect the Jewish population among students, estimated at upwards of 7,000. Not all are affiliated with congregations or are even observant. A significant number participate in functions carried out through Hillel. The Samuel and Jean Frankel Center for Judaic Studies, established at the university in 1988, grew to include 15 faculty members augmented by some dozen visiting scholars. Under the directorship of Professors Zvi Gittelman and Todd Endelman, between 800 and 1,200 students are enrolled in the 40 courses taught through the center each year.

The religious life in the city reflects the diversity in thought and philosophy among the community. In addition to Chabad, an Ann Arbor Orthodox Minyan under the direction of Rabbi Rod Glogower also serves those students and others who wish such an approach to Judaism. The Reconstructionist Havurah, emphasizing a more open approach to worship, provides both services as well as a K–8 religious school. The Jewish Cultural Society, dating from 1965 in Ann Arbor, stresses a cultural rather than religious approach to Judaism. A wide variety of programs and community functions for older children and adults have also appeared and grown over recent decades. A significant portion of the funding behind local programs is directed through the offices of the Jewish Federation of Washtenaw County.

The community remembers those who by their presence brought recognition during the long history of the Jewish community. During the 1930s, future playwright Arthur Miller attended the university. Raoul Wallenberg, the man who saved thousands of Jews in the Holocaust during World War II, studied architecture at the university. Jonas Salk is lauded as the developer of the first effective vaccine against polio, work he carried out at the University of Pittsburgh during the late 1940s and 1950s. It is often overlooked that during the early 1940s, Salk and his young family lived in Ann Arbor as he worked on an influenza vaccine for the armed services. Wilbur Cohen, among the architects of the New Deal, was a professor and dean of education from 1969 to 1978.

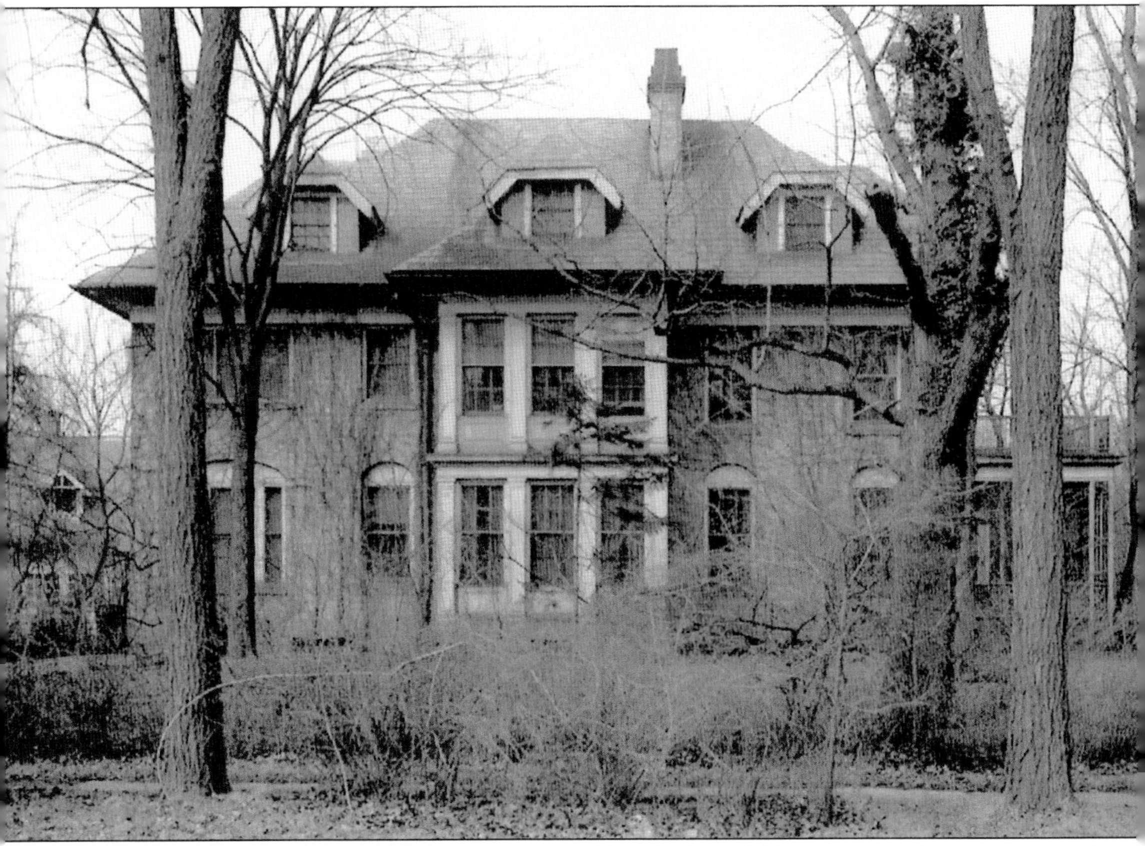

**1102 Oakland.** The Oakland Avenue site of B'nai Brith Hillel Foundation, close to State and Hill Streets, was used from the mid-1930s to mid-1940s. The first B'nai Brith Hillel Foundation established on a college campus was that in Illinois in 1923. In 1926, a chapter was started on the Ann Arbor campus, by then the third such chapter on a college campus. Rabbi A. H. Finkelstein became the first director, with Leonard Cohen as director of student activities. Over the years, Hillel was situated at various locations around campus. The location during Hillel's early years was at 615 East University Street (1926–mid-1930s), later moving to the Oakland site depicted here, with Rabbi Bernard Heller as director, and then to 730 Haven Avenue, near Hill Street. Directors who followed Rabbi Heller included Rabbi Henry Rabinowitz, Rabbi Jehudah Cohen, Rabbi Herschel Lymon, Dr. Herman Jacobs, and Rabbis Jerald Goldman, Joel Poupko, and William Rudolph. (BHL.)

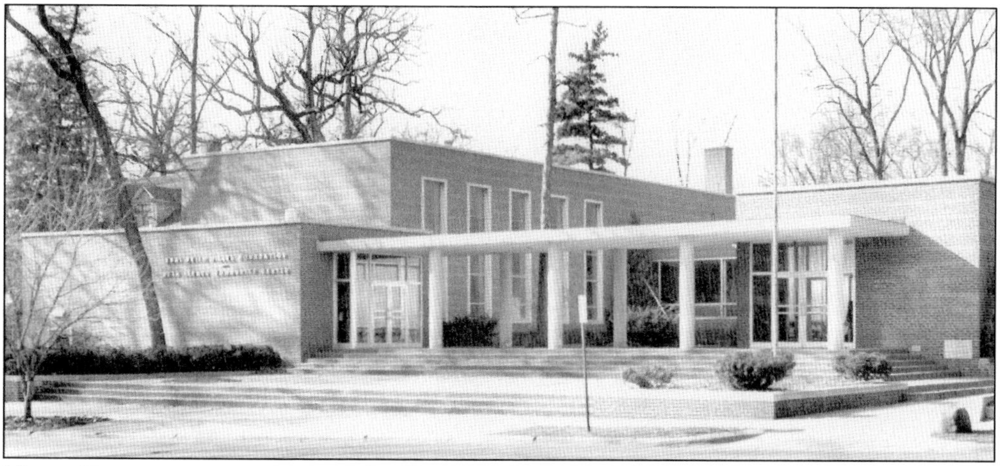

**HILLEL FOUNDATION, AROUND 1952.** The Haven Avenue property was obtained by the university in 1947 for the new business school, forcing Hillel to find new quarters. Through the efforts of Osias Zwerdling and Dr. William Haber, Hillel found temporary quarters at 2101 Hill Street, which it shared with Beth Israel. In 1952, it moved to its present location on Hill Street. (BHL.)

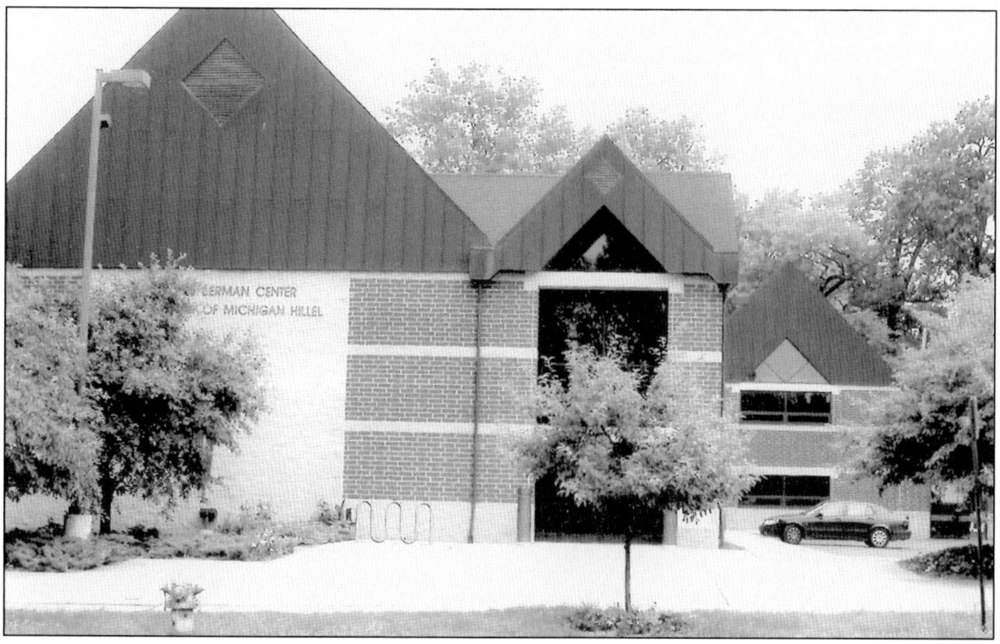


**HILLEL FOUNDATION, 1429 HILL STREET, 2005.** The first building was replaced in 1986 with the Mandell Berman Center, which is depicted here. The center now houses the Hillel Foundation, with Michael Brooks as director. (Authors.)

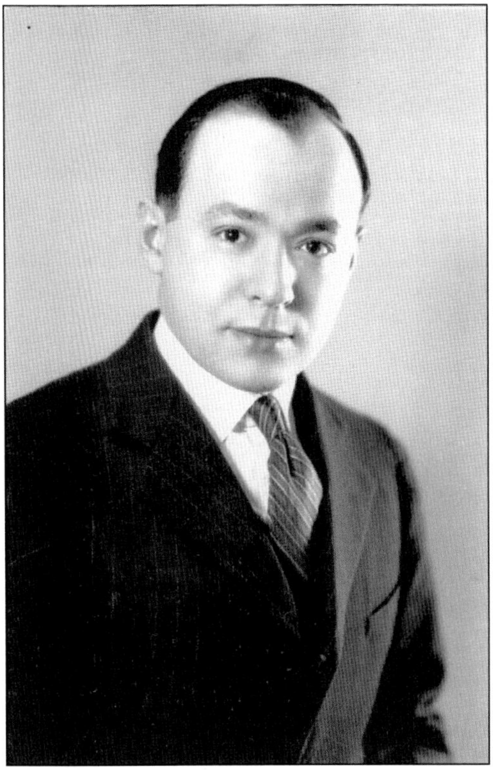

**REUBEN LEON KAHN (1887–1974).** Kahn was a major figure for decades in the field of immunology and serology. After serving as an immunologist for the Michigan Department of Health in Lansing, Kahn joined the University of Michigan in 1928; he remained with the university for 29 years. Kahn's most notable work was the development of the Kahn test, the standard testing method for the detection of syphilis. (BHL.)

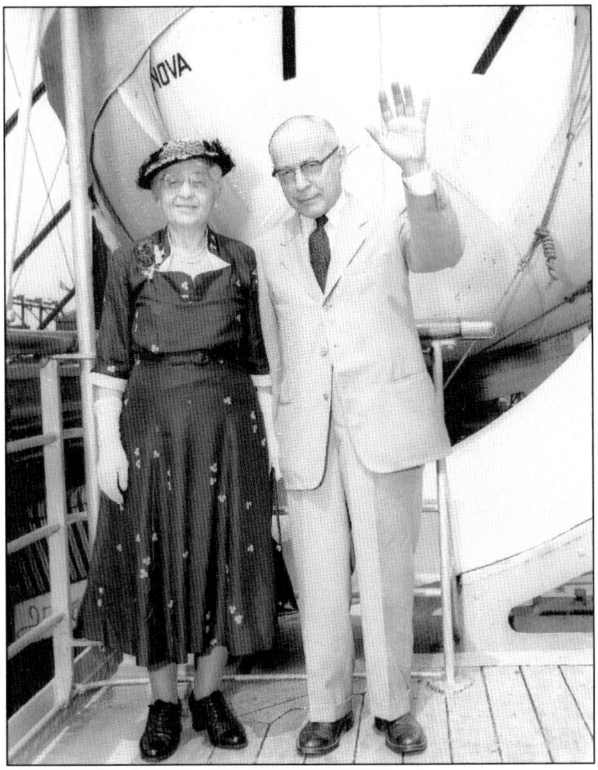


**REUBEN AND DINA KAHN.** Married in 1917, the Kahns had two children, Lyra and David. Dina Kahn (née Weinstein) was well known for her roles in philanthropic activities. For many years, she was one of the dominant figures for the United Jewish Appeal. It was said she carried with her a list of the Jewish residents of Ann Arbor and was not loathe to request donations from them if they crossed paths. Dina Kahn died in 1967. (BHL.)

**RAOUL WALLENBERG (1912–1945?).** The son of a Swedish naval officer and member of a distinguished family, Wallenberg enrolled at the University of Michigan in 1931, graduating four years later with a degree in architecture. Wallenberg volunteered in 1944 to travel to Hungary for the purpose of rescuing Jews designated for deportment and death. In 1945, Wallenberg was arrested by the Russians and it is likely that he died at their hands. (BHL.)

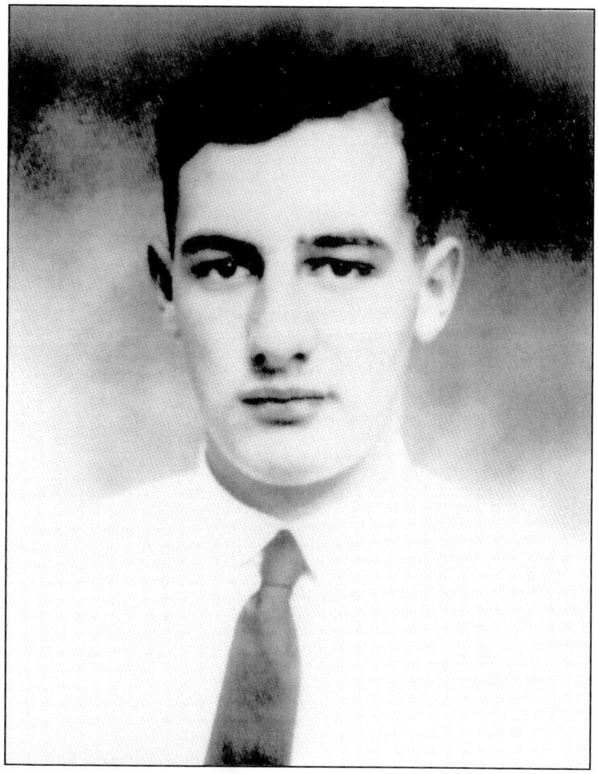

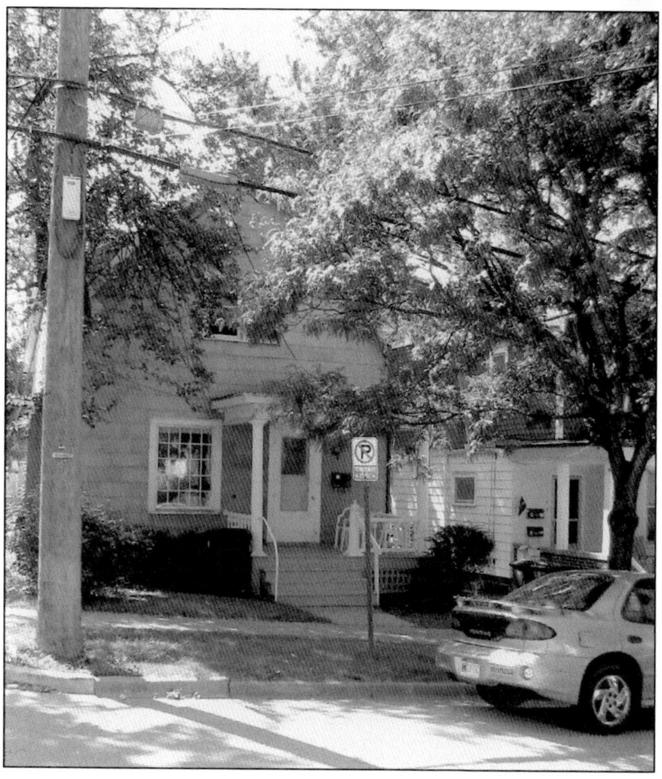

**308 EAST MADISON STREET.** Only one home in which Wallenberg resided during his years as a student in Ann Arbor remains. The house at 308 East Madison Street was Wallenberg's residence in 1931 and 1932. As many as 20,000 Jews designated for deportment and death may have been saved by Wallenberg during the last years of the war. In Wallenberg's honor, an annual lecture series, medal, and endowment were established at the university. (Authors.)

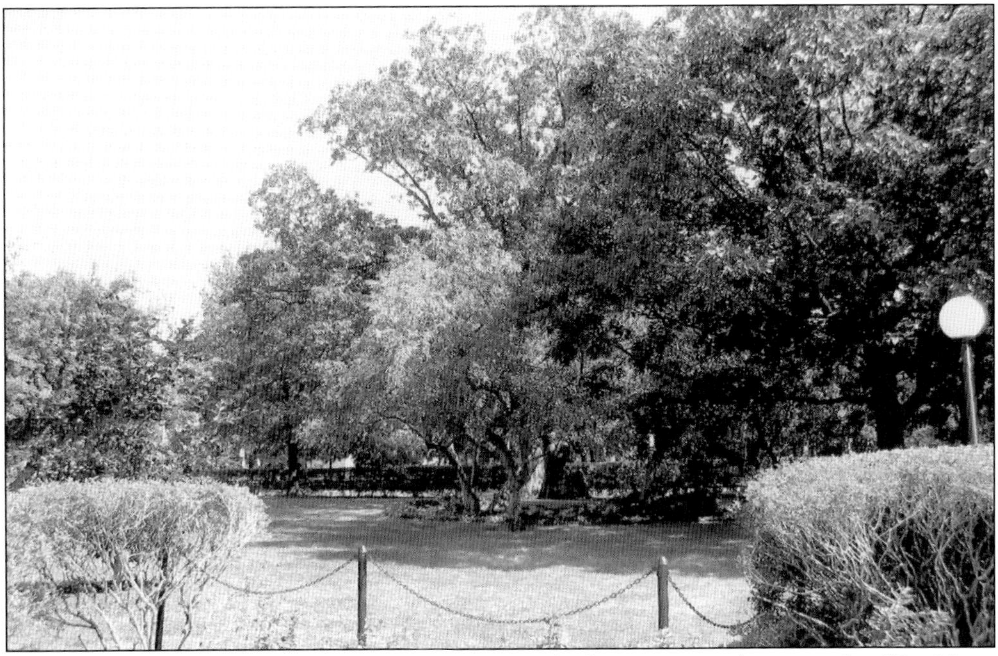

**East Side of Horace H. Rackham Building.** The lawn area on the east side of Rackham was at one time the site of the first Jewish cemetery in Michigan. The corner at Washington and Fletcher Streets is the site of the Holocaust Memorial, commemorating both the heroism exhibited by Wallenberg and the memory of the Holocaust itself. (Authors.)

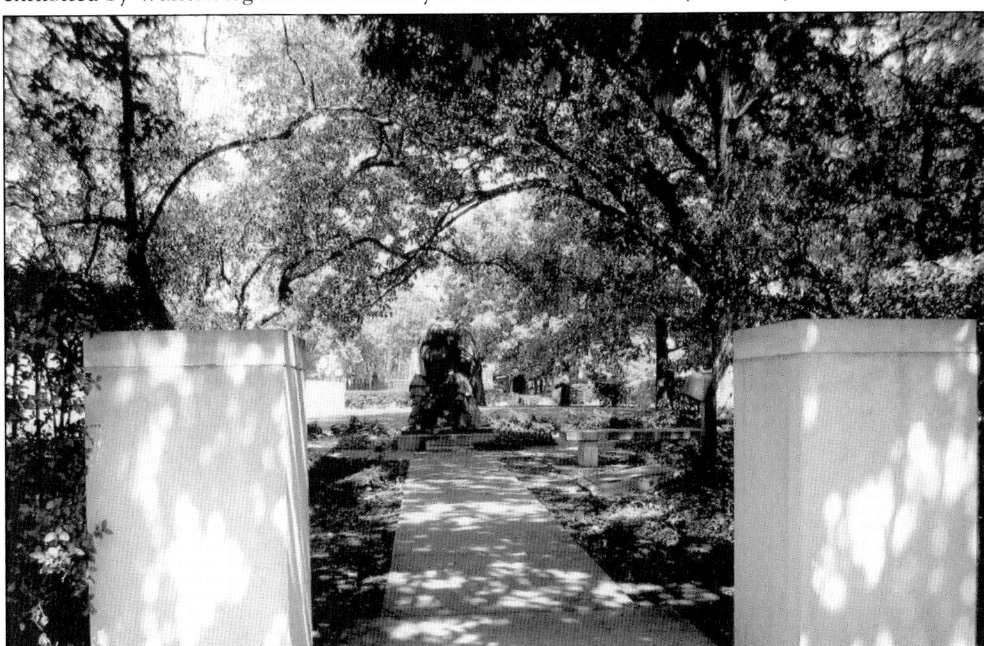

**Entrance to Wallenberg Plaza.** The small area designated as "the plaza" represents a place for contemplation, separate from the noise of campus and traffic. It is located at the corner of Washington and Fletcher Streets. The land was donated to the Jewish community for the purpose of the memorial. (Authors.)

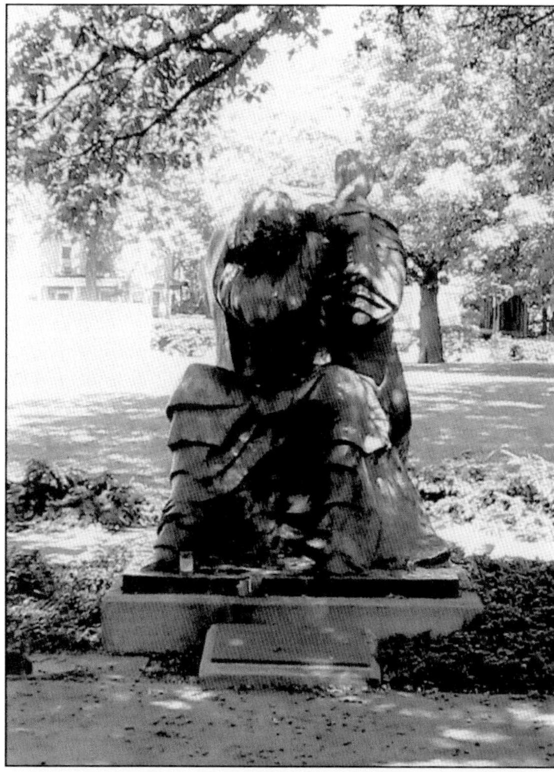

**Holocaust Memorial.** The memorial, designed by Leonard Baskin, was acquired by the university in 1994. Situated on the Raoul Wallenberg Plaza east of the Horace H. Rackham Building, the site of the first Jewish cemetery in Michigan, the statue depicts a figure wrapped in grief, and whose limbs depict both anger (closed fist) and mercy (raised hand). (Authors.)

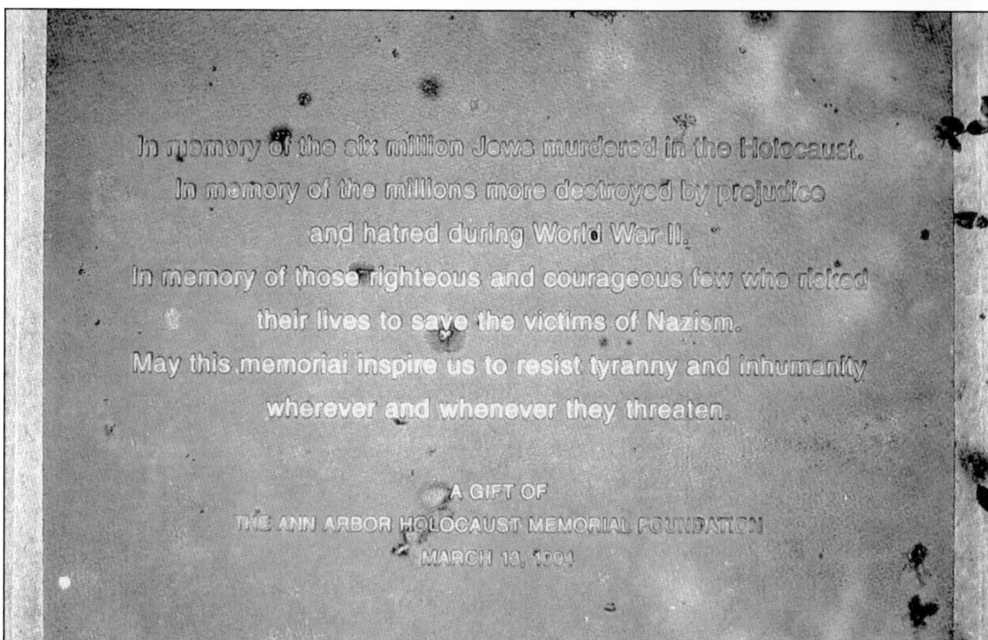


**Memorial Plaque.** "In memory of the six million murdered in the Holocaust. In memory of the millions more destroyed by prejudice and hatred during World War II. . . . May this memorial inspire us to resist tyranny." The plaque is situated in conjunction with the memorial. Shade and benches allow for quiet contemplation. (Authors.)

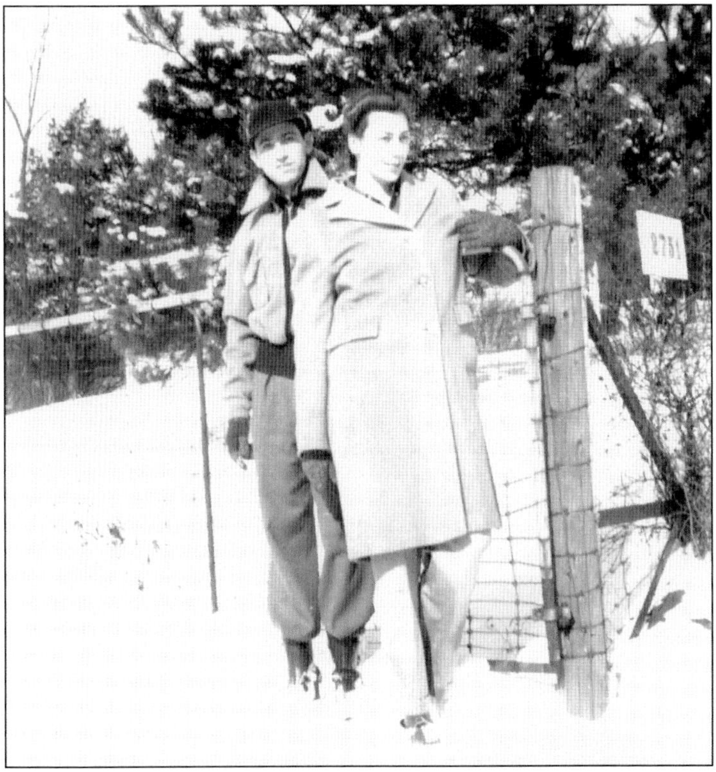

**JONAS AND DONNA SALK.** The Salks lived at the Craig farmhouse, 2751 North Maple Road, for several years. Married in 1939, the Salks came to Ann Arbor in the spring of 1942. Jonas's former mentor, Thomas Francis, was chair of epidemiology at the University of Michigan School of Public Health and offered Jonas a position. During six years at the university, Jonas developed one of the first effective influenza vaccines. (Darrell Salk.)

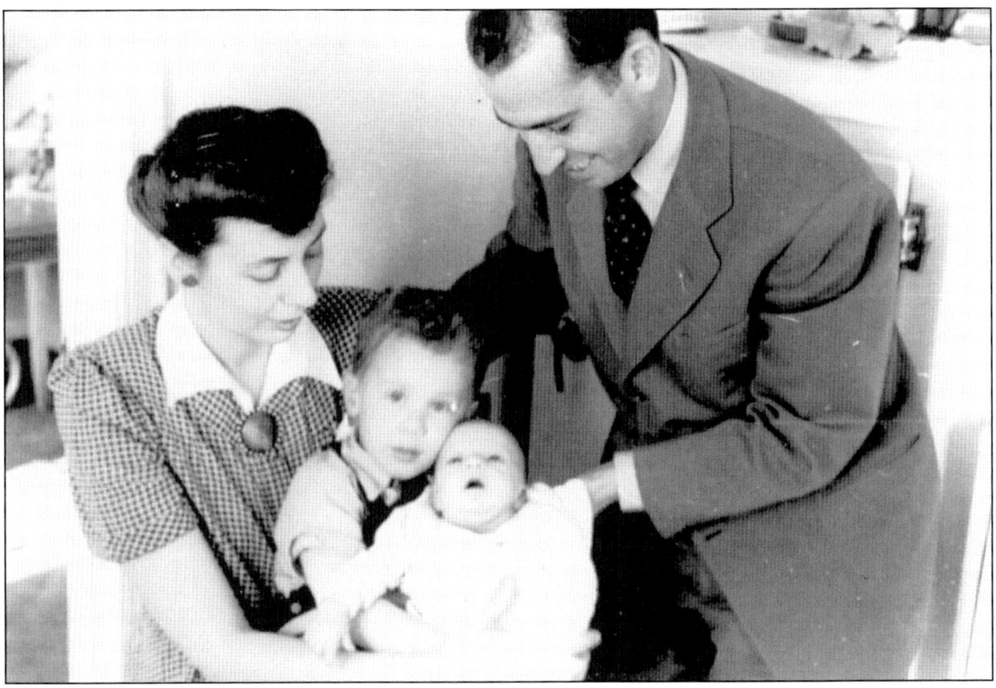

**SALK FAMILY.** This photograph was taken in 1947 when the Salks lived at the Pretz house. From left to right are Donna, Peter, Darrell, and Jonas Salk. The Salks moved to the Pretz house located at 575 West Delhi Road around 1946. (Darrell Salk.)

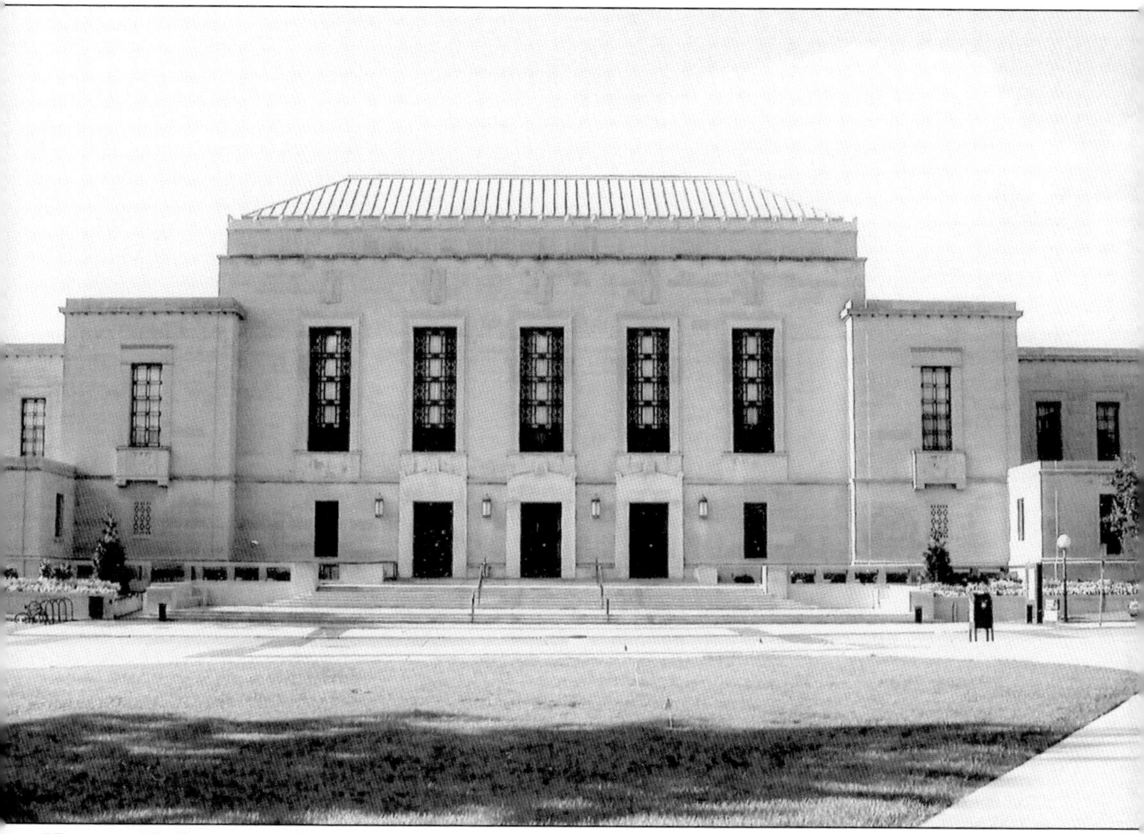

**HORACE H. RACKHAM BUILDING.** The site was originally purchased from the U.S. government by Thomas Charles in 1825 and was subsequently sold to Andrew Nowland. At that time, it became known as Nowland Farms. In 1834, the easternmost portion of the farm was sold to the town for use as a cemetery. The public portion of that cemetery is the current site for the Power Center for Performing Arts. In 1899, during a mortgage foreclosure sale, it was discovered that an agreement had been made some years earlier by the heirs of the Weils that the bodies which were present in the Jewish cemetery should be reinterred, upon sale of the land, in Forest Hill Cemetery at Observatory Street and Geddes Road. The same tombstones would be used. Horace H. Rackham Building was erected in 1935. It was here on April 12, 1955, that Jonas Salk released the results of the field trials testing the Salk vaccine. (Authors.)

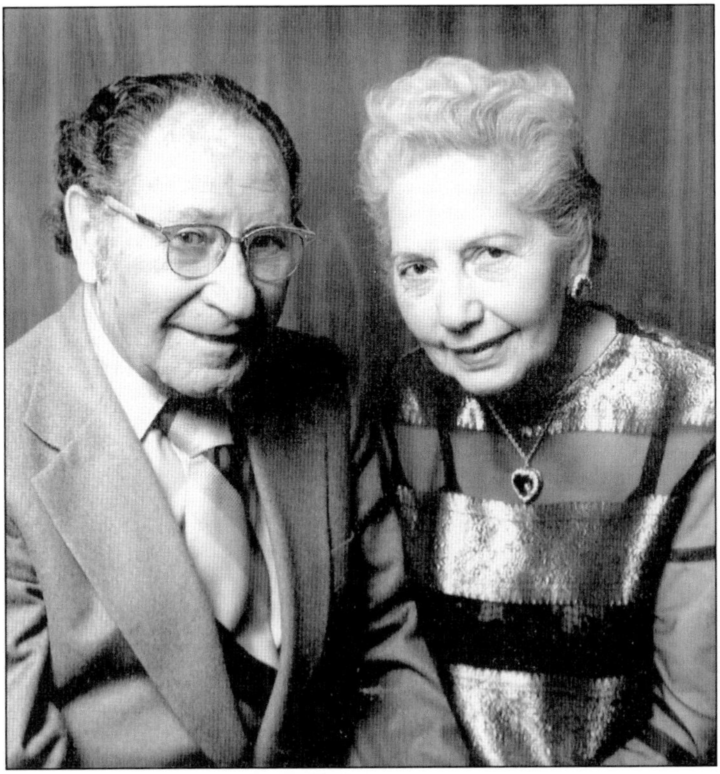

**WILLIAM AND FANNIE HABER.** Professor William Haber (1899–1988) was a primary architect in the rebuilding of European Jewry following World War II. A professor of economics at the university starting in 1936, he served as dean of the College of Literature, Science and Arts from 1963 to 1968. The William Haber Award, for contribution to Jewish campus life, and the Haber Professorship are among his legacies. (Alan Haber.)

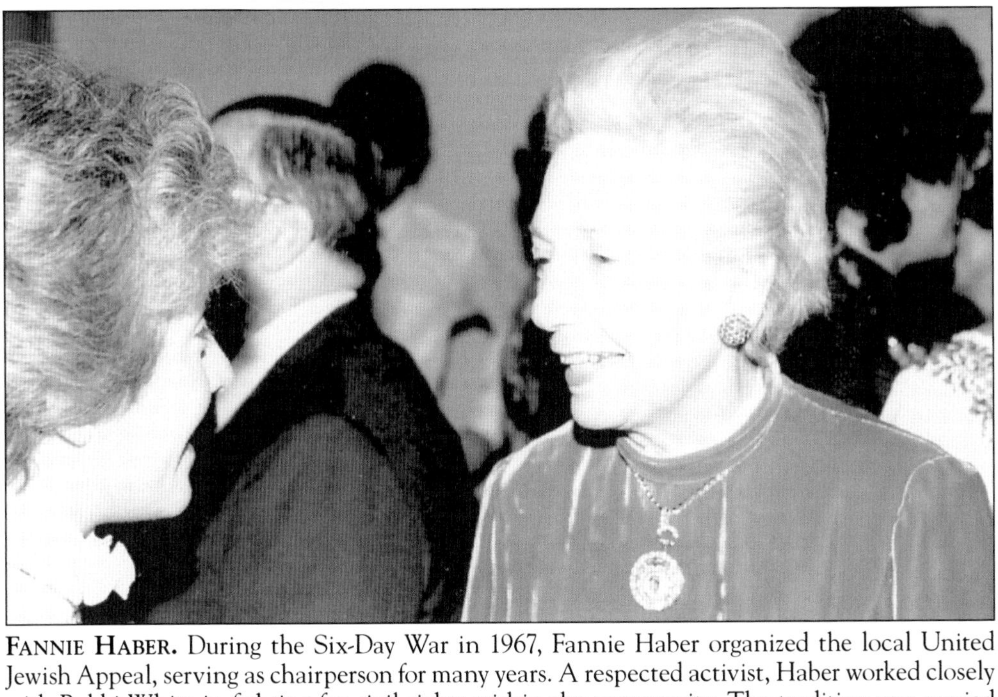

**FANNIE HABER.** During the Six-Day War in 1967, Fannie Haber organized the local United Jewish Appeal, serving as chairperson for many years. A respected activist, Haber worked closely with Rabbi White in fighting for civil rights within the community. The tradition was carried on by her son Alan, an organizer in the 1960s of the local chapter of Students for a Democratic Society. He is still active in the peace movement with the Megiddo Peace Project. (BIC.)

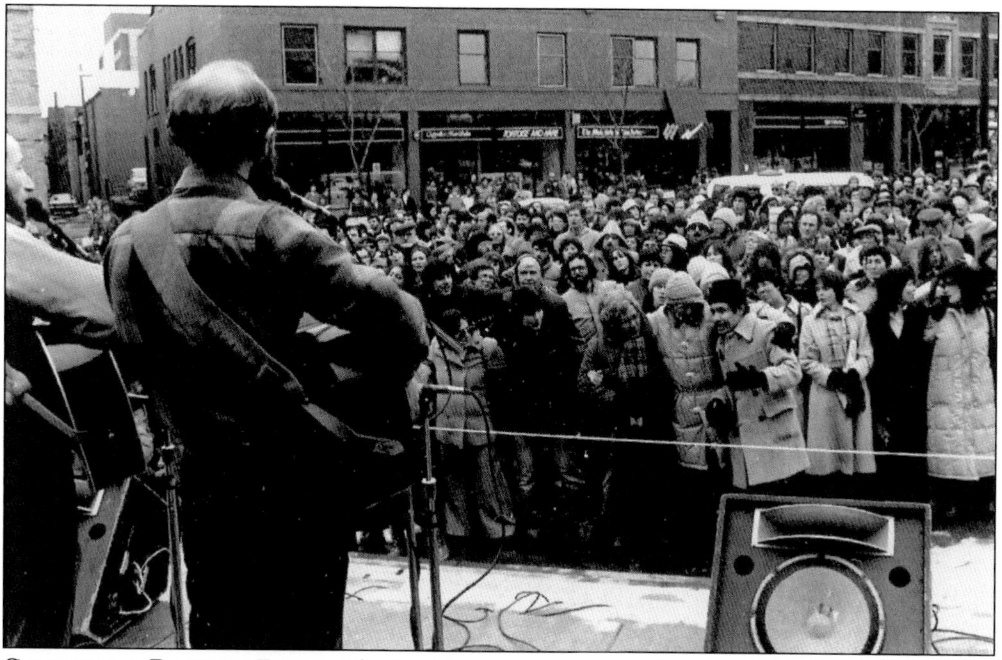

**COMMUNITY PROTEST RALLY.** The Jewish community has always been among the strongest advocates for civil rights as well as peaceful uses of atomic energy. This antinuclear rally, part of a national protest, was held at the Federal Building plaza on March 20, 1982. The rally included entertainment by the Detroit-area musicians Gemini, Sander and Laszlo Slomovitz. (BHL.)

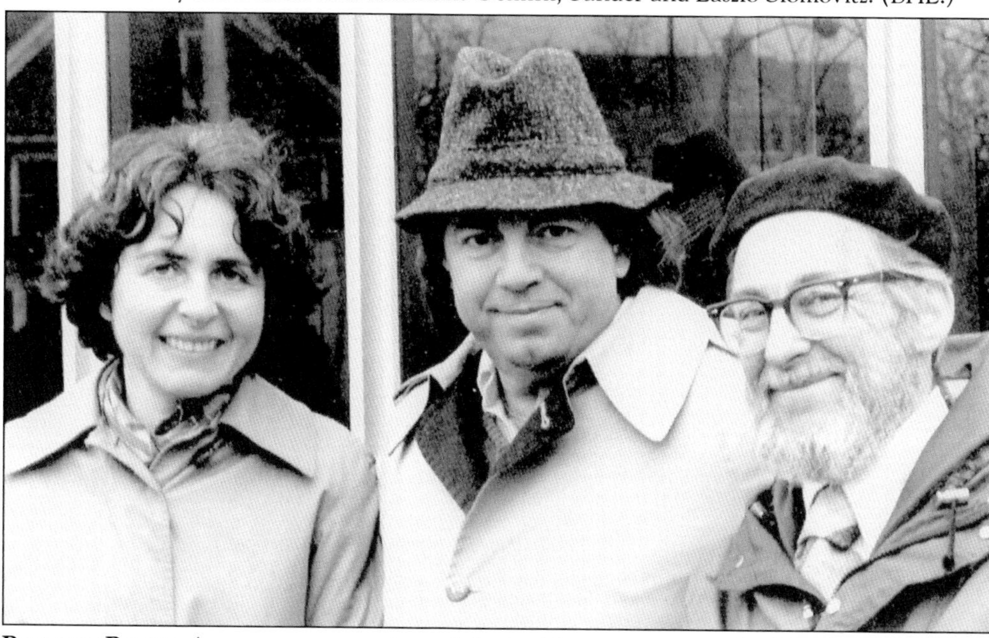

**PROTEST RALLY.** Among representatives of the Jewish community at the March 20, 1982, rally against proliferation of nuclear weapons were Elaine Pitt, president of the Jewish Community Council, for many years an agency that coordinated Detroit-area Jewish activities; Ann Arbor mayor Louis Belcher; and Syd Bernard (right), moderator and secretary of the Jewish Community Council. (BHL.)

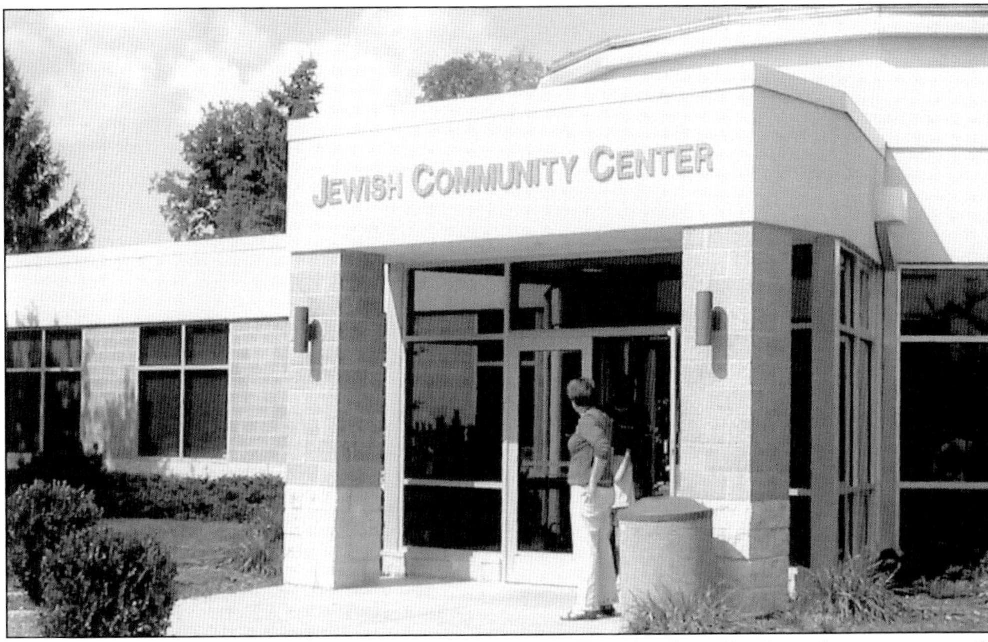


**JEWISH COMMUNITY CENTER.** In 1984, the site at 2300 East Stadium Boulevard was temporarily rented to serve as a common center for the community. Clinton School, 2935 Birch Hollow Drive, was purchased in 1987 and converted into the Jewish Community Center (JCC); Lawrence Smith was the first president. The building houses a variety of organizations, including the Hebrew Day School, the Jewish Federation of Washtenaw County, the Early Childhood Center, and the *Washtenaw Jewish News*. (Authors.)

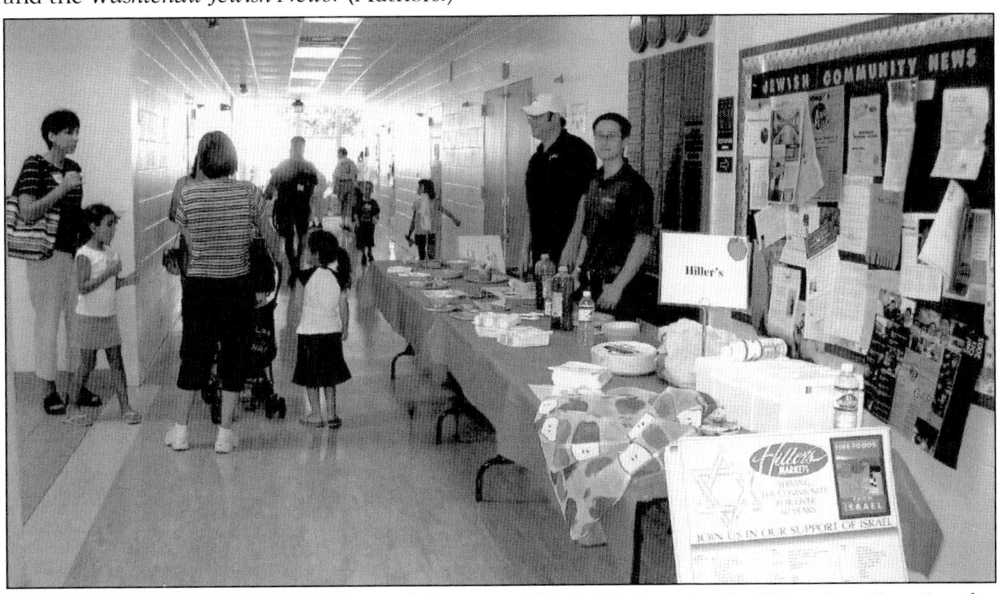


**"APPLES AND HONEY."** Each fall, in celebration of Rosh Hashanah, the "New Year," an "apples and honey" festival is held at the JCC. The program is among those throughout the year in which the varied community in Ann Arbor celebrates a common event. Hiller's Market, a strong supporter of the local Jewish community as well as the State of Israel, is frequently the primary sponsor. (Authors.)

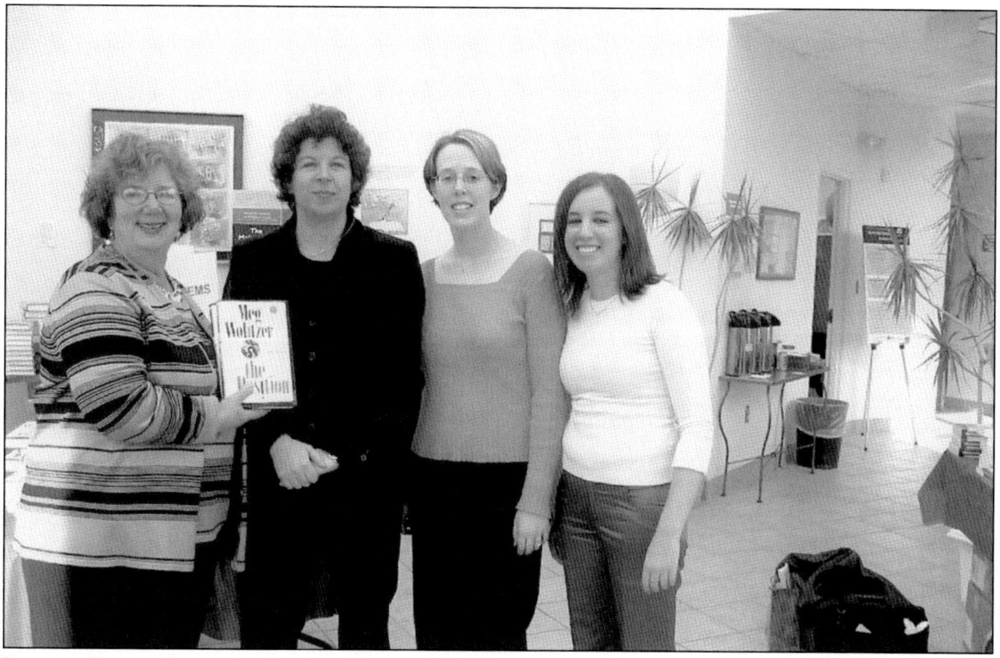


**Jewish Book Fair.** Each November, the Jewish community sponsors a "Jewish Book Fair." Housed in the JCC, the weeklong event includes a sale of relevant books or writings. Local authors are frequent speakers, while their books are provided a prominent place for perusal. The fair is also highlighted by a series of invited speakers. Profits are used for JCC activities. (JCC.)

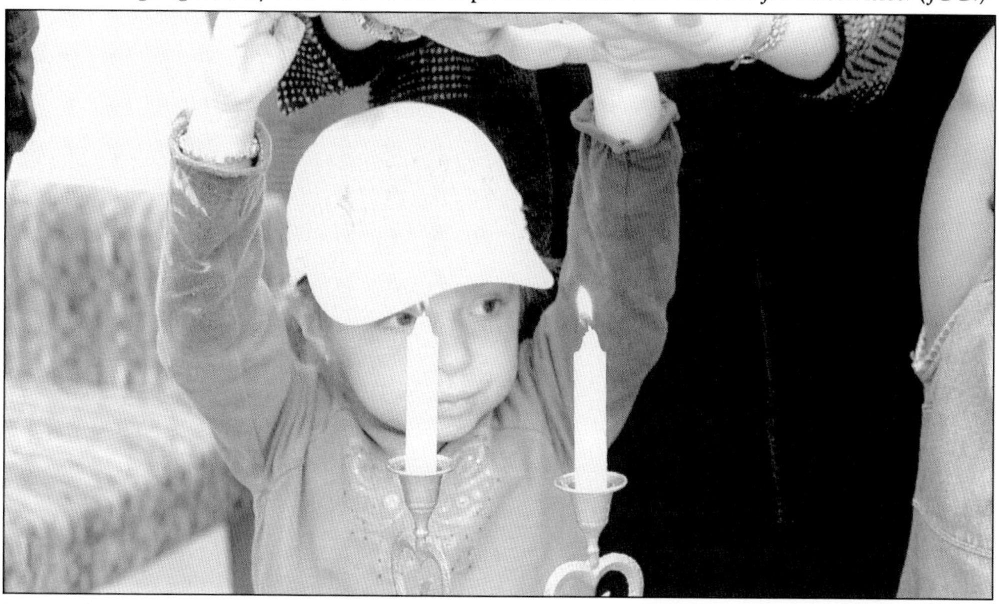

**Early Childhood Center.** The Early Childhood Center (ECC) is housed within the JCC. Originally the Beth Israel Nursery School, the ECC has grown to an enrollment of approximately 185 children, ranging in age from infant to pre-school. Noreen DeYoung is the current director of the center. Children have a wide range of age-appropriate activities from which to choose. The center is a state licensed and nationally accredited, quality early childhood education program. (Noreen DeYoung.)

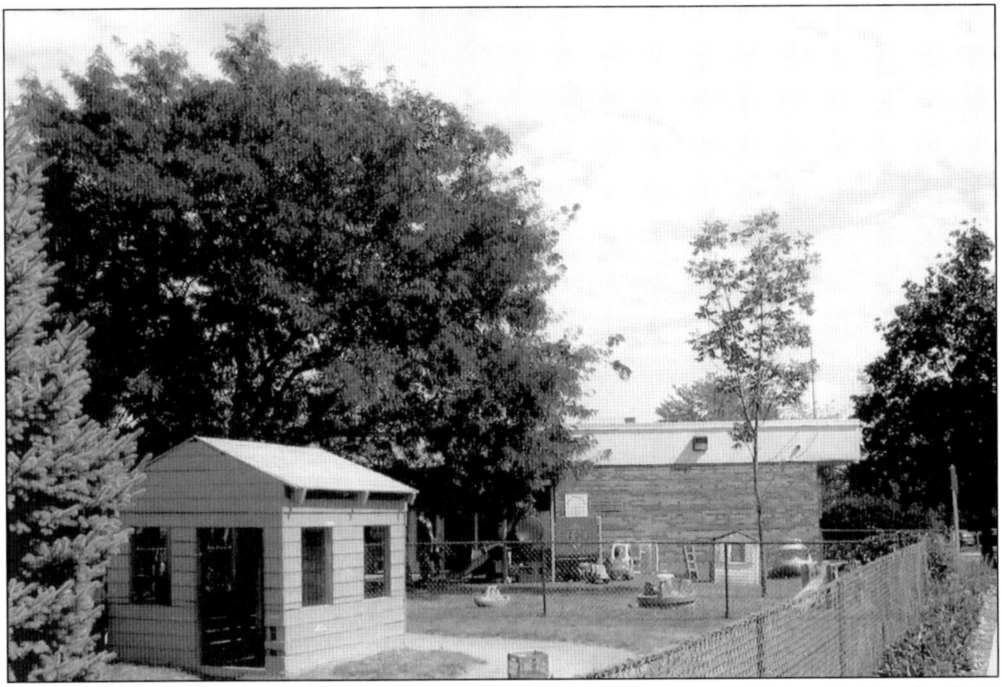

**EARLY CHILDHOOD CENTER PLAYGROUND.** Weather permitting, children enrolled in the ECC have a large playground outside the building where they can also play. Activities within the enclosed area may also include animals, which come to visit with proper supervision. Other activities associated with the JCC are also carried out in the area. (Authors.)

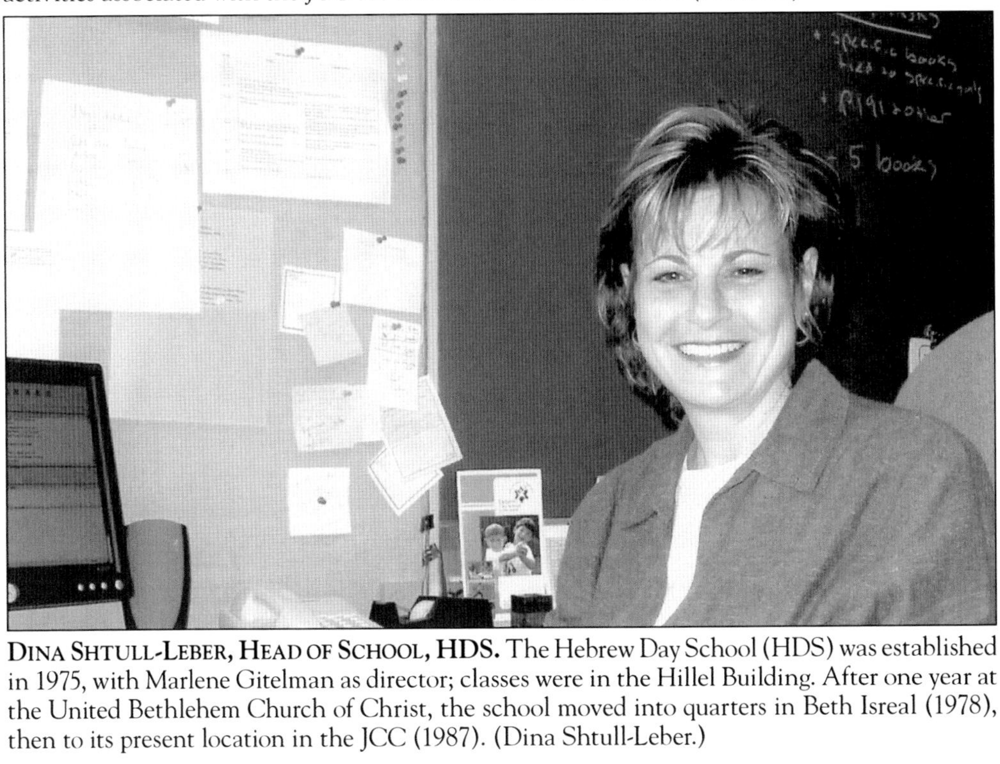

**DINA SHTULL-LEBER, HEAD OF SCHOOL, HDS.** The Hebrew Day School (HDS) was established in 1975, with Marlene Gitelman as director; classes were in the Hillel Building. After one year at the United Bethlehem Church of Christ, the school moved into quarters in Beth Isreal (1978), then to its present location in the JCC (1987). (Dina Shtull-Leber.)

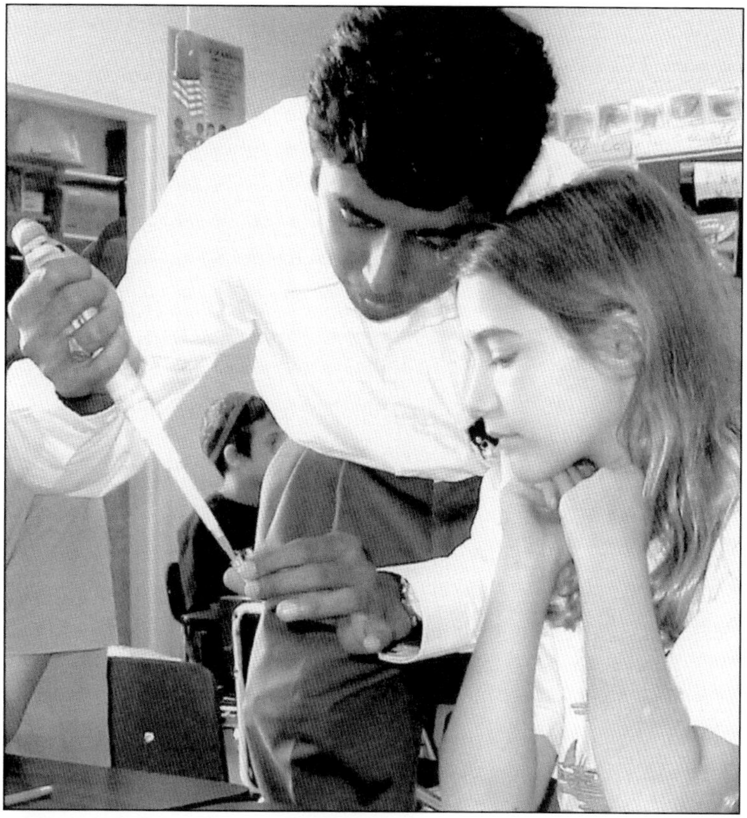

**HEBREW DAY SCHOOL SCIENCE ACTIVITIES.** The full academic program at HDS includes the study of science, as depicted in the aid provided children by visiting scientists. Visiting scientist Vishal Gohil, from the research laboratory of Dr. Miriam Greenberg, is shown demonstrating the technique of Thin Layer Chromatography while students carry out a hands-on approach to the work. (Dina Shtull-Leber.)

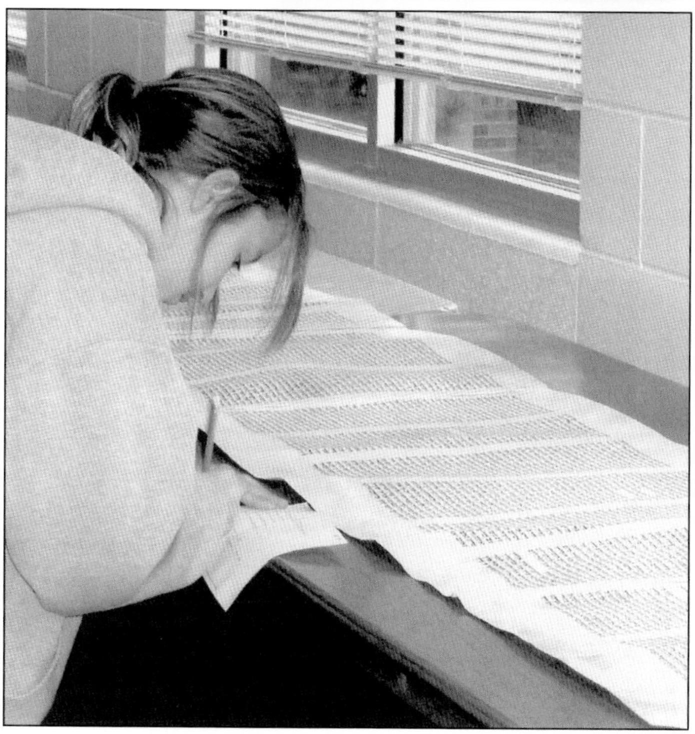

**HDS JUDAIC STUDIES.** The school is affiliated with the Solomon Schechter Day School Association. Students receive a strong Jewish education, as depicted in this scavenger hunt held in conjunction with the holiday of *Simchat Torah*. The student is attempting to locate a word or phrase in the Torah scroll, which was lent to the school by Rabbi Robert Dobrusin of Beth Israel. (Dina Shtull-Leber.)

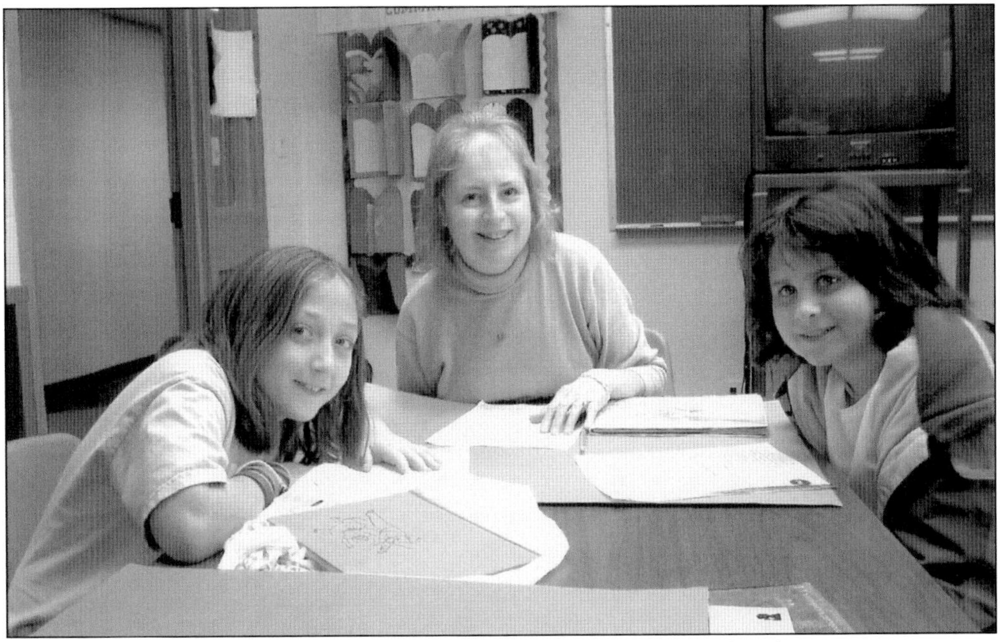

**BETH ISRAEL RELIGIOUS SCHOOL.** Religious education continues to be of primary importance in educating young persons in the Jewish religion. Carol Feldman is typical of the teachers from both Temple Beth Emeth and Beth Israel who have shown a commitment to quality teaching and training for the more than 130 students enrolled in grades K–8. In addition, a Madrichim program includes 37 high-school students working in the classroom. (Authors.)

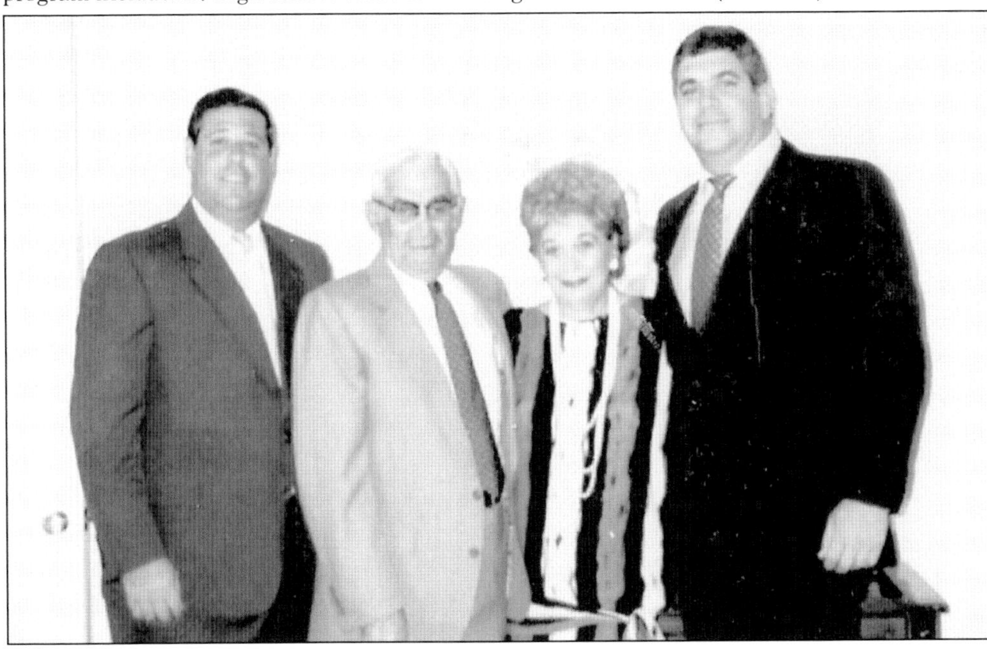

**MAX AND CEIL PEAR.** For 40 years, the Pears owned one of the few Jewish businesses in nearby Ypsilanti—Pear's Clothing Store. Ceil Pear was among the more active members of the women's organizations at Beth Israel, Hadassah and the sisterhood. Each was a contributing member of the Ann Arbor community. From left to right are Ed, Max, Ceil, and Michael. (Ceil Pear.)

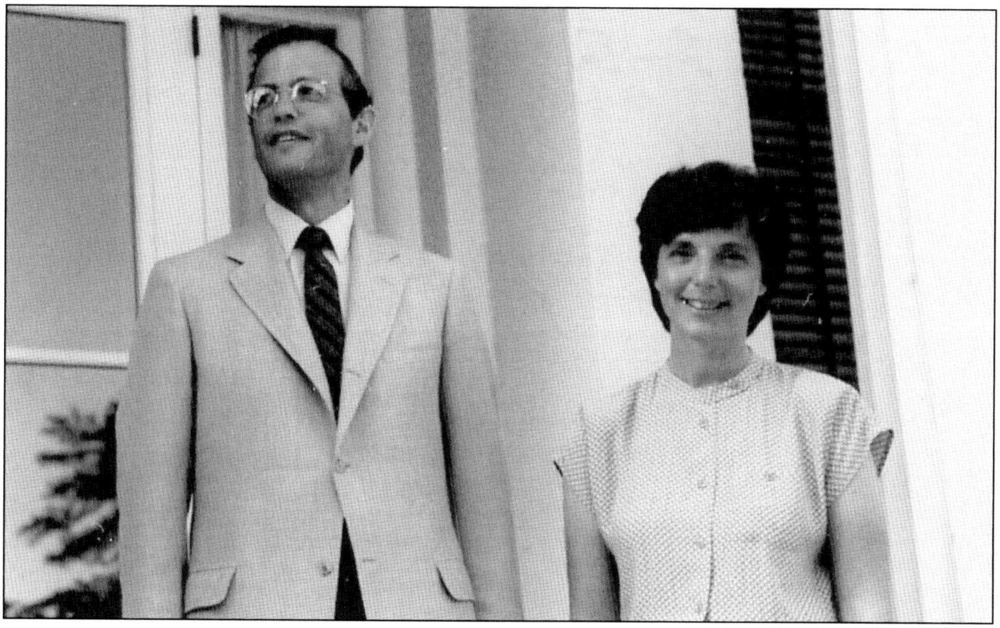

**PRES. HAROLD SHAPIRO AND VIVIAN SHAPIRO.** Harold Shapiro, president of the University of Michigan from 1980 to 1988, represented the first Jewish person to hold that position. Professor Shapiro joined the university in 1964 and remained a member of the department of economics through 1988, when he accepted the presidency at Princeton University. Both he and his wife were actively involved in the synagogue and local community. (BIC.)

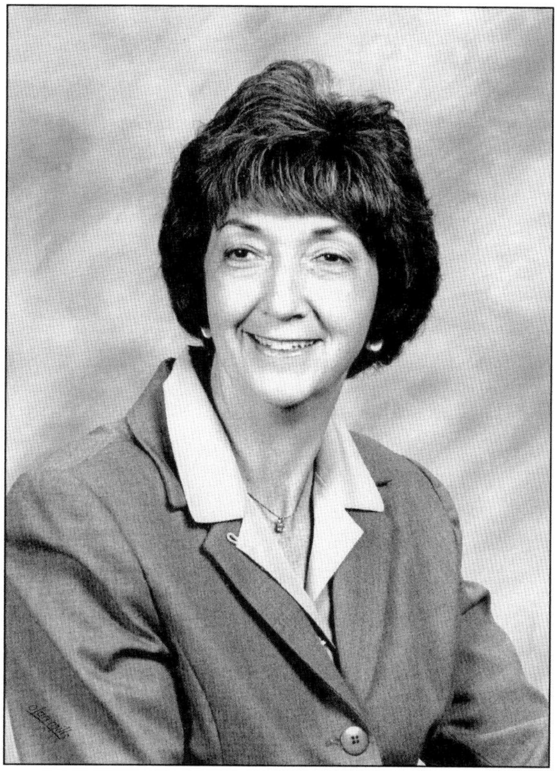

**MAXINE SOLVAY, PRESIDENT, ANN ARBOR HADASSAH.** Hadassah represents the largest Jewish women's organization in the United States. The Ann Arbor chapter includes over 450 members. (Maxine Solvay.)

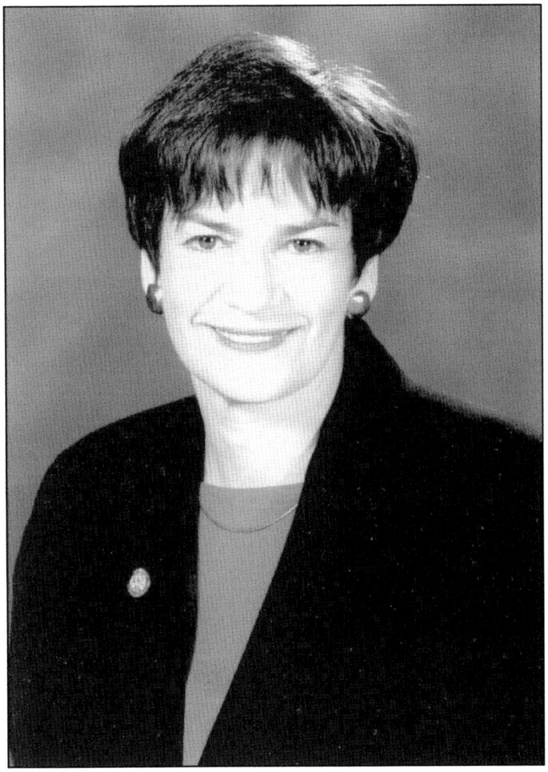

**Liz Brater.** Senator Brater entered politics in 1988 when she was elected to the Ann Arbor City Council. She was elected mayor of Ann Arbor in 1993, the first woman to serve in that position. Elected to the Michigan State House of Representatives in 1994, she served in that position until 2000, and as Chair of the Consumer Protection Committee. Unable to run again because of term limits, Brater was elected to the Michigan Senate in 2002. (Liz Brater.)

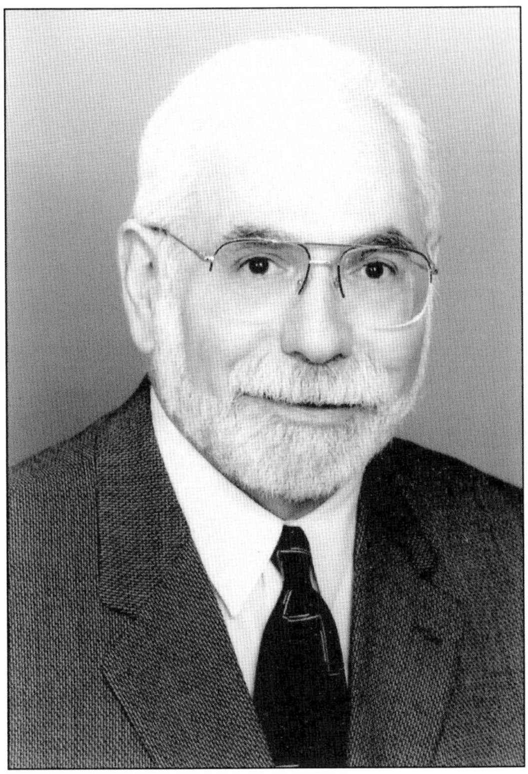

**Todd Endelman, Director, Jean and Samuel Frankel Center for Judaic Studies.** The Jean and Samuel Frankel Center offers both undergraduate and masters degree programs in Judaic Studies. A variety of public lectures are sponsored by the center throughout the year, most notably the David W. Belin Lecture, the Padnos Lecture, and the Derrow/Goodman Lecture, all in areas of Judaic Study. Endelman himself is a prominent author and speaker in areas of Jewish history. (Todd Endelman.)

# LEADERS

Congregation Beth Israel/Beth Israel Community Center

Spiritual Leaders/Rabbis
1918–1921: Pincos Grobstein (melamed, shohet, and hazzan)
1921–1924: vacant
1924–1932: Jacob Kamenetzky
1932–1934: Joshua Sperka (first ordained rabbi at congregation)
1934–1944: Isaak Goldman (melamed, shohet, and hazzan)
1944–1947: vacant
1947–1953: Herschel Lymon (director, B'nai Brith Hillel Foundation)
1952–1962: Julius Weinberg
1962–1968: Harold White
1968–1969: Joseph Krickstein
1969–1970: Mervin Tomsky
1971–1988: Allan D. Kensky
1988–: Robert Dobrusin

Presidents
1918–1958: Osias Zwerdling
1959: Morris Friedman
1960–1961: Jarvis Franzblau
1962–1963: Irving Copi
1964–1965: Keeve Siegel
1965–1966: Martin Sichel
1967–1968: Paul Pressel
1969: Saul Hymans
1970: Henry Gershowitz
1971–1973: Gerda Seligson
1974–1978: David Eduardo Schteingart
1979: Carl Cohen
1980: Paul Lichter
1981–1985: Susi Coran
1986: Irving Smokler
1988–1989: Robert Rosenblum
1990–1993: Steven Klein
1994–1995: Henry Gershowitz
1996–1997: Errol Soskolne
1998–1999: Richard Seid
2000–2005: Edward D'Angelo
2005–: Carol Finerman

Temple Beth Emeth

Spiritual Leaders/Rabbis
1968–1975: Bruce Warshal
1975–1984: Ralph Mecklenburger
1984–: Robert Levy

Presidents
1966–1969: Ron Tikofsky
1969–1971: Allyn Kantor
1971–1973: Paul Vanek
1973–1975: Steven Young
1975–1977: Gilbert Small
1977–1981: Marilyn Scott
1981–1983: Irving Fox
1985–1989: Alan Cotzin
1983–1985: Arthur Lindenberg
1989–1991: Steven Rhodes
1991–1993: Stuart Simon
1993–1997: Barbara Heilveil
1997–1999: Bette Cotzin
1999–2001: Patricia McCune
2001–2003: William Parkus
2003–2005: Gretta Spier
2005–: Wendy Lawrence

# BIBLIOGRAPHY


Aminoff, Helen. "The First Jews of Ann Arbor." *Michigan Jewish History*. Vol. 23, No. 1, January 1983: 3–14.

Aminoff, Helen. "A History of Jewish Ann Arbor." *Jewish Life in Washtenaw County 2005–2006*. Washtenaw Jewish News, 2005.

Attaway, Doris, ed., and Marjorie Rabe Barritt, ed. *Women's Voices: Early Years at the University of Michigan*. Michigan Historical Collections, 1935. Bentley Historical Library, Bulletin No. 47, October, 2000.

Ann Arbor News

Cohen, Irwin J. *Jewish Detroit*. Charlestown, SC: Arcadia Publishing, 2002.

Detroit Jewish News

Endelman, Todd. *A Short History of the Jews of the Ann Arbor Area*. Ann Arbor, MI: 1997.

Heineman, David E. "Jewish Beginnings in Michigan Before 1850." *Publications of the American Jewish Historical Society*, Vol. 13, 1905: 47–70.

Katz, Irving. *The Beth El Story: With a History of the Jews in Michigan Before 1850*. Detroit, IL: Wayne University Press, 1955.

Krohn, Nancy, ed., and Mary L. Liskow ed. *Washtenaw County, Michigan: plat maps 1856 and 1864*. Ann Arbor, MI: Genealogical Society of Washtenaw County, 1997.

Marwil, Jonathan. *A History of Ann Arbor*. Ann Arbor, MI: University of Michigan Press, 1990.

Michigan Argus

Reade, Marjorie and Susan Weinberg. *Historic Buildings, Ann Arbor, Michigan*. Ann Arbor, MI: Ann Arbor Historical Foundation, 1995.

Rockaway, Robert. *The Jews of Detroit. From the Beginning. 1762–1914*. Detroit, IL: Wayne State University Press, 1986.

*University of Michigan, Proceedings of the Board of Regents*. Bentley Historical Library.

Vanek, Linda and Rose Vainstein. *Temple Beth Emeth: The First Fifteen Years, 1966–1981*. Ann Arbor, MI: Temple Beth Emeth, 1982.

Washtenaw Jewish News

Weinberg, Susan. *Lost Ann Arbor*. Charleston, SC: Arcadia Publishing, 2004.

Weissbach, Lee Shai. *Jewish Life in Small-Town America. A History*. New Haven, CT: Yale University Press, 2005.

Young, Stephen. *A Program of Development*. Ann Arbor, MI: Temple Beth Emeth, 1973.